THE VIRGINIA BOOKSHELF
is a series of paperback reprints
of classic works focusing on Virginia
life, landscapes, and people.

Garrett Epps
The Shad Treatment

Donald McCaig
An American Homeplace

Ivor Noël Hume
*The Virginia Adventure: Roanoke to James Towne:
An Archaeological and Historical Odyssey*

Virginia Bell Dabney
*Once There Was a Farm . . . :
A Country Childhood Remembered*

Cathryn Hankla
A Blue Moon in Poorwater

Edna Lewis
In Pursuit of Flavor

Stephen Goodwin
The Blood of Paradise

The Blood

of Paradise

Stephen Goodwin

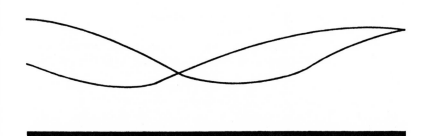

University Press of Virginia *Charlottesville and London*

Grateful acknowledgment is made for permission to quote from "Sunday Morning" and "The World as Meditation." From *Collected Poems* by Wallace Stevens. Copyright 1954 by Wallace Stevens. Reprinted by permission of Alfred A. Knopf, a division of Random House, Inc.

The University Press of Virginia
Originally published in 1979 by E. P. Dutton, Inc.
© 1979 by Stephen Goodwin
Foreword © 2000 by the Rector and Visitors of the University of Virginia

Printed in the United States of America

First University Press of Virginia edition published in 2000

♾ The paper used in this publication meets the minimum requirements of the American National Standard for Information Sciences—Permanence of Paper for Printed Library Materials, ANSI Z39.48-1984.

Library of Congress Cataloging-in-Publication Data

Goodwin, Stephen.
    The blood of paradise / Stephen Goodwin.—1st University Press of Virginia ed.
      p. cm.— (The Virginia bookshelf)
    ISBN 0-8139-1877-4 (alk. paper)
     1. Urban-rural migration—Virginia—Fiction. 2. Married people—Virginia—
Fiction. 3. Country life—Virginia—Fiction. 4. Virginia—Fiction. I. Title. II. Series.

PS3557.O624 B58 2000
813'.54—dc21

                             99-089088

For Eliza, in time

Shall our blood fail? Or shall it come to be
The blood of paradise? And shall the earth
Seem all of paradise that we shall know?

Wallace Stevens, "Sunday Morning"

The Blood of Paradise is the kind of novel you never quite leave behind. I know of no higher praise one can pay a novel, and I mean it exactly that way. I first read it in the winter of 1980, and I have been returning to it ever since. It is set in the early seventies—the Watergate hearings are on television; no one has heard of AIDS, there is drug use and casual sex going on, and not a word of the story has lost one iota of the freshness with which it first shone—the book itself, its psychology and insight, its distinctive vision, its brilliantly nuanced and authoritative prose, hasn't aged a minute in the roughly twenty years since it was first published.

Perhaps this can be said of every truly good novel, but the one I think about when I think about *The Blood of Paradise* is *The Great Gatsby*. We all know where that novel is set, and we follow its idiosyncratic cast of characters through their very specific landscape, under the eyes of Doctor T. J. Eckleburg, and every time, although it is clearly a young man's book (Gatsby and Carraway and everyone else—and by extension Fitzgerald himself—believe that five years is a *long* time), the charm of its prose wins us to it, convinces us all over again, and all the years and changes since we first read it fall away, and we are back there.

The Blood of Paradise has this same effect, and it is not, in fact, as obviously a young man's book as

Gatsby is. Its concerns are arguably less romantic, lean more toward a kind of wise melancholic grace, a *knowingness* about its characters and about life, that indeed suggests the experience of a much older man, a man not fooled by romantic images or conceits.

The Blood of Paradise is a grown-up love story rather than a romance; it is the story of Anna and Steadman, and their daughter Maggie, and it moves with tremendous authority from Anna's point of view to Steadman's and back. Steadman wants to write, and we are privy to some of his work, yet the usual writerly conflicts with existence, the usual sense of the world as being a part of the writer's emerging consciousness or art, never become the subject of the book; indeed, there are times when Steadman's writing seems no more important than the fact that the neighboring couple are sheep farmers. The same is true of Anna, who is an artist, and whose darkly shaded relationship with her destructive twin sister, Kay, makes up a good part of her portrayal. Anna's reality as an artist is only one facet of a very full and substantial *someone,* a created fictional presence that is utterly convincing, and wonderfully sympathetic.

The real subject of this novel, the real theme, is married love, and we come to know this young couple as well as we ever know anyone in life or in books; we become involved with them to the point of hoping for them, and we are completely under the spell of their complicated and evolving passion for each other, their relations with the other characters, their *lives,* rendered in Stephen Goodwin's sharp, intricately developed dramatic scenes, in dialogue that sparkles with the distinctive flavor of each person, all set against the backdrop of a rural Virginia that is beautifully and lovingly evoked on nearly every page. This fiction is, as Archibald MacLeish said poetry ought to be, "palpable and mute / As a globed fruit."

Here, for instance, is the end of winter, as perceived by Anna:

> The spring came on. Anna noticed the birds first. A pair of bluebirds nested in a hollow locust near the garden. Goldfinches sunned themselves on the power lines. The evening grosbeaks, always in a gang, always in a noisy yellow flutter, made dashing swirls around the trees, giftwrapping them. Birds were singing, and after the silence of winter Anna noticed it. Their songs sounded intrepid to her, and formidable, like so many small sweet drills loosening a glacial mass; she thought of the sheets of snow and ice that dripped for a while and then slid off the roof of the house with the rumble of avalanche. That is how she expected the winter, which was still felt in the air and still visible in the grays and browns of the mountain, to depart, in a rush and roar.

This book is a seamless tapestry of writing like that, and after you step out of the spell of it, you are simply amazed at its economy and grace, its precision, its poetry. Its perfection.

So. I will say that I cannot think of a series called "The Virginia Bookshelf" without thinking of *The Blood of Paradise,* and that is true—but the larger truth is that I cannot think of any series of books that could be called essential to a library, any library, without thinking of *The Blood of Paradise.*

RICHARD BAUSCH

The Blood of Paradise

One

"Please, no dog in the manger," Steadman said.

They were standing on top of Big Furnace Mountain and Anna was looking west, trying to take in three more mountains, long, gray, monotonous ridges. Was her sulking so obvious? She had not griped. She had spent the last week packing all their junk, the last two days on her knees with a scrub brush cleaning floors and fixtures in the apartment. During most of this time Steadman had been out buying a four-wheel-drive vehicle, which he said they would need, and this morning she had climbed into the new Blazer the color of rust and followed him out of Charlottesville. He was driving the loaded U-Haul truck and she didn't look at much but the orange sign in front of her, *Adventure in Moving*. The Blazer was such a tub she could hardly keep it on the road. Their daughter, Maggie, who had wanted to ride in the truck with Steadman, got restless and whiny in her safety seat and faked car sickness when they crossed the Blue Ridge. They drove through the Shenandoah Valley, through Staunton, where the stoplights were on hillsides, and Anna, who wasn't used to the stiff new gears or the clutch, stalled twice. A few miles out of town Steadman pulled off for lunch at the kind of dinky joint he always chose. This one was called Gosh's Hoot Mountain Inn. There were the usual wooden booths, the gallon jar of pickled eggs that always made Anna think of preserved fetal mishaps, the hillbilly music on the jukebox, the staring men in those shirts with the names stitched over the pockets. Besides the waitress she was the only woman in the place. And then, a few miles farther, after they'd crept around the curves to the top of Big Furnace and Maggie had finally fallen into a doze, he pulled off again at the scenic overlook. Up here on top of the mountain the green trash cans were overflowing and she could smell the rustic privy. Of course Maggie woke up the moment she stopped.

"Is anything the matter?" she asked Steadman.

"No. I just wanted to look."

So she looked too, or at least turned her face in the direction of the Alleghenies, and waited for him to get his fill. She hoped that he would not try to solemnize the moment.

"Anna, this is the first thing I've done for a while that feels right."

She knew that he'd turned from the mountains to her, waiting for her to say something. She shrugged.

"Please, no dog in the manger."

She could hear that he tried not to sound critical, she knew without looking that he was smiling as he appealed to her, and still she felt scolded. She was here now—wasn't that enough? He was waiting for her to reply, and before she really thought what she was doing she turned to him and barked, "Woof woof." Instantly she felt like a fool, but Steadman seemed to think she'd meant to be funny. Anyway, he laughed. Maybe it was funny, for in a moment she laughed too at how silly she'd sounded.

Back in the Blazer she followed Steadman again, down Big Furnace to a tiny white village—church, post office, store, a few houses —called Barger's Mill. The mill was gone but the great iron wheel was tilted up against the stones of the foundation. They turned onto a dirt road that ran along Prussian Creek. After a few miles the mountains closed in on both sides, Big Furnace on one side and Little Furnace on the other. The creek, way below them in a gorge, was all that kept the mountains apart, and the road was a vertiginous ledge. When the valley opened up again it was poorer and meaner. Most of the farmhouses were rundown and some were deserted. The windows were bashed out, whole walls were blown off, porches were peeled away. The roofs of listing barns sagged like hammocks, and old cabins were just compost heaps with chimneys. People had been leaving this place for years. Anna did see one recent cinderblock building, and she noticed here and there, shining in the woods, aluminum trailers and a school bus painted silver—hunters' camps. They looked incongruous out here, these tacky metal heaps. They looked as if they'd fallen out of the sky, the wreckage of orbiting satellites or spaceships. Maggie was taking an interest now; she was looking for what she called the Christmas house, a farmhouse with those lightning rods that were long black spikes sticking through glass balls. The place had a sign on the gate: *Cross Dog.* And when they crossed the iron bridge, the planks thumping under the wheels, Maggie grew expectant, eager: "There's our house," she said as soon as she glimpsed it.

"Yep," said Anna, and she looked too. The house was across the creek, crouched under Little Furnace Mountain. It was well back from the road but plainly visible in winter with all the leaves off the trees. Faded, red-roofed, small at that distance, very angular against the swell of the land, dominating its little colony of sheds, the house had always looked forbidding and defiant to Anna. Whoever lived there didn't want neighbors and didn't think much of the mountain overhead. The fields began at the creek, where the land was flat, but they were pushed right back into the mountain, past the point where the slope got steep. Above the line of cleared land the woods just hung, a curtain that could fall at any minute. And on the very highest point of cleared land, directly over the house, there was a rail fence around the graveyard in which generations of the Argenstills were buried. Anna might be superstitious but she did not like the idea of dead people watching over her. She did not like the swinging bridge, either, a few boards hung on spidery cables over the creek. That was no superstition, just common sense.

Steadman didn't pull off at the bridge but drove half a mile beyond it to the Obenwalds' house. Even Anna, who didn't know much about country things, could see how neat their farm was, and their house, with green shutters and fresh white paint, was reassuring to her. Steadman parked at the gate in the white picket fence and Anna parked behind him. They were expected. The two big dogs stretched and crooned, and Diana and Harry came out of the kitchen door. Diana babbled; her smile was something. Anna saw Steadman and Harry, who were old friends, shake hands in a way that struck her as formal and solemn. She was aware of the excitement all around her at that gate, and to her surprise she felt a little leap of it herself.

Steadman wanted to unload the truck right away. Harry got into the cab with him and they drove back to the swinging bridge. There was a ford just below it—but Anna couldn't believe Steadman really intended to cross it. He did. The water, a chill lurid green, churned over the tires, the truck lurched on the rocks and stalled. Steadman waded back to shore in Harry's hip boots—at least he'd foreseen the possibility of failure—and they talked it over and went back to the Obenwalds' house to phone someone named Duty Armstrong. Diana made tea while they waited for this person, whom Steadman seemed to know. Of course he'd come here far more often than she had, to go hunting or fishing with Harry, but she was nevertheless struck by how familiar he seemed with this whole predicament. He acted as if he'd spent his life getting moving vans stuck in creeks. "Why don't you unload the stuff in my barn?" Harry asked. And Steadman, who hated any hitch in his plans, just said, "It'd be better off there if it wouldn't be in your way. It'll be a lot easier to work on the house if it's empty."

Duty Armstrong arrived in a decrepit truck with a bulldozer on the back. Anna thought he had a tumor in his cheek—his tobacco. His teeth were stained, he wore overalls that were practically quilted with patches, and his speech, which twanged like a plastic ukelele, was completely incomprehensible to her. She thought she had never seen such—well, such a hillbilly. Yet when they were introduced, he made a dodging bow and yanked his cap without looking at her, and she realized that he was polite and shy. He and Steadman consulted for a moment, and then Duty scampered onto the seat of his bull-dozer and Steadman waded back out to the truck and hooked a winch cable around the bumper. Duty dragged the U-Haul out, and he insisted on helping them unload it in Harry's barn. He and Steadman talked as if they'd been neighbors for years, and when Duty kidded him about all the stuff he'd brought, and Steadman took the kidding right in stride, it occurred to her that these two men liked each other.

It turned out that Steadman was right; they were better off with the furniture in the barn. In fact, he was right about a lot of things, and seemed to know what had to be done to make the house habitable. The first thing was to clean it out—the scrub brush again, and more Lysol. The filth was astounding. She hadn't really noticed it while the house was full of Mrs. Argenstill's things, but now, empty, nobody could miss it. Cluster flies were an inch deep on the windowsills and on the floors underneath the windows. They hibernated in the walls, Steadman said, and on sunny days they came out and bumped sluggishly against the warm panes. The walls were alive with mice too, which did not hibernate but were always skittering around. The bottoms of the cupboards in the kitchen were carpeted with their scat. And after Steadman climbed up on the roof and cleaned out the chimneys with a gob of clanking chains, and scoured the cast-iron stoves with a wire brush, the house was full of a black sooty dust that kept settling for days. When Anna took her baths at the Obenwalds'—they were eating and sleeping there—the water turned black instantly. Anna had her moments of disgust, plenty of them, and even moments of horror—she watched a panicky mouse, whose nest must have been threatened by all the cleaning, relocate its almost full-grown babies. It carried them in its mouth, its teeth sunk into their napes, tottering under their weight, literally reeling across the floor before disappearing with them behind a metal screen that blocked a fireplace. Three times the mouse made this journey to safety, but the fourth time Anna could stand it no longer. When it went behind the screen she kicked the metal and crushed the mice, mother and baby both, flattened them between the screen and the stone. She didn't kill them. After the crunch there were pitiful squeaks and she kicked the screen again. That did it. She left the room. When she told Steadman and the Obenwalds about it at dinner, Diana said "Ugh." Harry offered to lend her a few of the cats. "They do a neater job," he said. There was not much sympathy for the mice. Anna felt almost proud of her nerve.

And on the whole she took a kind of satisfaction in cleaning and airing the empty rooms, especially in cleaning the windows. Once the bug spots and the soot were off them, the old irregular glass, warped and wavy, with little bubbles trapped inside, made a beautiful sparkle in the sunshine. Maggie, who put up with the drudgery very patiently, looked at one window Anna had just finished and said, "Gleams." Anna looked herself: a sheet of light, no color at all,

a transparent plane that flashed and shined: gleams. Sunlight gleam-
ing as it entered the house.

Of course they were lucky that the weather was good; it was bright
and warm for December, warm enough to do without a fire while
Steadman was cleaning the chimneys and stoves. He'd been cutting
firewood too, and she'd almost got used to the sound of the chain
saw. As long as he was off in the woods it was just a drone, soporific,
like bees. The house made its own shifting and creaking noises, and
sometimes, if a window was open or if she stepped outside, she'd
hear, from far across the creek, the bleat of the Obenwalds' sheep,
even a bit of conversation between Harry and Diana as they moved
among their barns and sheds. It was that quiet.

Diana came over one afternoon, though Anna protested, and
helped her scrub floors, and the next afternoon two women whom
she'd never seen appeared and went right to work. Their names
were Val and Laurie, and they lived at a place called Xanaduc a few
miles down the road. One of the men from the place, Zep, a tubby
bearded fellow, had been helping Steadman get in wood, and he'd
told them that Anna looked as if she could use a hand. "We thought
maybe we'd find the rest of the fortune too," Laurie said.

"Oh, that's right," Anna said, "you're the ones who found the
money in the barn." Steadman had told her about that. Lulu Argenstill, the widow from whom he'd bought the place, had been certain
that her husband had hidden money from her, and she wouldn't sell
until she found it. These two, Val and Laurie, had come over one
afternoon to muck out Lulu's barn—there was some vintage cowshit
out there, Anna was told. They knocked loose a stone of the foundation and found a money box hidden behind it.

"That got everybody around here digging for a while," Val said.
"There's some story about money hidden on half these old places."

"Did you know Mrs. Argenstill very well?" Anna asked, and from
their smiles she knew they found the question curious in some way.

"She had a real strange head," Val said.

"She was one of the church folks," Laurie said. "They don't
approve of us—you know, hippies. Dread narcotics."

Anna wondered, if these women in overalls were hippies, where
that put her. She was grateful that they didn't seem to be sizing her
up. Yet she couldn't feel altogether comfortable when these two

women she'd never laid eyes on started cleaning the hall, including the foul closet under the stairs. Anna worked alongside them, as did Maggie—Laurie hit it off with her right away—and kept offering them tea or coffee so frequently that Val grinned at her and made her feel like an airline stewardess. They really had come to work, not just to visit, though they did fill her in on Xanaduc. They made it clear that they did not want Xanaduc to be thought of as a commune. It was just a place where a bunch of people happened to live together. They'd been there since that spring, and they were getting into sheep, goats, and organic gardening. Laurie was a potter, Val a spinner and weaver, and everyone else at Xanaduc seemed to have a craft or two. When they got their shit together, they said, they'd each spend half a day at the chores and half a day at their own gigs.

In the middle of the afternoon they did invite Anna to share a reefer—the first time she'd heard that word for a while—and when she hesitated they didn't press her, though Val remarked that Diana didn't smoke either. The comment wasn't quite nasty, but it kept Anna from taking her turn on the reefer the next time it was passed. All drugs from cough syrup to coke had strange effects on her and she mostly left them alone, but she had been prepared to toke up with these new neighbors. Too late now, for Val said that they were afraid the locals were going to bring the narcs down on them, and in this matter, Anna realized, she was classed with the locals.

But even if the locals were suspicious, Val and Laurie had managed to collect the valley's gossip and tales. They told her about Arlie Argenstill, Lulu's husband, who had dropped dead in the middle of the swinging bridge, and they emphasized the detail of the story that was always emphasized: the water carried him a mile downstream and left him on the bank right behind the Panther Gap Chapel, but when they found him there wasn't a scratch on him, not a scratch or a bruise. Anna never knew what to make of this death that was not a transformation; somehow it always put her in mind of Millais' Ophelia, the gorgeous corpse in the lovely brook.

And so the afternoon passed, and Anna mumbled out thanks that were awkward and inadequate. The visit seemed to her truly generous; she could not imagine herself walking into a stranger's house and pitching right in. And they'd done the last really nasty job. In just four days the house was clean, not immaculate but no longer dismal. Four days, and Anna realized that this place was beginning to fill with its own sights and sounds, its own people, its own stories. The creek had gone down, and late that afternoon Steadman made the maiden voyage across it in the Blazer. He got some kind of sulfur bombs; they'd kill the flies, he said, and maybe even discourage some of the mice.

The next day, while the house stank of that disinfectant, Anna and Maggie went to town with Diana to buy groceries. Steadman was supposed to be moving stuff, mattresses and pots and pans, from the barn to the house. This was going to be their first night under their own roof. To Anna the day seemed endless. Diana had a hundred stops to make, and she couldn't make them without explaining each one in exhaustive detail. The one thing that fixed itself in Anna's mind was Bag Bomb, Bag Bomb, Bag Bomb. Diana kept talking about this Bag Bomb which was supposed to soften her milk cow's udder. "It just gets hard as a bowling ball or something, it must be like a big boil or abscess, I don't know, but poor Gertie gets so tender she can't stand for me to touch her." Anna was too dazed to ask what this Bag Bomb was going to do. By this time she had an image of the bag itself as a bomb that was going to blow into smithereens. When Diana actually got the thing, it turned out to be a tin of ointment, Bag Balm. "I kept thinking you were saying bomb," Anna said, "bomb, not balm, you know, something that explodes." Diana laughed politely, but she didn't really get it until a few minutes later. Then she did laugh, her good crinkled laugh, but Anna felt all day that they were off balance with each other. They both knew that they were expected to be good friends, and Anna did like Diana—but not the forced intimacy. And of course Maggie got sour halfway through the day; Anna went through a lot of rigmarole at different stores about her Charlottesville checks, and it didn't help when she said that her address wasn't the address printed on the checks; at the laundromat the clothes came out with stains all over them because Steadman had left a tube of stove polish in one of the pockets.

And then he wasn't there when they got back to the Obenwalds'. Anna saw the Blazer across the creek, up at the house, and Diana stopped at the ford and beeped her horn a few times. "He probably heard it," Anna said, for it was getting dark and starting to rain and she knew that Diana was anxious to get to her chores. Anna thought of walking across the bridge and sending Steadman for the groceries, and she wished she had when she'd waited half an hour in the Obenwalds' kitchen. It was almost full dark and raining hard when he finally came to the door, his poncho dripping and his wet hair sticking out in points. "It's getting cold out there," he said. "We'd better get going before this rain turns to snow." Anna felt a real bitterness: it was like him to act as if he'd been waiting for them. They loaded the Blazer with the boxes of groceries and the suitcases they'd packed that morning, but Steadman drove only as far as the bridge.

"Aren't we going to drive up to the house?" Anna asked.

"We'd better walk up."

"Why? Haven't you been crossing all day?"

"If it rains hard the creek'll come up and we'll never get the Blazer back over. It just makes it across as it is."

Anna didn't think of asking him to take her and Maggie to the house and unload the Blazer there, then drive it back across and make the walk up by himself, until she was already on the other side and too wet to bother. It took Steadman four trips to get everything over the bridge, and then it didn't all fit in the wheelbarrow. She had to lug one of the suitcases. The path was wet and slippery, the house hardly visible through the rain and dark. She kept changing the suitcase from one hand to the other. Halfway up the slope Maggie fell behind, then stopped altogether and refused to take another step. "It's too gooshy to walk." She stood there in her hat and slicker and refused to budge. She would not be coaxed. "We'll just have to leave you here, then," Anna said. "Nobody can carry you." But Steadman picked her up and perched her on top of a suitcase that was across the handles of the wheelbarrow.

"Won't she fall off?"

"Not if she holds on tight."

Maggie stuck her tongue out at Anna. Steadman laughed. Anna didn't feel angry but just crummy when she picked up the suitcase and sloshed after them.

Steadman reached the house before she did and picked Maggie up and set her down inside the door. Though Anna saw what was coming next, she was still surprised to find herself in his arms, carried over the threshold like a bride. The room was bright and warm—she saw the fire through the clove-shaped vents of the cookstove—and there wasn't even the sulfuric stench she expected. The mattresses were made up, pillows and quilts, the table was covered with an oilcloth. In the center of it Steadman had placed a blue jar filled with ocher and silver sprigs. He'd put down a carpet. She looked at the room, she looked back at Steadman. He kissed her. Both their faces were wet, and water was running over her brow and cheeks. She hoped he would mistake the dampness as some return of his ardor.

He said, "That's a wonderful fragrance, that cedar, isn't it?"

"It doesn't stink in here the way I expected."

That wasn't what she meant to say at all, but he put her down, and because Maggie had been watching them in a stern way, as she always did when she was left out, he picked her up and spun around with her, dancing with his daughter. Anna looked again at the welcoming room and then she stopped the dance by putting an arm around each of them. She pressed her face against Steadman's cheek. "A family smooch." He laughed. "A very wet family smooch. I think Anna's nose is the coldest."

"You went to a lot of trouble," Anna said, and to Maggie, "Doesn't the room look nice?"

Maggie, turning, broke the circle of their heads, and in a moment they had dispersed. Anna and Maggie shucked off their wet coats while Steadman brought in the groceries. Anna started to empty the boxes into the rust-flecked refrigerator Lulu had left them. While she was bending over, Steadman put his hand once on her neck, under her hair. She didn't feel pawed, not exactly, but she hoped he wouldn't try to drag out the momentary affection. He lingered over emotions and forced her into little deceits when he expected her to do the same. "I'll cook dinner," he said, "but first I want to sit down for a minute with Maggie. I haven't seen my girl all day." And as she watched him place Maggie on his lap to read to her, she became aware of something covetous in her attention. People said that Maggie looked like her, and she was dark-haired and dark-eyed, but she had Steadman's complexion, those Dutch girl cheeks with blooms in them. She had Steadman's innocent way of concentrating, too—their faces over that book were so peaceful.

"In a house in Paris . . ." Steadman read.

And Maggie: "All covered with vines."

"Lived twelve little girls . . ."

"In two straight lines."

Maggie couldn't read yet, but she knew the rhymes by heart and pored over the pictures at length. Steadman didn't hurry her. Anna couldn't even guess what took place inside her daughter's head, but Maggie's hand glided over the page as contemplatively as if it were printed in Braille. Anna found herself hushed so that she would not break the silences in the reading, and she felt guilty at her fascination. It was foolish, she knew, but she didn't want them to catch her staring.

"They smiled at the good . . ."

"And frowned at the bad."

"And sometimes . . . sometimes . . ."

"They were very sad."

The way Maggie said that word—minted it, Anna thought, remembering Steadman's phrase for Maggie's clarity of enunciation —the way her hand traced the picture of the soldier on crutches, the way she sat against Steadman's chest and arm—Anna was sure that what she felt was love, but why, when it came this way, unsolicited and irrefutable, did it always bring her to the verge of sadness?

"And a crack in the ceiling had a habit . . . had a habit . . ."

"Of sometimes looking like a rabbit!"

Maggie turned round and grinned at Steadman; that line always tickled her. And Steadman looked over Maggie's head at Anna. "Is her memory astonishing, or just normal?"

"Both," said Anna.

When they finished the book Steadman turned Maggie over to her. She was glad that he was going to cook—the big wood range with all its handles and throttles was still disconcerting to her. She and Maggie unpacked a few things from the suitcase, but they had only one drawer each in the small dresser Steadman had brought across. Anna tried to entertain her with another book, but Maggie was hungry now, and restless, and since her supper wasn't ready, she decided she wanted to look at the rest of the house. She evidently expected to find all of it transformed, as the kitchen had been, but as they poked with the flashlight through the chill damp rooms, which did smell of sulfur, she clung to Anna's hand. "It's ghosty, isn't it?" She didn't want to go upstairs. "How long are we going to stay here, Mama?"

"This is our house now. We're going to stay here for . . . a long time."

She had almost said forever, and as it was she might have lied. Yet her answer, surprised from her in the dark, startled forth a hope after all, and when they returned to the kitchen, and Steadman sat them down and poured them a glass of wine—he'd rummaged through the boxes in the barn to have the tulip-shaped glasses for the occasion —she didn't know how to check it. In all their talk about the Argenstill place Steadman hadn't said a word about their troubles, and neither had she. Their troubles had always been unspoken and insidious. But she'd understood all along that Steadman regarded the move as an opportunity to escape those troubles. Now, in this new place, with crystal, wine, a blue jar full of weeds—a winter bouquet, Steadman called it—she hardly knew how to form her own hope, but maybe these things were enough for a beginning.

When Steadman brought the food to the table she discovered that she had an appetite. She ate a lamb chop, noodles, beans, and after she'd cleared her plate Maggie studied it for a minute, knowing something was amiss. "You didn't leave any for Daddy." Steadman laughed and said he'd had plenty. Then, while they waited for the packaged tarts to brown in the oven, they stood in the doorway and looked into the sky, for the rain had turned to snow. Steadman cast the beam of the flashlight up into the darkness, and the half-frozen flakes, falling fast, wriggled through it dragging their short incandescent tails. They reminded Anna of something, but she didn't know what it was until Maggie said, "Tadpoles."

By the time they'd eaten dessert Maggie, a little wine in her, was nodding. Anna got her out of her clothes and into her nightie and spread the bright animal quilt over her. Tired as she was Maggie asked for the fox song, and Anna, singing, watched the flickers of sleep steal across her face.

> *Oh, the fox went out on a chilly night*
> *And he prayed to the moon to give him light,*
> *For he'd many a mile to go that night*

Before he reached the town-o, town-o, town-o,
He'd many a mile to go that night before he reached the town-o.

By the end of the verse Maggie was gone.

Anna went after Steadman then. His back was to her; he'd already begun to wash the dishes. She tapped him on the shoulder. He turned around, his soapy hands in the air, but she realized that she didn't know what she wanted to say. She put her arms around him, pinning his arms. "I'm going to try," she said. Her voice sounded fierce and combative. "I'm going to try not to be so backward." She was pressing him against the sink. She kissed him, conducting her ardor this time.

Two

This life in Zion County was like nothing Anna had ever imagined. To her the country was landscape, always fixed, always distant, placid with a vengeance. Paintings were more vivid to her than actual landscapes; she thought of scenes from Brueghel, of stupefied workers drowsing in hayfields, drugged not by beauty but by tedium. And in these pictures the aspect of nature was always absolute; things were always the same, always and utterly the same—as it was in the beginning, is now, and ever shall be. No wonder the workers nodded off. In the actual world, Anna knew, things did happen, seasons and crops, but the change was too slow to be visible as a process. The human figures in any rural landscape were just that, figures, tiny figures dwarfed by huge spaces. She knew that people worked outside, and thought of tractors forever going back and forth in fields. She wasn't too clear about what they accomplished. The one specific image of what might lie in store for her was milking a cow, which she'd seen Diana do. The barn stank, the cow shat, the flies swarmed. Anna didn't drink milk anyway. As for Steadman, she had imagined him carrying an ax, wearing a plaid shirt and a wool cap, looking like the illustration on a can of pork and beans.

But the paintings, after all, were paintings, and the other anticipatory images were so feeble that they did not clog her perceptions once she'd arrived. Anna was glad they'd come in winter, the blankest of seasons; she realized that in her conception of nature summer always prevailed, and that the outlines of things were obscured by a continuous green haze. On that morning after snow Anna looked at Big Furnace Mountain, the black lashes of the trees on a white plane—and the clarity was incisive. Anna, who drew, had never been able to do much with colors. Hers were always too splashy and indefinite. She had once tried to explain this to Steadman, who replied that the eyesight of the lesser mammals was confined to black and white—a joke, but she didn't forget it. The mountains under snow she regarded as the confirmation of a private vision. And when the snow was not present, the winter colors, browns, grays, dark greens, had a subdued depth that belonged in things, was not an accidental shimmer. Over here in winter the moon was the real moon, a chrome planet that rose over a ridge of the mountain; it wasn't a big gumdrop competing with a streetlight. And when Anna stepped out at night and squatted with her pants around her ankles to piss, and tilted her face to look at the stars, she thought of space as a lovely transmutation of light, a manifestation of color as it might be, purified, distilled, encompassing. The constellation she always looked for was the Pleiades, the Seven Sisters, the small close cluster. Steadman, who knew the constellations and their stories, had pointed it out to her; it seemed wonderful that the stars had names and biographies. One of the few aphorisms that had stuck with Anna was Pascal's—"The eternal silence of these infinite spaces terrifies me"—but now that she recognized Orion and the Dippers, now that the heavens were not just a gorgeous chaos, she was not so intimidated. And anyway she was usually pissing during her stargazing. The body's little functions undermined awe.

Over here the scale was new to Anna. She looked, couldn't help looking. The magnitude of the place was always calling sight forth. The mountains weren't big as mountains go, the skies only as large as the opening between the mountains, but to her everything was huge. She had grown up in the city, and she knew that her vision was selective; she was deliberate about not looking at anything when she was on the streets of Washington. She'd had enough run-ins with drunks, weirdos, and guys on the make to know that the best protection from them was to keep her eyes to herself. One glance was all it took to stir up some creep. It was a luxury to be able to stare, and the distances eyesight traveled seemed fabulous to her. Sounds traveled too, and some days she'd hear the clank of a bucket, Diana's or Harry's piping call, *Sheep sheep,* and raise her eyes to see, across the creek, over and through the branches of the trees, the bulky flock running toward grain in a field a half mile away. Seeing then was as good as motion. And sometimes when Steadman took his giant walks she looked at places in the mountains where he might be, and almost believed that she would see him. Before he set out he showed her his route on the survey maps—and she'd watch his big hand, the nail of the index finger tracing a specific contour line; she'd become conscious of her own bitten nails, the blunt naked fingertips, and tuck her hands under her arms—so that she'd know, he joked, where to send a search party. And then she would stand and look at the mountain where he might be and long to see him: if their eyes could meet across those miles of air, if vision could join them across such distances . . . seeing then became an emotion.

So the place was large, but she could still contain it in her senses —or so she thought until the weather changed. Everybody talked about the weather, and Steadman turned on the radio every morning at seven to listen to some cornball announcer who always sounded as if he was scratching his head. She and Maggie couldn't make a peep during the five-minute report. This was one of Steadman's country affectations, she thought, like the almanac calendar or the wintergreen snuff he carried—once in a great while he did stick a pinch of it under his lip—but she changed her mind after the first big storm. Trees crashed, roofs shuddered, streaks of sleet actually ran upward across the windowpanes, and she knew that what she could see and hear was nothing to the power that was loose. In the city storms had always seemed small and individual, broken up by all the buildings; out here she could guess at their mass and extent. When she looked out the window, she saw clouds the color of bruises and the size of mountains booming overhead. It wouldn't have surprised her if the house had gone up like Dorothy's house in *The Wizard of Oz.* It seemed unlikely that she could be safe inside, when inside was so tiny and outside so mighty. The very idea of inside, of these buildings plopped down here and there to contain their own climates against all this force, seemed optimistic. As a phenomenon the weather was colossal, even when it was ordinary

—which, she realized, it never was. It was only poised. It still filled the valley, overfilled it. Anna in the city had considered most days as having no weather at all; otherwise, like a puppy, the weather was either nice or bad.

The weather was practical too. Snow, rain, ice, sun—these made a difference in what they did, what they could do, on a given day. Theirs was the last road in Virginia to get scraped, and when it iced over they stayed put. Sometimes that damn bridge iced too, and Anna clung to the cables when she crossed it to the mailbox—she wasn't expecting anything in particular, and she never wrote letters, only notes on white index cards, but when the mail van passed at ten o'clock she bundled up and went down there. Sometimes that was as far as she went during the day. That pleased her too—out here people stayed home. They didn't get in cars and reshuffle themselves every morning. They stayed home where they had things to do. It wasn't like being cooped up in an apartment. Of course when they did have to go somewhere it took all day. The nearest store was in Silesia—Anna loved to hear Maggie pronounce it, Si-les-i-a, giving it four syllables, with a clean space around each of them—a tiny hamlet five miles away where Prussian Creek ran into the St. Margaret's River. Silesia was even smaller than Barger's Mill, and the store sold chewing tobacco, Vienna sausages, gas, and not much else. So they had to go to Staunton when they needed anything. Anna didn't much like the drive over the mountain, but Steadman, who always had page-long lists of things he needed, tools and fittings and connectors she'd never heard of, usually made the trip himself, and took Maggie with him, so that she had a day alone. She did what by now had become routine, she scraped or painted in the upstairs rooms, and she discovered right away that she had a taste for the freedom of isolation. Out here she could please herself—not that she'd ever attempted to please the world, but all kinds of expectations seemed to have fallen away, and she was aware of them in their absence. Some were specific—her mother's expectations, which were still vocal, for her mother phoned regularly, but irrelevant now—and some were just social, but whenever an external sense of what she was doing came to her, she put it out of mind. She might be putting on her goggles to keep the paint dust out of her eyes, or squatting under the stars, or simply walking down the slope to get the mail when she had a pang of self-consciousness and thought how peculiar her activities were—but nobody was looking, nobody but herself. Nobody approved or disapproved, nobody was judging. The sensation was so potent that she had been tempted more than once to test it; sometimes she skipped or danced a few steps in the empty rooms, and once on her way to the bridge she had stopped, put her hands on her hips, and shouted at Big Furnace, though not very loudly, "You hamburger." Nothing happened, nothing at all, and she laughed.

Meanwhile the house, after that first decorous evening, had turned into a mess. Between Steadman, who tore out a wall in the kitchen and kept knocking holes for pipes, and the electrician—a fundamentalist zealot who stopped his proselytizing when she told him she'd been raised a Catholic—who kept pulling boards off the walls, the entire downstairs was filling with debris and grit. The whole front part of the house was log, boarded over inside and out, but when the boards came off the chinking came out, mud and straw and lime, and covered everything with a powdery dust. The flies Steadman had killed in the walls came tumbling out too, and it was almost impossible to sweep with the litter of tools and materials. "Why did we bother with all that cleaning?" Anna asked, and Steadman replied, "Just a ritual." When Anna touched her hair, it felt like a collage, and Steadman said when they got between the sheets at night—they had moved the mattresses upstairs, which was relatively clean—that it felt like slipping into a sandwich of crunchy peanut butter. Every three or four days they did impose on the Obenwalds' shower, but Anna didn't really mind the squalor. She only worried, with all the sharp tools and exposed wires and nails sticking out, that Maggie might hurt herself.

This life was not exactly the simple life, not yet, but it was not as grim and primitive as it sounded when Anna tried to describe it to her mother, who called at least twice a week and advised her to leave Steadman immediately, or at least to make him hook up the toilet. Anna tried to explain that he'd had to unhook it—the Argenstills' toilet and basin had been slapped into the corner of a bedroom— so that he could build a proper bathroom. She said, knowing the effect it would have on her mother, that one night while she was pissing a rabbit dashed by her, pursued, a second later, by a fox.

"You live that way, Anna? You think that's funny?" "The fox wasn't after me, Mama." "Well, use the outhouse. You have an outhouse, don't you? Use it and shut the door." But during these interrogations, for her mother wanted all the particulars, Anna thought of her there in Washington, seated in her kitchen, a cigarette in her hand, a tray of pills in front of her, an eye on the television—and it was her mother's life that seemed strange, not her own. When Anna exaggerated inconveniences, she did not feel spiteful or dishonest, for her mother enjoyed vicarious grievances and forgot most of them between calls. Her mother was an obnoxious battery, Steadman said; Anna's father generated a head of voltage in her which she then discharged elsewhere, and Steadman knew that it was often directed at him. He was the one who usually answered the phone, and he signaled to Anna that her mother was calling by pumping his arms in what was supposed to be an imitation of Mrs. Ciccenberti fanning her ire, and was also a mockery of her name, pronounced by Steadman as Chicken-birdy. He always left the room while Anna talked to her mother, which was just as well; Anna couldn't have indulged in her harmless exaggerations if he'd been there, nor in her own sense of bravery. Her mother's exclamations made her feel that this life out in the sticks must be an adventure.

When she hung up, even though her mother did most of the talking, Anna felt like a windbag. She wasn't much of a talker, never had been. She was a twin, and her sister, Kay, did most of the talking for both of them while they were growing up. This suited Anna, for whom language had always been hazardous or worse. At home she'd heard Italian from her father and grandparents and English from her mother, and a mixture of the two when all the adults talked together, but she didn't know how confused her own speech was until she went to kindergarten. The other kids laughed at her every time she opened her mouth. The effect on her was to shut her up. They laughed at Kay too, but Kay didn't shut up. She just got louder.

Anna had admired Kay's quickness and depended on it in school and at home. It made them inseparable—Kay was her protector and translator—but it also put an end to the telepathic intimacy Anna believed she could remember. As children, as infants, their communication had surpassed any language. Their sensations, even their intuitions, had been shared without the need of speech, not merely shared but mingled as the elements of a single consciousness. Language, Anna thought, had been the undoing of that unity. She might, as Steadman had told her, have exaggerated that early intimacy to compensate for the loss she felt, but she knew that her first memory of terror was accurate and precise. *Anna,* Kay was saying and pointing at her. *Anna, Anna, Anna.* Kay was standing on Anna's bed, pointing down at her, hopping up and down in her nightie, a tiny, disheveled goblin. She was aware of the cruel power she had. Anna must have been three or four years old at the time, she certainly knew her own name, but until that moment she had not realized that it designated her as a being distinct from all others. The way Kay repeated it, in a savage chant, had made Anna feel that the identity conferred on her by language was a curse. *Anna, Anna, Anna,* Kay tormented her, bouncing over her, and the only sound Anna could make in reply was a dry friction in her windpipe. Perhaps she had cried, she couldn't remember, but she knew that for what seemed minutes she had been unable to breathe.

So their names, Anna and Kay, had come between them, as all language did. It was not a memory she had ever mentioned, not to Kay, not even to Steadman, who was the first man with whom she'd ever found anything like her own voice. That voice, she knew, was a mess of noises, gestures, and mumbles. Anna had never outgrown the feeling that she was translating, not from one language to another, but from tumultuous impressions into small vain chirps. Yet Steadman, when she first knew him, had professed to like the way she talked. He had ended by making her even more sensitive about it. She could see him diagraming her sentences, and sometimes, like the children at kindergarten, he taunted her by repeating her words to her.

One day that winter he asked her if she'd seen the pliers, and she heard herself say, "I guess they're over there on the floor by the pipes"—which could have been almost anywhere in the house. She had a perfectly clear image of two copper pipes with soldered ends beneath the sink, of pliers on the dusty floor between a pipe wrench and a propane torch—but she hadn't said that. She waited for Steadman to repeat her directions in a musing, mocking way. Then a wonderful thing happened: he just walked over and picked up the pliers. Of course she knew that he'd often understood her but pretended not to, just to throw her clumsiness in her face, but now, even when she didn't make any sense, he didn't get impatient—he just asked what she meant. She was still embarrassed that she explained things by making noises—she didn't know why, instead of just telling him that the scraper was getting dull, she said, "This thing goes kind of kuuuck now, and not krick"—but not only did he know what she meant, he smiled at the way she put it, just as he smiled at Maggie, as if he did not want to impose an awareness of his pleasure on her.

Of course he hadn't changed overnight, and neither had she. Two things he still noticed: her flapping bootlaces and her hairbrush. She just wasn't able to tie her laces in the morning, not until she'd been up for at least an hour, and even after she did tie them they kept coming undone, and she just let them drag. One night Steadman handed her a book, some kind of woodsman's guide, and told her to read it—two pages, with illustrations, on how to tie a bow that wouldn't come apart. As for her hairbrush, she guessed she must drop it when she was finished with it, and it never fell in the same place. She spent more time than she should looking for it. Maggie, luckily, was observant and often found it for her. One morning the brush was tied to a cord that was tacked to the wall. Maybe it wasn't such a bad idea—but how could Steadman care about that when the house was in such disorder? He did apologize, in his way. The morning after he showed her that book he went down on his knees at breakfast and tied her boots himself, and he took the brush off the string. She wasn't quite sure what to make of it. Did he hold her bad habits against her? She wasn't even sure if she held his attempts at correction against him.

Altogether she wasn't sure what to make of him. Naturally he liked being in Zion County, but she'd somehow expected his pleasure to be more grandiose. In Charlottesville he had been morose for days at a time—and suddenly turned euphoric. He had an antic streak in him, and behaved as if he expected her to be knocked off her feet by his clowning and his inflated spirits. Yet here he didn't spout or rhapsodize, didn't bully her with his moods, didn't have as many moods. He was more patient too, and didn't sail into rages when he worked. He swore sometimes, but he didn't throw tantrums—only one, when he cut a piece of Sheetrock wrong for the third time and kicked and stomped it into a crumbly mess. That was more like the old Steadman. Usually he seemed studious and thoughtful when he worked; he didn't regard the materials—except Sheetrock, which he called shit rock—as his enemies, and he didn't blow up when she asked him questions. That came as a real discovery. In Charlottesville it had got so that she was almost afraid to ask him about anything, for he always took her questions as criticisms, but one day without thinking about it she just popped out and asked him why he was going to put the bathtub against that particular wall. When she realized what she'd done, she braced for the consequences. She expected him to say something like, "You have a better idea?" But he explained something about the weight of the tub, the joists—she hardly listened, she was so struck by her escape. She began to venture other questions. Sometimes, it was true, she did try to disguise faultfinding in a question, and when he flared up she was angry at herself for not speaking out plainly. She didn't think he ought to put a closet over one of the windows in the bedroom that was to be Maggie's—and she should have told him so outright instead of asking in a dumb mincing way why he was putting it there. And sometimes he treated her like a nitwit for not knowing something that he knew, but almost every time he did he recognized it right away and made up for it with some bit of affection. He didn't like to apologize in words any more than she did.

Anna realized that she had taken to watching him as she watched Maggie; his familiarity, his simple presence had become just as mysterious to her as Maggie's. He seemed especially kind and patient and strange when they all took walks together through the fields or woods and he talked about the things he saw. His hunting she had never attempted to understand; she had a vague notion that he bashed through the woods shooting at things. It hadn't really occurred to her that woods were anything but just woods, that they were varied and intelligible, that he was noticing things all the time he was in them. But as he talked, mostly to entertain Maggie, she listened too. He knew the names of the trees, of course, and he liked to speak them, oak, ash, hickory, as if he found something stout in the words themselves. Hick-ry, he said, sassyfras, el-um instead of elm, cheery instead of cherry, trying the mountain accent on his tongue. He tried to get Maggie to notice things; he asked her what the twigs on one tree reminded her of, and she said needles. The tree was a pin oak. Another tree with shaggy bark—the only word Maggie could come up with was prickly—was a shagbark. He broke off a twig and asked them to smell it: lemon, they agreed. "But there can't be lemon trees here," Anna said. He laughed. The tree was a black walnut. He knew which acorns were sweet and which bitter, which trees were male and which female. Anna, to whom trees had always been big weird vegetables, paid attention. He'd thump a tree with the stick he carried—Bo-oum! She didn't know how he could tell they were hollow. Look at the base, he said, and see if the tree spreads out. He'd point out the tracks of deer, turkey, squirrels, the plants and berries and nuts they fed on. Anna was often glad that Maggie was along to ask the dumb questions. "Is this ka-ka?" Maggie said, pointing at the little green pellets they saw everywhere, and Steadman said yes, deer ka-ka. It was almost annoying how he could take a glance at a bird and identify it confidently. "A flicker," he said when she asked and he looked up just in time to see it speeding off. "A flicker? That's the name of a bird?" He swore it was, but she looked it up in the bird book anyway. She had a few sessions with that book, but she didn't seem able to remember any but the bright, gaudy birds, cardinal and blue jay. The third time she asked what the little gray bird was, she was answered disdainfully not by Steadman but by Maggie. "It's a junko."

It pleased Anna that he was so assured and definite. Her only previous experience with certainty had been the Baltimore catechism—and it had turned out that there was a difference between certainty and dogma. *Faith, like night to the intellect*—that was another aphorism that had stuck, and that one came from John Butler Yeats, the poet's father, the painter. Anna had studied art history at college, and without really meaning to be defiant, surprised by her audacity after her convent education, she had trusted her eye. She did not see in pictures what her professors did. They had remarked on her poor writing and called her perceptions "original" or "devious" or "naïve." She got mediocre grades. Only one professor, a ranting and erudite little Englishman who turned his head upside down when he looked at slides, had encouraged her. When she listened to him lecture, she sensed how learning could enlarge perception. But he knew half a dozen languages, and his encyclopedic learning, the only learning she respected, seemed beyond her. She didn't need it, the Englishman told her when he saw her drawings in a student show; he said exactly that. "You don't need us, my dear. Draw! Draw!" His praise, more than she thought she deserved, she nevertheless took as a justification, and she was left with the opinion that, except in rare cases, what passed for knowledge was either dogma or pompous cant. The descriptions of things had little or nothing to do with things themselves. And that was what impressed her about what Steadman knew: the events conformed to the accounts he gave. When she asked why she saw a pale moon in the sky one afternoon, he explained that the moon as it waxed and waned rose later each day in the east. She was looking at a first-quarter moon, a right-hand moon, he told her, and he cupped his right hand and held it up to the crescent in the sky. That week she watched the moon, and secretly measured it with her own hand—and it did exactly as he said it would. She realized that much of what he knew was just basic, and he didn't pretend that it was otherwise—he talked about Duty Armstrong as if the man were a genius—but still she was struck when he heard a rustle in the leaves and said, "A towhee," and sure enough a towhee flew up, or when he said that he bet squirrels lived in a tree, and she put her ear to it and heard them inside making a noise like purring.

She was learning from him, and she began to wonder, for the first time really, about his past. There was so much that she didn't know about him. She did know that he'd worked for his grandfather, a builder, and learned something about houses and tools, and that as a boy he'd spent hours in the woods with his grandfather, but that part of his life had never seemed to have much to do with her.

The night she met him, at the opening of a show of paintings at a gallery in Washington, she thought he was a fop. There was the usual mix of people at the opening, and Anna, an art student at the time, did not feel that she had anything in common with the fashionplates. Yet Steadman had come up and introduced himself to her and Kay—together they were flypaper to a certain kind of lecher—and made flattering remarks about their looks. In situations like this Kay took over. She was brutally sarcastic, but Steadman didn't seem to mind. In any case, he was equal to it and treated it all as pleasantry. Anna could tell that Kay was interested in him. At the end of the conversation he said, "It's been nice meeting you, Groucho"—that was Kay—"and Harpo." Anna was too confused to say anything. She felt as if he'd guessed her secret, for she believed that she knew exactly why Harpo was mute.

A few days later he called her up—called her, Anna. She recognized his voice, and yes, she remembered him. They chatted for a moment. She expected him to ask to speak to Kay, who shared the apartment. He didn't. He asked her if she'd like to go to a museum with him. She accepted. At the museum she watched him to see if he was faking an interest in the paintings. He wasn't. When he brought her home she was too backward to ask him in, and he shook her hand very courteously. That's over, she thought with regret. But a few days later he called again and took her out to dinner. She kept seeing him and tried to conceal from Kay how much she liked him. They made fun of his manners, his clothes, his rosy cheeks, his job as a congressman's aide.

Then Anna got pregnant—stupid. Steadman wanted to get married, and Anna didn't want an abortion. Kay told her she was a fool, a lovesick romantic fool. "You're out of the convent, Baby," she told Anna. "You won't go to hell if you get rid of it." Anna did not know how she held out against Kay. There were scenes, and they were always the same: Kay abused her while she sat passive and silent. And then, one night when she was in bed alone, Kay returned to the apartment and woke her in the dark. Anna thought that Kay was going to strangle her but she did not resist. Then Kay released her and there was a crash, a window breaking. Anna turned on the light. Kay was standing over her with a bloody arm. She smeared blood on Anna's hair, face, shoulders, breasts. Anna had the presence of mind to take her to a hospital. They stitched her up and confined her and asked Anna what kind of drug she was on. When Kay was released the next morning she asked Anna what had happened to her hand, and Anna did not know if her forgetfulness was real. That was Kay's last attempt at persuasion.

When Anna married Steadman, a Catholic wedding to please her family, Kay was her maid of honor. From the vestibule of the church she watched Kay hobble down the aisle—hobble, because her legs, hidden by the gown, were solid bruises. They were black and blue from hip to ankle. That affliction had come intermittently, once so severely that Kay was on crutches, but no doctor had ever been able to diagnose it. Kay called it her Blues.

But Kay, or that church ceremony, or the fact that she was pregnant—something numbed the feelings she'd begun to have toward Steadman. She had Maggie, and adored her, but Steadman had simply come to occupy a fixed place in her life, and she did not often think that he had come there differently from the others, her mother and father, who occupied similar places. She used to tell him she loved him, only to reciprocate his declarations, but it had been a long time since he had forced that word from her.

A long time, but here in Zion County the word often came to her unbidden. The trouble between them had receded, as had most of her past. Anna felt that she had cast off from it and was adrift now on the calm and benevolent surface of the present. Memories of Kay were still, sometimes, vivid to her, but vivid mostly as melodrama. It was hard to believe that she'd lived through such gory moments. Anna realized that she was content, and she wondered if she was changing.

She knew that her intimacy with Steadman had changed. They spent more hours together and they touched each other more often. Steadman was liable to put an arm around her as they walked, to pat her when he was near her in the house. On his part the contact seemed almost absentminded, but on Anna's it was anything but that. "I'm so touchy," she blurted out one day, meaning that she put her hands on him, meaning also, as she was sure he knew, that she was horny. What happened between the gritty sheets was not like what had come before, and Anna had never experienced a sexual urge so constant and consuming. Steadman's body felt different to her, hard as wood anywhere she touched it even under his bulky winter clothes—and she thought of the soft pouch of his balls, his soft dick, hanging between the solid legs, swinging there, queerly alive in her imagination, like a monkey in a tree. It was odd that Steadman, whose fair and rosy complexion looked as if it should yield to the touch, should be so hard beneath the skin, and odder still that at the center of him there was this tissue she could mold and shape with her hands. But she did not have to touch him or even look at him to think of his dick; that might happen at any time, and she visualized it not soft but hard as the rest of him, lengthened, its blue veins raised, into its hankering curve. His dick—she did not call it that or anything else, except to herself. She visualized it as a thing detached, as having in its engorged state as much to do with her as with Steadman, her own toy with which she could do as she pleased. Yet she was hardly present in her fantasies, if that's what they were. This imagined dick had properties of taste, touch, temperature that aroused diffuse longings in her actual body. It was more specific than she was, just as in their bed Steadman was more specific. Her orgasms were deep bucking shudders that came like visitations; they moved through her body but hardly seemed to belong to it. Steadman she could feel, his back solid and tense and muscled, as if the curve of him above her could duplicate the curve inside, as if the strength in the long arc of his torso could be transmitted to the smaller arc of flesh.

Why then, when his weight settled upon her, and his body was soft enough at last to give to her touch, when his dick was shrinking out of her as she clung to him, why could she not tell him that she loved him? And why did he say things that made tears start to her eyes, things about mountain air, as if feelings had more to do with the place and the weather than with either of them? How could he just plunge into sleep? His body, still at rest but completely isolated now, shuddered as he fell asleep, twitched with spasms like those he had just shoved into her. Trying to stay warm, knowing she would not wake him, she pressed against him, stranger to her than ever. She could hear her heart thudding in the pillow, feel Steadman's stuff oozing out between her legs. In the next room Maggie stirred, on the mountain there were barks and hoots and screeches. Fox, bobcat, owl—Steadman had identified the noises, and still they scared her a little as she lay awake, cold sperm on her thigh, the sound of blood in her ear. She lay awake beside her husband on those winter nights and wondered if they were in love.

Three

They went to Bristol for Christmas, though Steadman would have preferred to stay in Zion County. They had always spent Christmas in Bristol with his family, partly because they had seen Anna's family as a matter of course while they lived in Washington, partly because Steadman's grandfather, Watts, was a patriarchal bully who wanted family on hand at appropriate times of the year. "I don't see how we can get out of it this year," Steadman told Anna, though she had made no objection to going. That spring his grandfather had had a heart attack, and though neither his mother, Jane, nor his grandmother, Betty—he'd managed at last to stop calling her Bits—was willing to say that this might be Watts's last Christmas, they had nevertheless made Steadman aware that he'd better show up. Watts himself, who used to stay in touch by letter, for he detested phones, had not written lately and had not mentioned Christmas when Betty put him on the phone during her calls to Steadman.

They'd had a falling out. On the Fourth of July, Steadman's last visit to Bristol, Watts, who had always dominated the gatherings— and, as it seemed to Steadman, for whose sake the assemblies of kinfolk took place—refused to make an appearance. Watts, who always behaved on the Fourth like a campaigning politician, hefting babies and thumping their fathers and kissing their mothers, would not leave the house. His family, all the brothers and sisters, the nieces and nephews, all the in-laws and shirttail cousins, ate ham and watermelon on his flagstone terrace above the lake while he sulked in his room. Steadman, like everyone else, had been unable to keep from glancing at the windows, but he did not share the glee he sensed in some of his relatives. Because he'd been staying at the lake house, he was asked in whispers how Watts was doing—a natural question, but it seemed to Steadman that it was asked in a gloating spirit. "The old bastard's through at last"—nobody said it to him, but he had no doubt that things like that were said elsewhere on the terrace. And because he was his grandfather's favorite, and likely to be his heir, the professions of sympathy were like so much mulch and fertilizer banked around a seedling. Steadman thought poorly of himself for being too polite, and for taking a certain pleasure in the importance his grandfather's absence conferred on him.

All the same he felt that he'd been sticking up for Watts. He didn't give anyone the satisfaction of agreeing that Watts had declined. "How's old A?" they'd ask, for Watts was called A, or Uncle A; his given name was Estes Herschel Watt, and his nickname, Eh What, had contracted to the single sound Eh, or A. "He's just feeling ornery," Steadman said, pronouncing the word as Watts did, ahn-ry, meaning it as a tribute. And when Betty told him that Watts had asked to see him, Steadman supposed that his grandfather wanted cheering up, and it did not surprise him that he'd been sent for.

Almost the first thing Watts said to him was, "It's a pisspoor idea for you to buy that land in Zion County, and worse than a pisspoor idea for you to try to pass it off as some kind of investment. To pass it off that way to me, when real estate's been my business my whole goddamn life."

Steadman had just sat down on a blanket-covered sofa next to Injun, his grandfather's arthritic hound, who'd been taking a nap there for the last two years. They were in Watts's room, not his bedroom but a sort of private office and gun room, a room that smelled of dog, tobacco, powder solvent. It was the only room in this fancy new lake house, which he had designed himself, that Watts spent much time in. Steadman knew that the last two nights he'd even slept in there on one of the sofas. And though Watts had been subdued during Steadman's visit, they had got along more or less as usual. Steadman had mentioned the Argenstill place, which at the time he had looked at only twice. Watts had seemed bored. And so Steadman was not prepared for this attack. He said to his grandfather, trying to laugh, "Do you think I misrepresented it?"

Watts was standing in front of a window looking down at Steadman, breathing as if he'd made an exertion. He was wearing, as he did on all but the most formal occasions, a white shirt and khaki pants, but they were usually starched and pressed with military stiffness, and these were rumpled. He had a glass of whiskey in his hand, which he'd poured in Steadman's presence but hadn't touched—his defiance of doctor's orders. His mouth was open and the light glinted on his gold-filled teeth. The light bleached his skin and made him look frail, almost transparent, but there was nothing weak about his voice. "Misrepresented it. That's the first thing I've heard you say that sounds like a lawyer. I'd say you just plain lied."

After a moment Steadman said, "Is that all? Do you have more to say? Or shall I defend myself now?"

"Well, listen at you. Goddamn but you're reasonable. Maybe you'd make some kind of lawyer after all, but I'll tell you what it looks like to me—it looks like you're getting ready to quit law school like you've quit everything else. It looks like you're easing yourself into buying this piece of godforsaken land in Zion County so you can go off and live there and play writer."

"You know what a judge would say if you kept saying *it looks like.*" Even before the words were out of his mouth Steadman knew they were insulting, not funny. He felt his cheeks and throat begin to flush.

"This isn't a goddamn trial, and you better be glad it's not. I'd have your ass, boy. It's the fact that you quit working for me. It's the fact that you quit working for Congressman Biggs. It's the fact that you threw away money as soon as you got your hands on some to go live in It-ly. It's the fact that you been at law school one year and instead of keeping at it you knock off for the whole goddamn summer to write on some novel, which you haven't even mentioned to me. I got to find out from Betty what you're doing."

"I am trying to write a novel."

"I don't blame you for keeping it a secret, not if it's like that crappy story you showed me. Who reads that crap anyway but a bunch of women getting their hair dried at the beauty parlor?"

"I'll try to write something you wouldn't be ashamed to read at the barbershop."

"How much money did you make off that story? A thousand bucks? Well? You probably didn't even make that."

Steadman admitted that he hadn't.

"And that's what you're going to live on? You're going to shit in the woods and turn out the stories? Is that the idea? You're going over there and play writer."

"It wouldn't be play."

"Wouldn't be play, my ass. Who do you think would be paying for it? You know goddamn well who—me, the one who paid for everything else, and got you the job with Biggs, too, in case you forgot. Christ Almighty, you think I didn't know what you were up to when you started talking about this place? You know where the money comes from."

"I have the money to buy it."

"And where did it come from?"

"I didn't think there were strings attached."

"There's not any, but if you can't think of anything better to do with it than what you are doing, don't look for any more."

Steadman stood up. "Is that what you wanted to tell me? If it is I'll leave now."

"I haven't heard you defend yourself yet. Is that what you call a defense, getting your back up and walking out the door?"

"There's a difference between an accusation and a threat," Steadman said.

Watts tugged at his jaw. "Hell, Teddy, sit down. I need a little resistance. They all"—he made a cleaving gesture toward the crowd outside—"got it in their heads I can't stand an argument. And they'll be there a while yet. You got time to get back out there and be the life of the party." And then, after listening to them for a moment, Watts turned to him and said, "It sounds like starlings, don't it, all those children squealing. And goddamn, they multiply like starlings. It don't keep 'em from fucking that they're poor."

In spite of himself Steadman smiled, and Watts saw it. "Teddy, will you sit down for a minute and not be so goddamn headstrong? I got a proposition."

Steadman did sit down.

"I'll tell you why I'm not out there," Watts said. "You know why. They're just waiting out there to see how much kick I got left in me. Am I right? Ain't that what they're talking about?"

"You're giving them something to talk about," Steadman said.

"I'm not a goddamn exhibit, not yet. They can stare at me when I'm all waxed and rouged up and laid out—but I hear how I sound. Depressed. That's what the doctor tells me. The son of a bitch charges me a thousand bucks to tell me I'm depressed. This goddamn doctor they've passed me to now is about your age, and he tells me I'm depressed, and then he tells me not to worry about it, it's normal after a heart attack. He's got a cute name for a heart attack, a coronary event he calls it. Clever little fucker, ain't he? Teddy, I'll tell you the truth, what I am is flat-out disgusted. I'm disgusted with the doctor, and disgusted with Betty tiptoeing around and shaking her head every move I make, and standing there wringing her hands and looking a hundred years old, and disgusted with that whole bunch out there—Christ, Teddy, I've floated the whole sorry lot for so long now it's nothing but a goddamn debtors' convention when this family gets together."

He tugged at his jaw again. "I know how I sound, Teddy. I see how you look too, staring to the side."

Steadman had been unable to look at Watts, but he said, "You sound as if you've got plenty of energy left."

"Don't give me that. You know you don't have long to go when people start telling you how good you look. The worst of it is that I never been sick, never even had a goddamn headache in my life—wham! It was like getting hit by a goddamn bullet. I was sitting at breakfast eating a soft-boiled egg and I thought somebody'd put a slug in me. I didn't even know what it was. Betty did. She's been reading Dr. Diddlyshit's medical advice in the newspaper for forty years just waiting for this. 'Why, Estes, I believe you're having a heart attack.'"

Steadman laughed at his grandfather's impersonation.

Watts said, "You know what? Right now I'd trade that whole bunch out there for a young woman who'd screw hell out of me. I can still get it up, ain't that a bitch?"

Steadman didn't know what to say to that boast, and after a moment Watts said, "Teddy, come back and work for me."

The appeal was almost tender, and at that moment Steadman wished he could say yes. Afraid that Watts would ask again, he said, "I can't do that."

"Why not? You worked for me once, and you loved the work. You think I couldn't see that? You were raised for it, Teddy. You been looking at land and buildings with me since you were old enough to see. There never was any thought but you'd carry on with it."

"My father might have a different idea."

"Mason. Don't let him stand in the way, but let's give the son of a bitch his due, he knows how to make money. There's room for the Accountant—and if I been able to stand having him work for me for thirty years, why couldn't you stand it?"

"I can't, Watts."

"You'd be starting out with a hell of a lot more than I had. When I started buying land around this lake, back when South Holston Reservoir was nothing but a hole in the ground, I didn't have a pot to piss in nor a window to throw it out. If I'd had a pot I would have borrowed on it. When they started filling this lake up, I made more than a pisspot full of money, I made a shitload."

"I know you did," Steadman said, smiling again.

"It's no secret. They all know it." He flung his hand toward the crowd outside. "Come back here, Teddy. Forget about Zion County. Forget about law school—you can hire all the goddamn lawyers you'll need. And if you don't want to work for your father, we'll have some fun and kick his ass out."

Steadman said, "I don't know, Watts."

"You can't stay behind a desk any more than I could. You need to be out. Hell, Teddy, I know something about you. You couldn't stand an office. You couldn't stand all the farting around that lawyers do. You couldn't stand being a parasite like a lawyer, a tick getting swole up on some dog's ass."

"I don't see how I can come back."

"Come back for the joy of it. That's all I ever did it for, not for the money—as far as that goes, I never got up there with the Rockefellers. I worked for the goddamn joy and glory of it, of seeing something happen, making it happen. You look at the land around here, Teddy, and I'm all over it. The government takes credit for

the water, but by God I did my share of the rest of it. I put out,
Teddy. I flat put out."

"I just don't want to come back here and do what you've done."

"Want? You don't know what you want. You go from one goddamn thing to the next like a dog too dumb to remember where it
buried a bone. You'll go to Zion County and scratch your ass for a
year and then you'll be sick of that. Or if you do get yourself a law
degree, which I doubt it, it won't take long for the four walls to close
in on you."

"I suppose we all have to make our own mistakes."

"Want, shit. You don't know what want is. It's a goddamn passion, that's what it is, and you're further than you ever were from
finding it. Old Injun there is better off than you are—at least he can
remember it. I'll tell you what you reminded me of yesterday, when
I saw you coming up the lawn in that glorified jock strap you call a
bathing suit, coming up all muscles and pecker with that damn gypsy
you married beside you—you reminded me of the kind of worthless
hound that never learns to go. Put him in the back of the truck with
the others and he'll try to hump 'em all, but turn him loose and the
poor bastard doesn't have an idea. Passion—the poor bastard never
finds the passion he was born for."

Steadman was standing now and looking levelly into his grandfather's blue eyes. For the first time in his life he realized that he and
Watts, who had always seemed very tall to him, were exactly the
same height. And at the end of the curse—for that's what it seemed
to him at the time—Steadman said, "We weren't all born to chase
coons."

His grandfather looked at him—and laughed in his face. "Myself,
I'm just an old coon hunter. I never thought one of my pups would
turn out a genius."

Steadman left the room enraged and humiliated, and carried on,
louder and rowdier than ever, in front of Watts's windows. He did
not mention, certainly not to Anna, and not to Betty, who asked,
what had taken place. "He's just feeling a little low," he said, and
tried to believe that himself. Watts was old, confused, and frightened, and Steadman attempted not exactly to forgive him but to
indulge him. Watts was near death, he told himself, and he had not
contradicted him out of respect for an old man's delusions. Come

back and work for him—ha! Every summer and for a year after college Steadman had worked for Watts, not long but long enough to understand that Mason, his father, was running the company. Watts made visits to the construction sites, where he expected to be received like a king. All work came to a halt while he gave audiences to the masons and carpenters and plumbers, who called him A, if they were old enough, Mister A if they weren't. Steadman gathered that his job was to be a kind of equerry. He saw too that Watts, in order to impress him, made a show of bossing Mason around. Mason —the Accountant, Watts called his son-in-law, and Steadman had joined in that derision—did not complain. Steadman admired his father for his patience and, once he grasped the scope of the company's activities, for his success. Mason had turned a small-time building and real estate operation into a formidable construction company. Steadman tried awkwardly to apologize to his father for the nuisance his presence was creating. "We're past all that, aren't we?" Mason said. At no time did Mason attempt to include him in the management of the company's real affairs, and Steadman knew that he would have to leave.

And so it was ridiculous for Watts to ask him to come back—but the insults and the judgment struck deep. Steadman had practically grown up in his grandfather's house, where he had his own room; it had always seemed a duty to visit his parents. In all that mattered most to him—the sports, the hunting and fishing—Watts was present, not his parents. As a boy Steadman had been able to see that his grandfather, who drove a big blue Chrysler and wore a big gray hat, was more than a success, he was a figure. The only way in which Steadman did not wish to emulate him was in name, for he had been given his grandfather's name, Estes Herschel. When he was mocked —not quite mocked, for he was big and strong for his age—he simply stopped answering to the name. His third-grade teacher was almost as stubborn as he was. She kept calling him Estes and kept the backs of his hands black and blue until he smashed out all the windows of her car with a baseball bat. At the conference held in the principal's office to shame him, she folded her glasses and placed them on the desk. He smashed them. His mother and father were present, but so was Watts, who said, "I guess she'd better call the boy whatever he damn well pleases. I can't keep paying for all this broken glass." Steadman loved him for that, and tried to explain to him about the names. Watts just shortened Steadman to Teddy, but Steadman felt that the change of name, even though it had been absolutely essential to him, amounted almost to a betrayal. He was aware of what the name had bestowed. Estes Herschel Watt, Jr., Watts's eldest son, a pilot, had been killed in the war. The other son, Joe, whom Steadman remembered vaguely, had simply left Bristol. Steadman did not know why but understood that it was not to be discussed. He understood, also without discussion, that he was Watts's successor. It was years before he realized that in insisting that he be called by his last name he had only copied Watts again.

At a certain point in his life, when he began to understand the enmity that Watts had succeeded in fostering between him and his father, and began to suspect the ruthlessness his grandfather was capable of, Steadman had wondered about Joe Watt. He never had the nerve to ask Watts about it. At about the same time he started falling for girls. His father, with obvious distaste for this paternal chore, advised him to try to control the biological urge. Watts told him to fuck 'em and forget 'em. Steadman's feelings were more romantic, and they put a distance between him and Watts. When Steadman went to the University of Virginia, and the distance became physical, he told his fraternity brothers stories about Watts in which the old man was a super-hillbilly, and he was pleased, when Watts did show up in Charlottesville, that his friends found him a fabulous character. Steadman knew he would survive the embarrassment of having discovered that Watts was crude, vain, self-dramatizing. He thought he was beyond the old man's power.

And when he returned to Bristol after college and worked for Watts, he was sure of it. Of course Watts had told him that he was a fool to leave Bristol, but they had another, more bitter quarrel. That was 1967, and Steadman was called by the draft board. He took to his physical exam a certificate from an eye doctor stating that he had amblyopia, a lazy eye, and as he had hoped, the Army wouldn't take him. In Watts's opinion he became a draft dodger. Watts had been a buck private in the front ranks from Château-Thierry to the Argonne Woods—"from Shadow Tree to the Woods of Oregon,"— Steadman always thought when he heard that ritual phrase, for that is the sense he made of it as a boy—and he thought draft dodgers should be deballed. Steadman, who was not sure where to go from Bristol, was astonished when Bunny Biggs, the district congressman and a crony of Watts's, got in touch with him and offered him a job as a legislative aide. Steadman went to Washington and assumed his duties, which consisted mostly of placating constituents. He liked Bunny, who was an old hand in the House and who called himself a Jeffersonian, which seemed to mean that he venerated the Constitution and that he thought anyone should consider it a blessing to be poor in America. A kind of reconciliation seemed to take place between Steadman and Watts, and when Steadman pretended to have some political ambition, Watts started calling him the Governor.

Yet a discontent had set in. This was the time when, after a spell of real cunt-chasing—he didn't know what else to call it, and he'd had enough of it—he met Anna. He was not sure why, of the twins, he'd fallen for Anna, and even after he'd made his choice he was fascinated—and frightened—by Kay. He was aware of his own solemn appetite for emotion, for elation, for ecstasy. It was the only time in his life he tried to write poems.

> *Grave the vision Venus sends*
> *Of supernatural sympathy*
> *Universal love and hope . . .*

Those were not his words but Auden's, from a poem he learned by heart and repeated to Anna. *Grave the vision*—even then he knew that his adoration of Anna partook of illusion, but he didn't know who was responsible for it, Venus or he himself.

Illusion or not, he did adore her. Quiet Anna, so diffident and skittish, revealed and entrusted herself to him, and his sense of privilege was profound. He almost believed that she became real only in his presence, a being created for his delight alone. Poor Anna, she trembled, she sometimes actually vibrated, when they lay together in the darkness. "What is it with me?" she'd ask, and he'd say, "Just nerves." When she talked, often about her childhood and about Kay, her perceptions seemed singular and acute. She told him about that language she had shared with Kay, a language made up primarily of colors. She was certain that she and Kay had seen the same opulent spectrum, and more, that their colors had denoted moods and states of feeling. "How old were you?" he asked. "One," Anna replied. He laughed, not because he doubted her but because he couldn't remember anything before the age of five. When Anna told him that her drawing, and before that her painting, was mostly an attempt to recover some of that early language, he believed her. He couldn't doubt her, not when her statement was so obviously a confession. To Anna the mere attempt seemed a presumption. Steadman confessed not to a presumption but to an ambition: he wanted to write.

When they married and Anna had Maggie, Steadman doted on them both and felt that his own life, *his* as distinct from the life that had been mapped out for him, might have begun at last. After his twenty-fifth birthday, when a trust fund came into his hands—a relief, for he believed that Watts was capable somehow of revoking it—he left Bunny Biggs and took Anna and Maggie to Europe for six months. They spent most of the time in Italy, looking at pictures and eating. Steadman also produced two stories, both of which he managed to sell after he returned and entered law school, and law school, which had demoralized him from the first day, began to seem intolerable to him. It wasn't so much his classes as his classmates, and in particular their briefcases, that he found obnoxious. One day he carried his books to class in a monstrous leather suitcase. No one commented on the joke, if it was one. Coming to law school had been a blunder, worse than a blunder, a failure of nerve. Steadman was contemptuous of himself for making it, even more contemptuous that, having made it, he did not know what to do about it— except write his book.

His book. It had a title, *The Making of the Mountain,* and it had a hero—Watts. Steadman had been writing the book since his sophomore year in college, when he was encouraged by his writing teacher, Rufus Howell, a novelist who was notorious for beating his wife and his cruelty to students. Rufus not only encouraged Steadman but took him on as a drinking pal—they got bombed regularly not at the college beer joints but in the honkytonks. And Steadman finished his book, a cracker comedy with ecstatic landscapes. That was Steadman's own description of it after two publishers returned it to him. He fooled with it now and then in Bristol and Washington, and in Europe he thought he began to see how it could be made into a wonderful book. In the first version that character based on Watts was a gusty fool; in the new book the hero would have all of Watts's power and passion. Passion—Steadman intended to use as the epigraph of his book a question from Warren's poem, *Audubon:* "What is a man but his passion?" His hero's passion would be to transform a mountain from an Appalachian slum into a land of bounty; and he would accomplish this transformation not by an infusion of federal funds but through his own ingenuity and energy, particularly the contagious energy of his delight. A fantasy, but still the only model for his hero was Watts.

Passion. Nothing could take away from the severity of Watts's last charge. Steadman had spent hours in the woods with his grandfather, and their moments together were nothing like what he'd seen on TV —the wobbly grandfather, the cane fishing pole, the plastic bobber, the sullen little shitass who won't stop pouting until his grandfather buys him the chewing gum he covets. Watts at the age of sixty could walk Steadman's legs off in the mountains, and Steadman at the age of seven, when he first went, without a gun, into the woods with Watts, had no doubt that if he did not keep up he would be left behind. His grandfather spoiled him, but not in the woods. Several times Steadman had found himself on the forest floor with a head numb from the blow he just took. "Don't you do that again, you dumb mutt," Watts would say, and Steadman wouldn't do it again. It didn't occur to Steadman to get angry. He accepted the cuffs and the abuse as the treatment he deserved in the woods. If he spooked a deer they'd stalked, or startled a wild turkey into the air after Watts had called it to them, a smarting ear was nothing to the mortification he felt. Steadman learned how to hide, how to walk, how to see, for Watts, who hardly left the mountain where he was raised until he went to war in France, underwent a feral reversion in the woods. The difference between Watts in the woods and Watts in town was apparent to Steadman, and he had a notion, confused but persistent, that these hours in the woods were the source of all his grandfather's energy. Above all else Steadman as a boy wished to be accepted by his grandfather as his equal in the woods.

Almost the only memories Steadman trusted completely were those memories of time in the woods—and Watts, who dominated those memories, told him he would never discover his passion. After that Steadman got nowhere with his book. He could ignore Watts's remark about his story, but the book seemed false, no longer a fantasy but a farce. His passion, if he had one at all, was to write; he loved language and books, loved especially stories, and knew that when he believed in his own writing he was capable of a rapt concentration he would have called passion. Now—because of Watts, he thought—he did not believe in it. That summer he was alone in the apartment during the mornings, for Anna went to a studio and Maggie was at a day care center, but almost the only report he could give of his hours was that he watched the potted tomato plant on the concrete balcony wither in the exhaust of the air conditioner. In August it finally died, apparently of the effort to bring forth two fruits as hard and shriveled as walnuts.

He did not know what to do.

And he thought of the Argenstill place. Harry Obenwald had told him it might be for sale when he went to Zion County in May to fish, and he looked at the place. He went back again—to fish again, he told Anna, and mentioned the Argenstill place in the most offhand way. In August, after that meeting with Watts, he went back a third time and walked over the property. He did not feel covetous; he regarded the place as something he'd already lost. At the end of August he asked Anna to look at it with him, but he didn't expect her to like it. She hardly opened her mouth as she followed Mrs. Argenstill through the house and outbuildings. "What do you think?" he had to ask her as they walked down the slope from the house. Anna hiked up her shoulders, wedged her hands into the pockets of her jeans. "It's kind of rundown, isn't it?" And then she said helplessly, as if the words had slipped out by accident, "It's terrible." And she ran down to the bridge to keep Maggie from trying to cross by herself.

On the other side of the bridge Maggie came upon something in the road and fled back to her parents. Steadman took a small grim satisfaction that she ran to him, not Anna, for protection. Frightened, panicky, Maggie was able to say that she'd seen a snake. "Oh God," Anna said.

Steadman insisted on carrying Maggie back to where she'd seen it. She squirmed up onto his shoulder but she pointed out her serpent right in the middle of the dusty road—an ordinary wriggling earthworm.

"That's just fish bait, sweetie," he said to Maggie, and tried to make her laugh with the rhyme. "The worms crawl in, the worms crawl out, the worms play pinochle on your snout."

But he blamed Anna for Maggie's exaggeration of a worm into a snake. When he first knew Anna he'd tried to take her to the woods, but she couldn't conceal her apprehension. And that apprehension showed not only in the woods; her heightened perception, he'd come to believe, was nothing but apprehension. She was just scared of things, and she was so inward and passive that her fears were all magnified and distorted. Even in Italy, among the sites she has always expressed a longing to see, Anna was subdued to the point of torpor. Steadman ordered their meals and booked their rooms in his meager phrase-book Italian, for Anna was too self-conscious to speak. One afternoon, after a woman in their pensione had shrieked at Steadman—for leaving the door unlocked, it turned out, but Anna was too pained by the scene to explain that to him until they were back in their room—he lost his temper. He let her have it—a zombie, he called her—and she walked unsteadily to the bed, where she lay down and hid her face in the pillow. For a time after that he tried to apologize by being affectionate, but he couldn't disguise—either from her or from himself—his disappointment in her.

That summer in Charlottesville the disappointment turned into disgust. Her habits, even her appearance, repelled him. Anna had large dark eyes with a rim of white showing under the iris—sanpaku, she called this, and once told him that it was supposed to be a sign of estrangement. He suspected that she was proud of this condition. She had quirks that had come to strike Steadman as deliberate. She couldn't eat—that is, she couldn't sit down and eat a normal meal. She liked to think of herself as being in a perpetual fast, and she nibbled nuts, raisins, figs in amounts that were small enough not to break the fast. Her chief nourishment seemed to be her own fingernails and cuticles. If she ate a piece of meat she was sure to make some remark about the disturbance to her chemistry. She had a skulking, furtive walk—had she walked into a wall, her shoulder would have hit it first—as if she had never adjusted to being visible.

She came home from the studio with compulsive designs drawn in ink on the back of her hands. She was forever checking her pulse as if that was the only way she could verify that she was alive. So the heightened perceptions were just apprehension and these distasteful habits, her wierdnesses, as she had once called them.

That August was probably the worst month of Steadman's life. Every movement Anna made, every word she spoke, offended him. He couldn't stand her mumbling, her skulking, her messiness. She never picked up her clothes, and he made a pile of her dirty laundry in the front hall. She just stepped around it and didn't notice it until Maggie pointed it out to her. The kitchen was a mess, always a mess; Anna didn't eat and couldn't cook either. Her ideas of housekeeping were as primitive as a starling's. She did make one effort: she bought some kind of urinal cake and hung it in the toilet tank, but she couldn't stand the blue it turned the water. So she removed it and left it sitting in a wad of toilet paper on the windowsill in the bathroom. A blue stain like a fungus was spreading down the tile. Steadman wouldn't touch it; he was waiting to see how long it would take Anna to notice it. During this month before law school opened again, Steadman hardly spoke to Anna and was conscious of her watching him—watching him, he thought, the way a grouse, crippled but not killed by the shot that has knocked it out of the air, watched.

Kay came to visit. She slept on the big sofa out in the living room, and Steadman, in bed late at night, heard her and Anna talking and laughing. He couldn't sleep. When Anna still hadn't come to bed at two o'clock he slammed out of the bedroom to fix himself a drink. "Come to join us?" said Kay, who had on nothing but her panties and who did not bother to try to cover herself. He glared at her righteously. She laughed at him and said to Anna, who hung her head, "I guess hubby's on the rag." And after Kay had left, Steadman asked Anna, "Do you still speak the same language? Still see those fabulous colors? I'll bet Kay sees them, with all that speed she's doing." Anna just looked at him but he couldn't stop. "It was never a language. It was the opposite of a language. It was a fucking hallucination." Anna edged away from him, moving backwards, bumping into things. He realized that she was afraid he was going to hit her.

His dog was run over. The dog wasn't much more than a puppy, a pointer given to him by Watts when he moved to Charlottesville a year ago. Watts had named the dog Zack, short for 'zackly, because the pup looked exactly like his sire. Steadman, driving home after registering for his classes, found Zack on the road near the entrance to the apartment complex. His hips were completely smashed and his guts were all out of him, but he wasn't dead. He tried to rise when he recognized Steadman. Cursing and weeping, Steadman picked up a rock and threw it at the next car that passed. The car stopped. Steadman was kneeling beside Zack and stroking the pup's head when a woman in boots and jodhpurs walked up to him. After a moment she said, "It's your dog?"

"What do you think, you fucking idiot?"

"He's done for," she said. "I have a pistol in my car."

"Well, bring it to me."

And there at the roadside Steadman blew out Zack's brains, the only act of charity he seemed to be capable of. The woman patted him on the shoulder as he stood there weeping. "I've had to do it to horses," she said. "You'll be okay."

In his mood Steadman blamed Anna for letting Zack out when traffic was heavy. He couldn't help it. He knew how unjust it was and knew that something terrible would happen if things kept on this way, and so he stayed away from the apartment. Classes had begun, and he tried to work in the library at night. Sometimes he went to drink with Rufus, whose wife had left him. One night an undergraduate student of Rufus' turned up, a blond girl who smoked dope while they drank. Her hair was parted in the middle and fell over her face, leaving a clear space not much wider than her nose. Now and then Rufus noticed her and told her she looked as if she was in an all-but-nasal purdah. She evidently expected to sleep with Rufus but he passed out cheerfully in the midst of a diatribe against Airstream trailers. Steadman and the girl didn't move for a few minutes, and then he groped. When her clothes were off she actually said, "Please be tender," but he fucked her anyway.

Next afternoon he went straight home after classes and played with Maggie. She asked him where he'd been all night but Anna didn't. After Anna put Maggie to bed, she did ask him if he was going to stay home that night. "I thought maybe if you were I'd go to a movie. I just feel like getting out for a change."

"Sure, I'll be here. What movie are you going to?"

"I don't know. Maybe *Women in Love.*"

He said, "Why don't you read the book? Then you might understand it."

The pause then was awful and dangerous. Steadman thought that one more word from either of them could make it all come apart. But Anna just said, "I guess I'll go, then."

And when she was gone, when the door shut behind her, Steadman went down on his knees and rocked back and forth with his head bowed. He knew, after all, this hatred was something in him, not in her.

The next day he went to Zion County and went fishing in the St. Margaret's River. He drove along Prussian Creek but did not stop at the Argenstill place. He fished a tumbling stretch of water just above the village of Silesia, beneath the bluffs of Little Furnace, and he stayed on the water till dark. He stopped in the Silesia store for a Dr. Pepper. The usual men were there; Steadman knew some of them by name, and they knew him as the friend of Harry Obenwald's who was interested in the Argenstill place. One of them, a man named Other Byrd, told Steadman that Lulu had found her treasure at last. Steadman, by then, knew that she believed her husband had hidden money from her. A real estate agent had been calling on her. On his way home that night Steadman stopped at the Obenwalds' to ask if they knew anything about it. They'd seen the man's car but didn't know if Lulu was going to list her property. Steadman crossed the swinging bridge and called on Lulu herself, and she told him that the real estate agent, Glenn Swink, had bought the place from her for $30,000. No, she hadn't got the money yet, only $500 of it, and hadn't signed the papers. Steadman knew exactly what was going on. Swink was going to resell the place in his own name for whatever he could get and pocket any amount over $30,000. He did not try to explain this to Lulu, who regarded Swink as her benefactor. He had promised to take her to her sister's in Harrisonburg.

The next morning from Charlottesville Steadman made a few phone calls and found out that Swink had a reputation as a widow swindler. He decided to buy the place. He went to Harrisonburg and spent two days trying to convince Lulu that she was being cheated by Swink and that it wasn't illegal to sell to him. He failed, but he hired a lawyer who did convince her by drawing up an agreement of sale for $33,000. The amount was a little less than half of what remained in Steadman's trust. Mrs. Argenstill promised to say nothing of the transaction. Then Steadman read the Staunton paper, waiting for Swink's ad to appear. He had never met Swink, whose motto was *When you think property, think Swink,* but he became familiar with the man's prose, and Swink outdid himself in the ad for the Argenstill place.

PARADISE LOST

can be yours! Peace is the theme of this picturesque property majestically nestled in the mountain kingdom of Zion County. 94 acres of mature timber specimens and undulating bluegrass meadows in the breeze, fronting on one of Virginia's unspoiled crystal streams, commanding views and outbuildings. The house is the traditional L-shaped home with porch of the family's who settled this rugged land awaiting the tasteful hand of restoration. A property truly worthy of the discriminating buyer who hearkens to the call of nature.

Steadman read that with satisfaction, phoned Swink, and set a time to meet. He couldn't have asked for a better day: a harsh, gray, chilly October rain was falling. He took Anna and Maggie along with him, for they were necessary to his plan. Swink had invited them to lunch at the most garish restaurant in Staunton, and Swink himself was exactly the kind of organism Steadman expected. Slimy, overweight, dressed to kill, he exuded self-complacency as if he were equipped with a special gland to secrete it. After lunch Anna did her bit; she refused to ride over the mountains in Swink's car because it did not have a child's safety seat. Steadman, who knew well enough that to characters like Swink the car is the great totem, had tried to act enthusiastic during the meal so that Swink would fear the loss of a quick sale if he didn't consent to ride in his client's car. Swink did consent. Steadman drove west, over Big Furnace, through Barger's Mill, into Prussian Creek Gorge. It was pouring. Swink, he'd noticed with pleasure, was wearing no raincoat and cheap greenish loafers. He stopped the car in the wildest part of the gorge. There wasn't a house for miles. He showed Swink a copy of the agreement of sale he and Lulu had signed. He waited for the facts to sink in. He watched Swink gulp and flush. And then—he put the bastard out. He put him out in the middle of Prussian Creek Gorge and left him wallowing there in the downpour.

Maggie was the first one in the car to speak. "He's going to get wet."

And Steadman began to laugh. He had been tense during the little drama he'd arranged, but it had gone off perfectly and he began to laugh. It was all over now, all over and done, and he laughed till Maggie and Anna joined in, laughed till he had to stop because he couldn't see to drive. His eyes were all fogged with tears, and his face was running with them, and Anna was watching him with concern.

And after all the business of clearing out of Charlottesville—breaking the lease on the apartment, trying to get his money back from the law school, making the bankers let go of the money in the trust, all the packing and cleaning—and moving into the Argenstill place, he found he still hadn't finished that laugh. There was a place he and Maggie found on the slope in front of the house where they got a magnificent echo from Big Furnace. "Uffizi," Steadman would roar, and the mountain roared back, "UFFIZI IZI IZI IZI." "Piero della Francesca." The mountain had trouble with that one. "Dr. Pepper." "DR. PEPPER EPPER EPPER." And Maggie: "Me!" "ME ME ME ME." The mountain would say whatever they commanded it to say, but the sound it reproduced with most gusto and with absolute fidelity in the clear winter air was the sound of laughter. Steadman's ho ho ho's sprang off the mountain like tumblers off a trampoline, and Maggie's more delicate notes plucked it like a harp. They got into the habit of calling the echo Hector Protector, after the hero in one of Maggie's books.

Anna didn't call on Hector, but she stood by while they did and seemed to be amused by the ruckus. Steadman knew how hard the move would be for her, but since that first night in the house when she had promised to try, he had been moved by her willingness. When she came down from an afternoon of scraping or sanding, her hair all flecked, spitting sawdust out of her mouth, he wanted to thank her—but didn't quite know how to, since his thanks were for the past and not for the present only. At times he stopped whatever he was doing in the house and listened to her; he liked to hear the sound of her overhead, the boards under her feet, the eternal scraper in her hand, her fragmentary conversations with Maggie. These seemed to be in the very walls of the house, and listening to them was like dreaming. Steadman knew that he was inclined to swamp Maggie with talk, but Anna deferred to her. Sometimes Maggie's voice had an assertive tone as she told Anna what was what, and Anna would reply, "I guess so," or "That's a pretty good idea." Maggie regarded these conversations as confidential, for if Steadman interrupted one of them she put a hand over her mouth and looked guiltily at Anna. And at times Steadman caught glimpses of Anna— the straight nose, the cast of the cheek against the black hair, the habitual gesture of her hands that looked like the turning of a knob and left her palms cupped and open—when she seemed so much herself, so finished and complex, that any emotions he felt toward her were for a second held in abeyance. She was simply present, and it was enough to see her. The emotion that usually followed such a moment was something like shame, for he did not forget how these same glimpses of his, gestures of hers, had galled. And still, sometimes, galled, though his revenging pettiness seemed to be over. He knew, anyway, that the effort he had expected to have to make here in Zion County was hardly an effort at all. There was no housekeeping yet, and he did most of the cooking; and suddenly he and Anna, whose two subjects of conversation in Charlottesville had been Maggie and dinner, had more than they could talk about. The weather, the woods, Xanaduc, the Obenwalds, their neighbors, their house —of course it was all new, but there were moments when this ordinary domestic palaver struck him as miraculous.

They were together in this new place, and now, with mountains on either side of him, he was content to stay home. As a boy the month of November, when the hunting seasons opened, had been the climax of the year, and later, at college and in Washington, when he couldn't get to the woods very often, he began every fall, as Glenn Swink put it, to hearken to the call of nature. The days he did spend in the woods, because they had to stand for the whole season, were exhausting binges. Now, though he still knocked himself out with his long walks, he waited for the good days. The mountains would be there tomorrow. And he did less hunting than walking: these mountains were not familiar to him, certainly not in winter, for he'd come to Zion County mostly in the summer and mostly for the fishing. He was exploring, really, and his hikes gave him what he was after, the freedom of the mountains. It was something to stand on a ridge and know that his legs would carry him to any place that his eyes could see. And it was something to realize that the one fixed point in that domain he was marking off with his legs and eyes, the center to which he always returned, was the house that contained his wife and daughter.

December, their first month. Steadman felt that he was just learning his way in a new place, and he did not want to leave it. That trip to Bristol to face his grandfather was more than he wanted to risk just then. He had fulfilled Watts's prophecies, quit law school and bought the Argenstill place, and he supposed that he was due for another curse at Christmas. This one he was braced for.

In Bristol it took only minutes for him to see that Watts had changed. He looked slack, smaller, even shrunken. He was wearing his formal blue suit and there was hardly enough of him to fill it—Watts, who'd always filled a room with his presence, didn't even fill his suit. At first Steadman felt a relief that was almost comic, felt like a cartoon character who charges with all his might at a door that suddenly opens and sends him sprawling. But after the greetings, after the bags had been brought in, after a few minutes of conversation, Steadman realized that he had braced for the wrong thing. His grandfather was going to die. He stared at Watts with helpless, horrified fascination; until that moment he had never really succeeded in believing that Watts was old, and now he was dying.

For all his staring it was difficult at first to focus on the changes. This man before him was so different from the Watts he remembered that he could have been an impostor. For one thing, he was sitting. He sat in a wing chair in the living room, his hands inert on his thighs, his posture studied, as if a small effort of determination was needed to keep him from slumping. Steadman could not remember Watts sitting. He was standing, always, and moving, and his hands were in motion, thumping and whacking whoever he was talking to. And he was always talking too, not nodding as he was now, nodding at Steadman's and Betty's commonplaces about the weather and the drive down to Bristol. He did not seem to be listening particularly, just nodding; his attention, once so outward and overflowing, was now entirely inward. He did ask a few abrupt questions, one about the Blazer, another about the house in Zion County, but when Steadman replied he had nothing more to say. He seemed almost to forget that there were others in the room, talking around him. Once when Maggie was near him he was about to reach for her; he lifted his hand an inch from his trousers and it began to shake. The movement toward Maggie stopped. He watched his hand as if it was not his own and returned it to his trousers. Then for a moment he did look at the others to see if they had noticed; his eye met Steadman's, and Steadman turned away.

Later that afternoon Watts took a nap, and Steadman had a chance to talk to Betty. Yes, he was weaker, Betty said, but the doctors didn't know why. They had done several tests; they thought there might be a blood disease. "He's just not himself," she said, but Steadman saw, as she moved about in her kitchen, that she was going to carry on as if he were.

That night, Christmas Eve, some of the family came out to the lake house to sing carols. Steadman's parents were there, of course, and his sister, Carol and her husband, Billy, and all of Watts's brothers and sisters and their families, and some of Betty's people. Watts came out and sat in the wing chair. There was a piano in the room, which Betty played; there had always been a moment when Watts said, "Limber your fingers, Betty, and let's get the singing over with." And then the music would be handed out and Watts would say, "When it comes to music I'm about like Robert E. Lee. I don't know but two tunes, and one is 'Dixie' and the other ain't." But they all knew that he had a strong true voice and that they'd damn well better pipe up themselves.

This year the signal was not given. The time for it came, and Betty stood near the piano bench, where she was asked about her stiff fingers. Some of the children already had their sheets of music. Watts's youngest brother, Clem, asked if Watts had practiced any or if he was going to croak the way he usually did. Finally Steadman's mother, Jane, said to him, "Daddy? Daddy, we need you to lead the carols."

Watts looked bewildered for a second, and then, with a memory of his old force, he said, "What the hell's the matter with the rest of you?"

And so Jane led them and Watts never left his chair. And though nothing could have been more foreign to her, she tried to imitate Watts's spirit and bluster. She was a large woman, but self-effacing; for years she had taught in a school for the handicapped, and she had been among blind children so much that she had copied their movements. As she led the singing, her hands, like theirs, floated through the air in motions both wayward and sensitive, looking as if they could have detected and held a shadow.

In bed that night Steadman said to Anna, "My mother did well, didn't she?"

"Yes," Anna said.

"You did too. You must be getting used to my family."

"Well, I've figured out that they're talking to me when they say *Anner.*"

"You're going to have to come up with something new to tell Carol. You can't tell her every time you see her that she has a new hairdo."

"It's always true," Anna said.

Steadman smiled. In the dark room he could hear Maggie, asleep, stirring. "Visions of sugarplums," he said.

"Steadman, it's pretty bad with Watts, isn't it?"

"It looks that way."

"Oh Steadman, I'm so sorry," she said, and he turned to her.

In the morning Maggie shredded open her presents in such an orgy of greed that she had to be admired. The other presents were just merchandise, all but one, Watts's gift to Steadman. The moment he lifted the long slender package, wrapped in brown paper and tied with a string, he knew that it was a gun. It was not in a box but in a new sheepskin case, and Steadman said, "I hope the gun isn't this fancy. This case is enough." "Open it," Watts said. Steadman did, and he had the gun unsheathed before he recognized it. It had been blued, and the stock had been refinished, but it was Watts's Stirlingsworth, the one gun Watts had never swapped or traded.

"Don't hold it like a goddamn baseball bat."

"You shouldn't give this to me."

"You'll get more use out of it than I will. It wasn't made to hang on a wall."

Steadman looked at the gun, the colored lights of the tree reflected in the deep luster of the barrels. He opened the breech,
closed it again, heard the tight delicate *chock!* The dark burl of the
walnut, the silver knuckles of the breech, the clean taper of the
barrels, the balance and solidity of the thing—it was no gift but a
legacy.

He did not try to thank Watts until that night. The day was slow
and dreary enough, and the meal, in the silence Watts created, was
awful; Steadman heard, and was sure everyone else heard, every
clank of knife and fork on the china, every shiver of ice in the water
glasses, every swish of the stockings of the burly corseted woman
who served and cleared. Halfway through the meal Steadman
started to spout, knowing that he sounded like Watts, knowing that
he could not bring it off—but it was better than the silence. He
talked about Zion County of course, about the legendary mountain
men with names like Forty-Four Hammer and Cub Gwin, about deer
and grouse and turkeys, about his own struggles with plumbing. At
one point his father turned to Anna and asked, with a dour attempt
at humor, "Do you share this rural bliss?"

"It's not exactly bliss," she said, and looked across the table at
Steadman. "It's not—well, it's not quite that bouncy."

And so they got through the meal—*bouncy,* Steadman kept thinking, and it made him smile every time—and that night Steadman
found Watts alone in the gun room. They talked for a while about
dogs. Steadman wanted Watts to advise him about a dog to replace
Zack. Watts was diffident and distracted. Steadman tried to joke
about his shooting.

"Still can't hit a grouse?" Watts said.

"I can't hit anything with feathers on it. Maybe I'll do better
now."

"That Stirlingsworth shoots straight, Teddy."

"I'll take care of it."

"You goddamn well better."

"Thank you, Watts," Steadman said, and then he blurted out, "I
hope you'll forgive me."

For just a moment Watts gathered all his wavering, uncertain
attention. "Forgive? That's not in my line." That seemed to be all
he had to say, but he added, "It would be strange not to forgive."

Then they talked about dogs again.

Steadman left the next morning. When the bags were packed, and all the Christmas loot was in the Blazer, he went back into the house to find Maggie. She was in the gun room, on Watts's lap. "Time to leave," Steadman said. Watts gave her a kiss and Maggie came. Steadman, still at the door, was about to enter to say good-bye, but Watts rose from the sofa and stood with his back to Steadman. His jacket was off; against the window, Steadman saw the tawny, lucent outline of white sleeves, white shoulders, white hair. "Go on, Teddy," Watts said, not harshly. "Go on now."

They had been on the highway for an hour when Maggie said, "Sometimes Watts is very sad," and Steadman realized that his grandfather had turned away because he was crying.

Four

New Year's Eve. They were invited to a party at Xanaduc. They received an invitation that someone had taken the trouble to write out in florid script in sepia ink: Gala at the Feelgood Lounge.

Anna didn't know what to wear, and when she went to the Oben-walds' barn and poked through the suitcases still over there, Stead-man kidded her about having a little crisis of vanity. It wasn't exactly vanity, Anna thought; she'd been in enough life classes, and studied enough heads and bodies, to have a pretty good idea of her own. Her face was narrow and rather long, and all her features were too big. They didn't match either; her eyes were round, her nose long and straight, her mouth long but full. She had too much jaw and not enough forehead. Her torso, even though she was thin and didn't have much of a chest—Steadman's whole hand almost fit between her breasts—was thick through the ribs. Her arms and legs were disproportionately long; she was fairly tall, and all her height was in her legs. As for her extremities—well, she'd ruined her hands with her nibbling and her feet were like a monkey's. She had dark skin and hair, and Steadman had once told her that she looked like a Modigliani—and he was right, but she didn't take it as a compliment.

All the same Anna knew that she was not ugly and she knew that people noticed her, and she worried about her clothes. She did not dress to attract attention but to prevent it. She had boxes full of iridescent blouses and dresses that her mother had bought her and she'd never worn. Her usual outfit was jeans or other drab trousers and some kind of sweater or plain top. And shoes—she did not relate to shoes. They all looked like little caskets to her. She was thankful that in Zion County everyone wore boots. When she had to get dressed up she usually wore a black sweater with one of her two pairs of good pants. One pair was dark green, the other brown, and she thought they were both too tight across the ass. Her only pair of good shoes, plain brown with low heels, she bought in a thrift shop years ago. She did not wear makeup, though her mother screamed at her that she ought to do something about the circles under her eyes. She did not wear much jewelry either, no rings or bracelets.

On New Year's Eve she put on the brown pants and she fastened a silver chain with a pendant around the neck of the black sweater. She felt a little peculiar dressing that way in the unfurnished house by the light of a single lamp on the floor, and after a month in boots and work clothes—she even wore long underwear, for she was susceptible to cold—the getup felt as flimsy as tissue. But Blanche Hammer, the widow who'd come to baby-sit—Steadman had called her, for Anna was reluctant to ask someone she didn't know, and he'd brought her across the ford to eat dinner with them so she could talk to Maggie before bedtime—told her she looked real pretty, and Anna was pleased. She found herself wishing that Steadman would say something too.

When she walked into the house at Xanaduc, she felt like one big rhinestone. Denim, corduroy, flannel—everybody there looked as if they'd just come in from the barn. One of them whistled at her. "Real uptown," Val said to her, "that's real uptown." She was introduced to people—Stan, who was beautiful in an ideal, vacant way; Rod, who had a black beard with hairs as straight and stiff as porcupine quills; a man with a frizzy ponytail; a woman with a shiny face; two or three more, but she didn't get the names straight. The hugest dog she'd ever seen—a wolfhound, somebody said—wandered up and sniffed her. It had a bristly reddish muzzle, and its name was Marx. And then she went into another room, where she was glad to see Diana Obenwald in a long skirt and gold shoes. "You two are at the same party anyway," Harry said. Laurie too was wearing a long skirt, plain gray wool but long, and Zep had on a blue military jacket with epaulets. Anna felt a little better.

She sat down on a straight chair and talked to Diana for a few minutes, mostly about Blanche Hammer. She noticed that food had been put out around the room, a few loaves of fresh bread, some cheese, vegetables. The music—Jimmy Buffet, then cowboy songs by somebody Zep called The Great Wailin'—was very loud. The sound equipment looked like a miniature airport throbbing with blue and yellow lights. There were shelves sagging under the weight of records. In one corner of the room there was an iron bed, and on it there was a person who had not moved since Anna sat down. Steadman was talking to Harry about the hubs on the Blazer. Laurie was talking to Diana about lambs. There were two other people in the room sitting down and not talking. Zep was present but not sitting; he moved a lot and said the movement was gatoring. Anna noticed obscene objects placed here and there. Next to one of the loaves of bread was something that looked like another loaf but turned out to be a large plastic hot dog bun containing a large plastic hot dog smeared with yellow plastic mustard. On the mantel stood a moldy stuffed owl wearing panties and a plaster cast of an erect penis with a pair of red wax lips stuck to it. And on the floor next to the cast-iron stove was the most gigantic shoe Anna had ever seen, a wing-tipped cordovan, a real shoe about three feet long, and there was a carnival Kewpie doll lying in it with her head propped up on a tiny lace-edged pillow. It gave Anna the willies. She sat there for a half hour or so waiting for the party to begin—and then she realized it had begun.

"So how do you like the Feelgood Lounge?" Zep said to her, or somebody, and gatored across the room again. Anna gathered that he considered himself a kind of host or doorman.

"This is Zep's—creation, I guess you'd call it," Laurie said.

Anna didn't seem to have to comment.

"I got an idea," Harry said. "Let's read the phone book."

Anna thought that was one of the funniest things she'd ever heard, even though it turned out that Harry meant it. He went somewhere and came back with a Zion County phone book that was no thicker than a comic book, and he and Zep and Steadman carried on about

names. Duty Armstrong. Other Byrd. Anna had thought Steadman
was kidding when he told her that such a person existed. He was
now pretending to be Mrs. Byrd looking at her son, her eighth son,
and trying to come up with a name. Olin? Glavis? Kermit? Delbert?
None of these would do, for she'd already given a son that name.
She wracked her brains but all the names were taken. And so she
gave up and just called this one Other. Anna could tell that Steadman
was beginning to feel the bourbon he'd brought. He didn't care
much for dope—low energy, he called it—and he'd stoked himself
with a couple of huge drinks.

"Other is the watchdog of Prussian Creek," Harry said. "He
knows more about my place than I do."

Anna hadn't spoken to Other yet, but she'd seen him, always saw
him, driving back and forth along the road to Silesia. Several times
he'd passed her while she was at the mailbox. She asked, "Does he
always scowl?"

Zep said, "If bullshit was music, Other would be a brass band."

"That's his natural expression," Harry said. "When he just
frowns, he's grinning."

"I know what you mean," Diana said. "I was scared to death of
him at first. I thought he was going to gobble me up—"

"That would be quite a meal," Harry said.

Diana looked at Harry and batted her lashes at a prodigious rate.
"Please. No comments about my figure."

Then she and Anna fell into a conversation about Other and his
wife, Mavis, who, Diana said, was just a real nice friendly country
girl. Anna knew that Other and Mavis had the only child on Prussian
Creek, a little girl named Hope, who was anywhere near Maggie's
age, and she said she supposed she should try to get them together.
Diana offered to take her to call on Mavis.

Harry continued to read in the phone book. "Bland Bedwell
. . . Lucius Cakes . . . Dewey Delano Deel . . ."

But Harry wasn't forceful enough as a showman, and Zep and
Steadman were too wound up to wait for him to read through the
columns. "What about you, Zep? Are you in the book?"

"Fuckin A. I'm under Xanaduc. We gotta get one of those multi-
ple listings."

"How'd you get that name? Is Zep an alias?"

"Trim Eagle," Harry read. "René Eye."

"Named myself," Zep said. "Looked in the mirror, a full-length mirror, till I had an inspiration—Zeppelin. It just came to me." He was large and lozenge-shaped.

"That's how the Indians did it," Zep said. "They waited to see how the kid turned out before they hung a name on him. And what names—dynamite! Sitting Fucking Bull. Hiafuckingwatha. Geronifuckingmo." Zep was gatoring as he spoke the names.

"They all had the same middle name?" Laurie asked.

Zep had a jovial fat man's laugh that sounded as if it might be cultivated.

"Jess Folks," Harry read.

"That's not true," Steadman said.

"Here it is in the book. Call him up and ask him. And listen to this one—Please Ginger."

"Hey, what about you, Steadman?" Zep yelled. "What's this bullshit about initials? E. H. Steadman—are you a fugitive from a bank?"

"Yeah."

"Come on, what's the *E* for? Let's hear it."

"Estes."

"Estes! Es-tess, Es-tess!" Zep roared. Uh-oh, Anna thought.

"Man, that one came straight out of the coon's ass, didn't it? What about the *H*?"

"Horace Howdyshell," Harry read.

"Herschel."

"Too much, too fucking much. Es-tess Her-shell. Oh fuck, that just wipes me out. Es-tess Fuck-ing Her-shell." Zep got into a bebop routine to go with his chanting.

"That's why I don't use the name."

"Why's that, Es-tess?"

"Because it makes assholes like you hysterical."

Anna heard that Steadman tried to sound like he was joking, and Zep was too tuned to take it otherwise. "It makes your feathers fall, huh, Es-tess?"

"What about my name?" Anna said. "It ought to qualify."

"Anna?" Diana asked.

"No, my maiden name—let Steadman say it. He gets a bang out of it."

And Steadman said Chicken-birdy, and Zep flapped around the room, and Anna spelled her name for Laurie and Diana, and dogged Harry kept reading, "Ferry Huff . . . Israel Hurt . . ."

Laurie asked Anna how she was making out, and they talked for a while. Anna knew she made it sound as if Steadman had dragged her to Zion County, and she was glad he was talking to Zep. Anna asked about Xanaduc, and Laurie volunteered information readily enough. Other people had come into the Feelgood Lounge by now, but only five people lived at Xanaduc: Stan, the beautiful one, was Laurie's old man; Rod, the prickly one, was Val's; Zep didn't have a mate. The motionless person on the bed was Stewie, who had lived there for a while but didn't have a country head, and the girl with the shiny face was Sue, Stewie's new old lady who'd come down with him from Philly for the holidays. They were all from Philly, but Laurie had gone to college at Hollins, and when they started to get their earth trip together they came to Virginia, since that was the place Laurie and Stan knew.

Anna was listening, but she heard Zep and Steadman too; they were talking about writing. Zep was describing a novel he wanted to write, a story about a missionary fur trapper who deals drugs to the Eskimos, and she heard Steadman say, "Writing's getting very democratic now, the national pastime." So he was still peeved.

"Guyotha Liptrap . . . Lert Lotz."

"It took us a while to get it together," Laurie said. Anna noticed that language—earth trip, country head—and thought Steadman was sure to make a crack about it. But she heard that Laurie put the slightest droll emphasis on these phrases. Laurie's face didn't show anything; it was all broad open planes. Laurie had very light gray eyes and a way of glancing with them that Anna recognized—she didn't like to get caught looking. She told Anna about the trouble they'd had buying Xanaduc—and she and Stan put up the money, Anna gathered—from the scattered heirs. A family named Heitz had lived there, one of the old German families who'd settled Prussian Creek, but the last ones were loonies. The man's name was Carl, but they called him Digger because he had a thing about the creek—the fields there were low and he spent his time building dikes to keep the water out of them. Well, there was a flood and Digger tried to save his dikes and got washed away.

"Made a meal for those big catfish in the James," Zep interrupted.

"That's what they say around here," Laurie said. "They never found him anyway."

"What the fuck is this?" Harry exclaimed. "Mazroor Kizelbash."

So Digger's widow, Mad Maud, stayed on the place, and when the creek got up she'd walk along the bank with her lantern looking for Digger. Around here there was a superstition about drowning, something about the ghost getting out of the body in the water. Anyway, Maud's kids all left, and Maud started keeping her animals in the house with her. Talk about a mess—Anna should have seen Xanaduc when they moved in. And poor old Mad Maud died in the house, and her pets ate most of her before they found her.

"How can you live here? What a terrible story."

"It's not much worse than your place," Laurie said.

"Haven't you seen the ghost yet?" Zep said, and made haunting noises.

"What ghost?"

"Old Lulu used to see it."

"Arlie's ghost?"

"That's what she said. That's what she told Blanche Hammer."

"But Blanche is there tonight with Maggie."

Laurie did look at her then. "Do you believe in this stuff?"

"Gideon Meek . . . Smoky Nipper."

Diana said, "Those old people really had an imagination. Have you heard the twins screech yet?"

"The twins?"

"Oh, I forgot—you're a twin, aren't you?"

"Far fucking out," Zep said.

"It's a real old story," Diana said. "Lulu told me—she said she didn't believe it, you know. With me she always acted like she was above those superstitions. She thought they weren't respectable."

"What about the twins?"

"I can't even remember now. One of them killed the other one, I think. What is that story, Harry?"

"He shot him. That's all I know."

"Anyway, they say there's a screech up there sometimes that's supposed to be one of the twins. And sometimes you do hear something screech, but Harry says it's a bobcat."

"It is a bobcat."

"When did all this happen?"

"Oh, a long time ago, I think."

"Where's Steadman?" Anna looked around, but he'd left the room. "I never heard about this."

"Last one," Harry said. "No, last two. Buford Scaboo and Selah Sweet. What a place." He closed the book.

Soon after that Laurie went out of the room and Sue came in and took her place. Anna tried to talk to her but she was stoned, like Stewie on the bed. Anna had actually seen him move once or twice when a reefer traveled in his direction. And she was glad to be next to Diana, for Diana made a face as if she had ka-ka on her nose every time a joint was passed to her, and Anna didn't feel that she had to take a hit either. She had smoked plenty of dope at one time, when she didn't mind what it did to her. But it did shake her up, as all pills or chemicals and even some foods did, and she just didn't want that now. Then Val came and spoke to her for a while and she saw that she was in for a serious conversation. Val had learned from Diana that Anna drew and that she had majored in art history, and she wanted to talk about pictures. Zep had the music, reggae now, up as loud as it would go. Anna could hardly hear. "I don't draw much now," she said, "not with Maggie."

"Yeah, that can be a real bummer," Val said, but that wasn't how Anna meant it. Then Val wanted to talk about Georgia O'Keeffe, whose pictures Anna didn't much like. She thought the distortion in them was too calculated, but she said she didn't know much about her. Val was wearing a scarf on her head; it was tied so that it rose from her eyebrows and went back like a huge domed forehead. Anna kept thinking of dolphins. They talked about other coffee-table artists for a while, and Anna felt stingy and snobbish; she just didn't believe that Val had connected with any of the pictures she mentioned. Anna worked the conversation around to some of the painters she liked, and felt pretentious when she said Mondrian was trying to catch light in his grids; light collected in all the corners, she said, like frost on the windowpanes. "Far out," Val said, and when Zep passed out the noisemakers and turned on the radio to the countdown in Times Square, she said, "This has been real neat. We'll have to rap some more."

At this point the Feelgood Lounge contained, Anna guessed, just about everybody in Zion County who smoked dope. Steadman had never come back into the room, and Anna wished he would when Zep reminded them that the ladies were expected to put out on the stroke of midnight. He took down the plaster penis with the wax lips and waved it around. "Can you dig it, ladies? Can you dig it?" Anna didn't imagine that anyone took Zep very seriously, but when he said to Sue, "Am I going to get a feel of those big knockers?" she roused from her trance and put her arms across her chest and with great wrath said her first words of the night, "Not on your fucking life."

In Times Square and in the Feelgood Lounge there was a hullabaloo as a new year began, and just then Harry came into the room with Rod, who was all black—black coat, black hat, black beard—and carried a reaper's scythe. "You recognize this gentleman," said Harry, "the Spirit of '72. Too late for you, pal. Out, out, out." Boos and hisses as Harry picked up a book and drove and kicked the reaper from the room.

"And now, making a personal appearance right here in our very own Feelgood Lounge, that rosy-cheeked baby fed on mother's milk, a bright-eyed bouncing boy weighing in at about 190 pounds, may I introduce, ladies and gentlemen, the Spirit of '73!"

In he came, wearing a diaper and nothing else, nothing but some kind of cap with furry earflaps. He had a cigar in his mouth, and the biggest bottle with the biggest nipple she'd ever seen. Cheers greeted him and he strutted around with his arms aloft like Muhammad Ali. He kissed Diana, and he kissed Laurie, and then in his diapers he came and kissed his wife, Anna.

"Who thought that up?" Anna asked when they were driving home in the Blazer.

"It was spontaneous," Steadman said. "That party seemed like it could use a lift."

"It wasn't too bad."

Trees, woods in the headlights as they drove through Panther Gap. "We're in the country, all right. The rural scene—what do you think Fielding would have done with Zep?"

Anna said, "You don't think you're Tom Jones, do you?"

Five

The Obenwalds' story was all bad luck. Anna kept thinking she'd heard all of it, but when the lambs began to come that January she realized that it was ongoing. Lambing—Harry and Diana had looked forward to it with such infectious hope. To Anna baby animals—puppies in their blind filmed stage, wallowing and drooling on newspapers—had never seemed cute, but she let herself believe that lambs would be frisky romping fleecy darlings just as they were in Maggie's rhymes and picture books. She was almost as impatient as Maggie for them to arrive. Diana had told Maggie that there would be more than two hundred lambs, and Maggie imagined, Anna could tell, something splendid.

The first lamb they saw was dead. Harry was carrying it out of the house by its rear legs, and it was so long and black that Anna didn't recognize it at once as a lamb. It dangled in Harry's hand, limp and slack, long black knobby legs, long bloody cord, long carcass in loose skin that bunched around the neck. That much Anna took in at a glance, and then Harry tried to hide it with his body so that Maggie wouldn't see it. "What happened to it?" she wanted to know, and Harry said, "It just didn't make it." Diana asked them in for cocoa. She had been crying, and she sniffled a little while she made it. She didn't know why the lamb hadn't pulled through. It had been born that morning, the mother had cleaned it up—"She owned it right away," Diana said—and they got the ewe and lamb in a pen but the lamb wouldn't feed; Diana took the ewe's first thick milk, the colostrum, and heated it and tried to get the lamb to take it from a bottle; the lamb kept shivering and they brought it inside and put it near the stove; they shoved the tube down its throat to get the milk in it; and it just died. Watching Diana fix cocoa, listening to her voice as the clog in it loosened—"It just died," she said, as if that was the most natural thing that could have happened to it—Anna did not know how she did it. How could anyone get used to it? And when she and Maggie left the house, she saw Harry tending a small fire behind one of the sheds, and realized that he was burning the lamb.

Till then she hadn't quite believed in the bad luck. When Steadman told her about the Obenwalds, she suspected that he exaggerated as he usually did when he talked about people. About trees he was reliable, but he always tried to turn people into memorable characters. Before she met Harry, Anna had pictured a defiant hulking brute who was always raging, but Harry was quiet, and not large, and precise in his gestures. His hands were never far from his body. Anna had once watched him and Steadman splitting wood: Steadman made a big loop with the maul with his arms extended, but Harry lifted the maul straight up and swung straight down again. There was something contained in his manner too, and in his face, the dark blue eyes under the bony brow. In his round-shouldered green wool jacket, his short dark hair close to his skull, he looked very compact and integral—like a polished stone, Anna thought. Diana was almost as big as Harry, almost the big plush woman Steadman had prepared her for, but not quite so placid, not so padded, not just a big pudding. She always moved a little faster than Anna expected. And both Harry and Diana seemed so healthy and so busy—they never hurried exactly, but it always stunned Anna to watch them work, to see how much they got done in just a few minutes—and the farm and house were so neat that she didn't see how bad luck could get to them. Troubles had always seemed to her to get started in the mess of things, in clutter and squalor and confusion—but the Obenwalds did not tolerate mess. They didn't make a fuss about it, but there were never dirty dishes on the counter, and the garbage cans weren't running over, and the enamel in the bathroom was always spotless. Even the sheds and barns were neat. Bad luck—Diana talked about it as if it was like weather, too big and indifferent to do anything about.

Yet the glimpse of that first dead lamb, and of Harry and Diana afterward, shook Anna. She was in Zion County because Steadman wanted to live there, but still it felt as if either of them could choose to leave; for the Obenwalds being here seemed permanent. Diana's parents had both died in a car crash when Diana was three years old; she'd been raised by an aunt and uncle who had five children of their own and made Diana feel, as she told Anna, "sort of like Cinderella." This uncle was a salesman and money was always short. Diana had always wanted to live with her grandparents, on their farm. When they died, a developer bought the place and Diana came into a lot of money. They were her father's parents; the aunt she lived with was her mother's sister. The uncle threatened to take her to court to try to recover the money he'd spent on her. Diana was eighteen then, and bewildered; she went to college at VPI and spent her vacations with friends or with the banker who'd refused to let her uncle get his hands on the money. All this time she had been planning to marry a boy she went to high school with. He was killed in Vietnam. And then in her last year at VPI she met Harry in something called the Artmobile, a trailer that was set up on campus outside the library. She was looking at a picture of a flock beneath some willow trees, and his first words to her were, "Do you like sheep?" She said yes.

Harry was then a graduate student in biology, but he had already decided to give it up at the end of that year. When Steadman knew him first at the University of Virginia, he was an engineering student —and that Anna could see, Harry with his slide rule—but he switched to English and then to biology. Anna had heard about the Stuffed Olive, the English professor who drove Harry to biology; this sleek, round professor had a head that protruded from his shoulders like the pimiento from an olive that has just been squeezed. He was baldish, and a red flush rose from his collar to his scalp when he told off-color stories, as he often did. The students at the university at that time were all male, and the Stuffed Olive liked the atmosphere of the locker room; he was one of those people, Steadman said, who can't talk without pursing their lips. One day in class —it was a drama course and they were reading Jonson—the pimiento oozed upward and they knew a corker was coming. "The fundamental kiss is the very antithesis of art," they heard. Harry, playing dumb, raised his hand and asked, "The fundamental kiss— does that mean kissing somebody's asshole?" Steadman still made remarks now and then about the fundamental kiss, but Anna could tell that Harry didn't care for them. Since she'd had problems of her own in college, she guessed that some principle had been at stake for Harry. He just wouldn't submit to people whom he found des- picable. Steadman, who was pliable enough to get an A from the Stuffed Olive, said that Harry was afflicted with massive integrity, and for once he probably wasn't exaggerating. Harry lived in Zion County, Anna thought, because—well, because he didn't want to kiss any fundaments.

It must have been hard for him to disappoint his parents. Anna had met them just after Christmas when they came to visit; they were quite old but very handsome, cultivated, and distinguished-looking. They both had slight German accents and formal manners. Harry's mother was Jewish, and they had left Germany just before the war; they went to Canada first, then to Detroit, then to Richmond, where Harry's father, a chemist, taught in a high school. His mother gave violin lessons and played in an orchestra. Despite their courtesy, it was clear that they were bitter and that they had expected Harry, their only son, born just after the war ended, to do better than this, a sheep farm in the mountains. They liked Zion County, and Harry had found his way there because his parents, both of them sturdy walkers and amateur botanists, and intrigued by the German place names in the region, had brought him there to hike. Harry's father said that Zion County was not like Prussia at all but like the Black Forest, and when he described that place, Anna realized right away that it was a landscape with peasants.

Harry and Diana were married the month Diana graduated from college. They had already found their farm and they bought it that summer with Diana's money. That was inevitable, Anna thought; they were almost the only people of her own age whom she could not imagine doing something other than what they were doing. There was nothing tentative or hesitant about their decision. Right away they bought sheep and cattle. Within months the cattle were quarantined and the sheep had foot rot. The cattle—their disease had a name Anna couldn't remember, but it was the one that caused bangs in people—had to be destroyed. A government vet gave them lethal injections of curare and a bulldozer opened a pit, shoved them in, and covered them up. To save the sheep they had to run them through daily footbaths of formaldehyde. Diana described how the infection ate right through the hoof and up the leg, how the sheep grazed on bloody knees—and said it was lucky they'd started off with a small flock and that their farm was big enough so that they could keep rotating the sheep from field to field.

Their sheep died, were always dying. Rams had killed each other with their butting, had literally bashed each other's brains out, and ewes had electrocuted themselves by chewing through the cables in the barns. Others had been struck by lightning, shot by hunters, strangled in fences, drowned in floods. They died of kidney stones, pneumonia, and overeating, they died sometimes like turtles when they got on their backs and couldn't get up again, and sometimes, like that lamb, they just died. Anna had heard Diana repeat something Other Byrd said: "I do all I can for 'em, and then I tell 'em, All right now, just you lie down and die." To Anna the sheep, and particularly the ewes when they were all puffed up in their pregnancy, had never looked as if they had a very strong hold on life. Deer, or rabbits, or even groundhogs, were alive in every bristle, alive to their whiskers, but sheep were suffocating blobs. Their bleats sounded like the dry heaves to her, they came right up from their bellies and made their purple tongues clap.

And yet she could see that both Harry and Diana liked to handle and doctor them, and that they allowed for all the deaths, which were just ordinary. The only deaths Diana singled out were the deaths of her pets, lambs she'd raised by hand or others that had become special favorites. To her sheep had personalities—and this Anna had to take on trust. Not all of the sheep were named, and they all had big red numbers daubed on them, but Diana had named plenty of the ewes. There were Lucille, Yvonne, Demure, Dumpling, Glucose, Chanel, and Sugartit. Harry's rams were Glands, the Phantom, Buffalo, and Beethoven. The other animals around the place were named too, Gertie the cow and Luther Emmanuel the rooster, the setters Wig and Thump, and all the cats, whose names seemed to change according to whim. Several times, Diana said, she'd sworn never to name another animal—it was just asking for it. Harry had given her a purebred ewe as a wedding present, and they named it Eve; it died on their first anniversary. They thought it had probably eaten nightshade or wild cherry, both of which were poisonous. Then Harry got an expensive ram, the Moor, and it got stuck in a saltbox and broke its neck trying to get out—on Christmas Day. Another ewe, Eve the second, died on their second anniversary, and while Harry was out burning her Diana was in the house having a miscarriage. "There were so many coincidences like that," Diana said, "that sometimes I just felt like everything was bound to turn out wrong for us." But they had stayed put, and Diana had conceived again, and miscarried again, and talked of herself as if she was a ewe whose failures were just shirking.

All these events would have been portents to Anna, but she thought of them just as Diana described them, as coincidences— until that first dead lamb. And after that, when the lambs began to come in numbers, and they were more mischievous and just plain wild than anything in the books, she wondered if her apprehensions were silly. The lambs were so rowdy and exuberant that it was hard to believe they'd turn into big dull slugs of sheep. They were all over the place, even in the Obenwalds' house where they pranced around on hoofs that sounded like typewriter keys. Harry had set up a teeter board for them in one of the fields, and they loved to bump each other off it. On any little mound there was likely to be a game of King of the Mountain under way. Even Anna laughed when a pair of husky twins decided simultaneously to go for the dugs and hit their placid mother with such a whump they lifted her hindquarters right off the ground. They were merciless to the ewes; they'd see one down and decide in an instant, a whole gang of them, to pounce on her, and they'd just bury her. Anna had once seen a ewe rise from under such a heap, a bold lamb riding upright on her back. But what gave her most delight was the sight of one of those little creatures suddenly flinging itself into the air in an astonishing stiff-legged lamb-leap, as if it had been bounced right off the earth by some high thought of joy.

And the Obenwalds were happy too, even though they were worn out by the hours they kept. They seemed to be up most of the night checking on the ewes and lambs, and Anna had seen other funeral fires—but they said they were having a good lambing. Diana must have bottle-fed hundreds of lambs by that time, but each time Anna saw her do it Diana looked up and giggled. Maggie loved to feed the lambs too, even though it was a contest to see which one of them would end up in possession of the Dr. Pepper bottle with the nipple on it. And with the lambs Harry forgot his dignity. He allowed himself any excess. He'd lie down on the floor and let the lambs clamber over him, and he talked to them in a dopey Elmer Fudd voice: "You wike it inside, wittle wammies? You tink it's wewy wewy comfy by de stove?"

Animals were his medium and Diana's too. They were not Anna's. The cats she didn't mind—Steadman had brought home two from a man named Doc Hiner who had twenty or so around his place; where there got to be too many of them, Doc had his brother Junior drown a few—and they did catch mice, but they were sly, savage things, not like the sheep. And though Anna often brought Maggie over to the Obenwalds' to see the lambs, she was careful not to look too closely at the fields where they were penned. There was blood on the ground, blood and shit and slush, and when the days were warm enough to thaw it, there was a stench in the air and all the stains ran together in one pool of green muck. Maggie went with Diana out to the barns, but Anna looked at the lambs from behind the fence. That was close enough.

At the end of February Anna made maple syrup. It was supposed to be a joint venture with the Obenwalds but she got stuck with most of the work. The men always had something more important to do, and since the lambs were still coming Diana just threw a log on the fire now and then and went back to the sheep. Not that Anna minded; some of the work was tedious but there was plenty to keep her busy and she couldn't get over the idea that this rich delicious syrup came out of nowhere. It came out of trees, of course, but at that time of year the trees looked so dead and bare that it was the same as nowhere. It still surprised her that she found the spiles running and the buckets full when she made her rounds. The weather was changing and the days were warmer—they felt balmy after the blue cold of winter—and she thought of her activity when she boiled down the sugar water as creating a manifestation of this change. Maggie told her once that she looked like a witch—she didn't have a kettle but a long flat pan, and she did keep stirring the fire with a long metal poker—and that tickled her. She was possessive of her caldron; she knew how to tend the fire so that it kept the brew boiling and bubbling, and she didn't care for it when Steadman or Diana wandered up and chucked a log on it. She was developing an eye for the finishing too, the trickiest part of the whole process, when the syrup was just about to crystallize into sugar, was just a busy film on the bottom of the pan. She needed help getting it off then, and at night, when her hair was stiff from the sugar in the steam, she filtered it and decanted it into green and blue jars, her potion.

The pan and the barrels were set up on the Obenwalds' side of the creek, and Diana and Maggie, who'd become Diana's sidekick, for she preferred lambs to syrup, came out of the field one day to check the boiling. After they'd stood around for a few minutes, Diana said, "There's a ewe acting real funny—but maybe I can wait till Harry gets back."

Harry and Steadman had gone to Staunton together, and Anna knew she was being asked for help. "What's the matter with the ewe?"

"I don't know. She just doesn't look right to me. There's something hanging out of her, but it's not the right thing—she doesn't want me to get too close to her."

Anna poked her fire. "Well, what do you think you ought to do?"

"Actually, I wondered if you'd come up and help me hold her. If she's got a lamb ready, I'm just going to take it."

So it was evident to Diana how Anna felt about the sheep. Anna thought, I've got to do this. And somehow she did do it. She went back out to the field and she tried to pick her way through the ooze while Diana and Maggie splashed through it in their rubber boots. "That's the one," Diana said, and Anna saw a ewe with a bloody membrane hanging out of it. It skittered away but Diana grabbed it. "You hold her head," she said, and then, "We'll have to throw her. Reach under and grab her leg, all right, and we'll just throw her down." Anna reached down and put her neck and cheek against the fleece that was wet and muddy. "Ready?" Diana bucked the ewe over and it landed with a splashing thud. "Now try to hold her head up if you can, on your knee, so she can get air—and keep her legs out from under her so she doesn't try to get up again." Anna put the ewe's head on her knee; there was white froth all over the mouth and jaw. "There," said Diana to Maggie, "you see it? It's all ready to come if its mama will just push a little." Maggie watched intently. A trickle of fluid ran out of the ewe's nostril onto Anna's pants. "Push, dearie, push, that's right," Diana said, and Anna felt the clogged weight of the head on her thigh, heard the clogged groan that didn't seem to come out of the mouth but out of the body itself. "There it is, I've almost got it. Push again, dearie, and it'll be all over." And Maggie said, "Push, dearie." Another groan, heaving, and for a moment a glimmer in the dull bloodshot eye. "There it is," Diana said, and Anna looked and saw the thing, wet and flopping, soaked with a yellowish mucus. She let the ewe up, and it turned and nuzzled the thing and began to lick off the mucus and licked too at the puddle of blood in the runny ground beside it.

"Well, she owned that one," Diana said, "but it looks like she's going to twin."

And so Anna went back to the pan and stoked her fire and waited; she did not know if she could do it again. An hour later she did. This time it took longer, and then the lamb wouldn't start breathing. Diana slapped it and swung it in the air and put her finger down its throat; she wiped off its muzzle and covered it with her own mouth to try to start it. The lamb, its eyes sealed with mucus, twitched convulsively. "Its heart won't go," Diana said. And Anna, listening to the slapping, aware of time passing, became conscious of where they were, two women and a child and a stillborn lamb in the middle of a field. Still kneeling at the ewe's head, Anna was looking up at Diana, saw a red roof behind her, the gray mountain, the sky with thin slaty clouds that broke the light into flat bar-like rays. As simple as that, Anna kept thinking, as simple as that. Diana shook the lamb as if she were drying lettuce in a wire basket. The ewe stood up and began lapping blood and fluid off the ground. Diana set the lamb down and slapped it between her hands, listened for its heart, swung it again. And Anna thought she saw the little black mouth open, and Diana stopped, the lamb was just dangling there, suddenly it was shivering, it looked as if it was trying to wipe its eyes, it looked as if it was waking up, exactly as if it was waking up from a snooze. Diana laughed and said, "God, I didn't think that one would ever go." She put the lamb before the ewe, glanced between its legs, said to Maggie, "It's another little girl." And then she put her arm around Anna and said, "Don't feel bad about it. I've cried in this field plenty of times."

Six

The spring came on. Anna noticed the birds first. A pair of bluebirds nested in a hollow locust near the garden. Goldfinches sunned themselves on the power lines. The evening grosbeaks, always in a gang, always in a noisy yellow flutter, made dashing swirls around the trees, giftwrapping them. Birds were singing, and after the silence of winter Anna noticed it. Their songs sounded intrepid to her, and formidable, like so many small sweet drills loosening a glacial mass; she thought of the sheets of snow and ice that dripped for a while and then slid off the roof of the house with the rumble of avalanche. That is how she expected the winter, which was still felt in the air and still visible in the grays and browns of the mountain, to depart, in a rush and roar.

And flowers: during those mongrel days of March, and into April when the great display came forth, Anna tried to draw them. Whenever she had a few hours to herself, she'd walk along the edge of the woods where they grew and sketch them. Steadman, she'd discovered, was not infallible about wildflowers, and she carried a book with her so that she could identify them, bloodroot and cinquefoil and the early trilliums, the Stinking Willies. At first the drawings were aids to memory, a way of fixing the names to the things, but she was pleased with them and began to aim at a stark, literal accuracy. Every serration of every leaf, every vein and fluting, every

division and dint of blossom—these details she tried to draw exactly
in hard true lines, and the more she tried, and succeeded, the more
abstract the drawings became. They still resembled specific flowers
but they were also, to her eye, exposed or discovered forms, the
conceptions of flowers, symbols of flowers. It seemed ironic to her
that simple looking, a simple effort to recognize and identify, should
lead from the things to their conceptions. When she talked about this
to Steadman, who said the drawings were lovely, he looked distrust-
ful until he said, "Do you mean the flowers are symbols of themselves?" "I think that's what I mean." "I didn't understand you at
first. It's always easier to see things as symbols than as things. You
can let the symbol stand for whatever you want and forget about the
thing." "Well, the drawings stand for flowers," Anna said, and,
surprised at her immodesty, "They're—like ideographs, aren't
they?" And the best of them were. But not all of them pleased her:
some had a dogged, determined quality, for it took an effort for her
to keep the point of the pen on the paper through a continuous line.
Her drawings—they were too imitative of Van Gogh's, she thought
—had always been full of short wiggly lines, and they always looked
insubstantial and ephemeral, as if everything were on the point of
dissolving. They were drawings not of objects, really, but of the
shimmer made by light as it struck objects. These flat drawings were
more solid, she thought, even though wildflowers were the briefest
apparitions, and she realized that drawing was intriguing her as it
hadn't for a long while.

Maggie was four years old in March. She wanted a birthday party,
and her guest list was Diana, Val, Laurie, and Hope Byrd. She
thought of asking Zep and Harry, but she decided against boys and
tried to explain her decision to Steadman so that he wouldn't feel
hurt. "Don't you wish there were more kids out here?" Anna asked
Steadman, but he said, "Why? To make her a brat?" And Maggie
wasn't much of a brat, but she had become so self-reliant, even
stoical, that sometimes she hardly seemed like a child. Anna could
not help comparing Maggie's solitude to that equal, cozy compan-
ionship she had experienced with Kay—but she did not mention this
to Steadman. "You're just worried that Maggie's getting away from
you," Steadman said, "now that she has language, memory, will,
imagination, all those complications." And that was true, Maggie

was more complicated and Anna was afraid of losing her—and still she felt that childhood should not be so solitary and severe. Maggie did like to go visit Diana and Laurie, and she played with Hope Byrd two or three times a week—always at the Byrds' house, though Anna had often asked Mavis Byrd to let Hope come visit Maggie. "You'll have a little time to yourself," Anna said, and Mavis said, "Lord, I don't know what I'd do with it." Maggie spent a lot of time with Steadman too, who was good about taking her when she got crabby. So Maggie wasn't that much of a chore out here; she could sit for hours with her books, and with all the stuff lying about the house she made fantastic tenements for her dolls and animals; she made up stories for them and did not like to be interrupted in the privacy of her play.

Her birthday came, and the party could have been worse. Mavis Byrd brought Hope across the bridge for the first time, and she stayed for the party too. They all had hats and balloons and cake and games. Steadman's present to Maggie was a television antenna. Anna was touched, for he liked to think that Prussian Creek was one of the last places in America beyond the reach of TV. The nearest stations were in Roanoke, and the mountains set up powerful interference. But Maggie had complained that she missed her programs. While the party was going on, Steadman was on the roof of the small log barn, the building highest up the mountain, where the huge aluminum antenna looked absurd. He brought the wire in the window and hooked it up to the TV, and the first picture they saw was of "Sesame Street," Big Bird talking to the grump in the garbage can, and they all cheered.

They had a visitor that spring, Rufus Howell. He stayed the night, got drunk, made a half-hearted pass at Anna, asked Steadman if he was writing at all, and when Steadman said no, Rufus said, "Nature is to art as drink is to sex—it increases the desire but takes away the performance." After the visit Steadman was somber and talked about a time, coming soon, when they wouldn't have so much to do on the house, and they could do what they'd come to do, write and draw. He talked of moving the log cabin, once a slave cabin, from the lower field to a site near the house and fitting it up as a kind of studio for her. The roof of it was collapsing anyway, and he didn't think it would be much of a job to put it on a different foundation.

And he mentioned money: they were going to have to do something to make the place pay. Anna did not want to confess how opposed she was to sheep. She knew that the lambs had delighted Steadman and that he'd been as fascinated as Maggie by the obstetric details. "We don't want so many that we end up as their valets, like Harry and Diana," he said, but all Anna said was, "I don't think I'm too good with animals." He didn't press her. The restlessness he felt didn't have to do with animals, she thought, or with money or with her; it had to do with his own ambition. She didn't care much for Rufus, who was a swaggering loudmouth, and she hated the way he treated Steadman, calling him an "author trainee" and "apprentice genius." She was sure that Steadman didn't really like him either, but he envied Rufus his success. He longed for his own success—but about his talent Anna truly couldn't judge. He seemed to have to endure a rite and ordeal to get words down on paper, and then the work had to amount to something, had to be public. She suspected that he cared too much about what others would think of it. His stories struck her as efforts to charm. She never quite believed them. They were too smooth, too neat, didn't have edges. Because she'd had to say something about them, she told Steadman that the language was beautiful, and she meant it, but she was aware that this compliment was insufficient to him. He had not asked her to read any of his novel.

Rufus's visit had disturbed him, and she pitied him in his spell of doubts. She wished that she could get him to talk, for talking was more important to him than to her, but about this matter she didn't trust herself to speak. The only thing she could think to say was, "I don't care if you never write another word." Sometimes their silence brought her to the verge of tears, and at night he teased her about her passion. "You used to be so shy," he said, but he never seemed to guess how she wished that their lovemaking would open other intimacies. It didn't; it was merely nocturnal and mostly silent. Anna was surprised, even shocked, at the way they fucked now, the way she wanted to fuck. There was nothing dainty about it. She put her hands on his perineum to feel the hard bulge where his dick ran back inside him, pressed his balls against her perineum. She wanted his thighs to close around her when she sucked his dick, something she had rarely done before, until he came in her mouth. "Your stuff

tastes like apricot nectar, like electric apricot nectar," she told him
—and that seemed to be the only kind of remark that either of them
was able to make. She still could not tell him she loved him—after
such a silence as theirs the words just wouldn't come—and she still
couldn't sleep. Steadman made fun of her. "Poor Anna, you haven't
closed your eyes for five years." When he had his bad nights, he
didn't even seem to remember them the next morning.

Then he bought himself a dog, a glossy German shorthair that
looked as if it had been dipped in chocolate. He named it before he
brought it home—Otto. "I don't want to put the puppy through that
trauma," he said. They weren't very good at coming up with names.
It had taken them weeks to name the cats Shoo and Scat, and then
they didn't really name them, those were the words applied. But
Otto was right for this puppy who was already two months old,
brown and leggy and shiny, somewhat dopey and nevertheless dig-
nified. When Steadman and Maggie laughed at him he paced off and
had to be appeased before he'd clown again. Anna could see what
a boost he gave Steadman.

And the toilet was flushed for the first time on April Fool's Day.
Anna wasn't quite sure why that was funny, but it was, to all of them.
They invited the Obenwalds' over for a bath, and they came, but
didn't bathe, and Harry presented them with a notched bar of Ivory
soap—a notch, he said, for every bath and shower they'd taken at
the Obenwalds' house. Steadman kept humming the *Water Music.*
And they had dinner in the big kitchen, which still wasn't finished
—no cabinets yet, and bare bulbs, but there was a new gas stove, a
new stainless sink, butcher block built into the counters. The walls
had been painted, the floor sanded and refinished, an enamel wood
stove hooked up to the flue where the old iron monster had been,
the big pine trestle table moved from Harry's barn. Steadman had
cooked a pork roast and made a *crème caramel,* and he and Harry
talked, as they always did at meals, about food, and they ended up
in their usual argument about Italian versus German cooking, the
pasta versus sauerkraut debate. Anna slipped outside to pee—and
had to laugh at herself when she realized what habits she'd acquired.
And she was glad she'd come out: the lighted windows, friends at
the table, her daughter, a comfortable, complacent household. From
outside it was desirable and beckoning.

She reported the household improvements to her mother, who still phoned regularly and who reluctantly gave up a few of her grievances. Of course she still told Anna that she was throwing her life away—but the matter had become almost philosophic. It was Kay's turn to be the horrid daughter. That was chronic: Kay, the older twin, had always been more resolute and defiant than Anna. Kay was still in Washington, and her mother was sure she was living with a man—a man always answered her phone, and she'd seen Kay with this wild man in a store in Chevy Chase. "But you probably know all about it," she said to Anna, "you never tell me anything."

"No, Mama, I don't hear much from Kay, just a postcard now and then."

"Well, I saw this man, Rick his name is—God, if your father saw him!"

Anna didn't think her father would want to see him. He treated his daughters like dolls, and it was easier for him if he didn't know anything about them.

"Anna," her mother said, lowering her voice as if the line was tapped, "she's on drugs. I'm no fool, I know you and Kay had to try all those things, but you should see Kay, she's just a skeleton, she looks terrible, she's a wreck. You two would never eat right, either of you."

Anna didn't pay much attention until her mother said, "She's had that leg trouble again, too." That leg trouble, the Blues, the same trouble she'd had when Anna got married. Kay had not mentioned that in any of her cards, and it worried Anna, even made her feel guilty. It didn't seem right to her that she should be so nearly content if Kay was not. Sometimes she almost believed that she and Kay had been issued one ration of happiness, and that she was claiming it all for herself—but that was ridiculous. Kay would not envy the banal contentment of a country wife. Anna wondered what, exactly, she would make of it. She would probably think it was corny—and Anna had to smile to herself, because it *was* corny. She realized how much she missed Kay, and without telling Steadman about it she wrote her and invited her down for a visit. It took her a long time to get the invitation to sound the way she wanted. She was afraid Kay would get the impression that she was trying to save her.

In early April Steadman planted the orchard. He came home one day with a bundle of switches all corded together—not switches, trees, Anna had to think. They were all tagged, apple peach pear plum, and packed in moss, a fragrance of humus and nitrogen clinging to them. When she asked if they were alive, Steadman nicked one of them with the nail of his thumb so that she could see a crescent of green bold as arsenic beneath the bark. He set them out where the old orchard had been. There was only one twisted, tilted apple tree standing; the others had all been blown down in a windstorm. This new orchard was to be laid out quincunxically, according to the design Steadman showed her in *The Garden of Cyrus,* which he plucked from the book boxes. From the house Anna watched him dig the holes and move the rich black soil from the old hogpen; she went out to help him set the trees, she saw how carefully he spread the roots out in the dirt, watched him trim all the bruised or floppy branches so that the little trees had a tight spiky strength. "You have to set the longest root to the west," he said, "into the prevailing wind. We want these things to stand." Otto was trotting around near them, and Maggie was trying to help with a kid's shovel Steadman had bought her, and when all the trees were straight and tamped at last, Steadman smiled at her. He was flushed from the work, damp, and crumbs of black dirt stuck to his forehead and in his sandy hair. He was holding a shovel and mattock. He smiled and made a gesture, not assertive but hopeful, and said, "The orchard."

Anna had to turn away. *Where,* she almost said. Leafless stems in a weedy field were not an orchard. But she checked herself; she knew that perverse question was formed only to keep her from crying. She didn't know why she was turning into such a weeper, or why all this drippy, sappy, corny stuff moved her so, or why the emotions could take such a sudden hateful twist.

"It's time you went up Little Furnace," Steadman said to her at the end of April. Real spring had come by then, green grass and leaves. Steadman had been going up to the top of the mountain almost every morning before daylight and coming down again in time for breakfast. It was spring gobbler season, and he'd killed one turkey, but he kept going back. Anna wasn't sure she wanted anything to do with hunting. "Isn't it dangerous?" she asked. She often heard shots on the mountain, and there were stories of hunters mistaken for turkeys. "What about snakes?" she asked, for Other

Byrd had reminded her that it was time for the copperheads to start crawling and told her they made their dens in the limestone up on the mountain. "What'll we do about Maggie?" But Steadman wouldn't let her off. He asked Diana to keep Maggie, who was excited about spending a night in a different bed, and that afternoon he and Anna set out.

Anna couldn't keep up with him. He wasn't walking fast, she knew, and he was not trying to press her, but he just walked straight up. She was used to having Maggie along on walks, to ambling and stopping every few steps, but Steadman climbed right up to the old logging road, the highest she'd been, and right across it without a pause. Anna was determined not to say anything. He was carrying the sleeping bags and the pack and his gun and he wasn't even puffing. She heard herself grunting. She was hot. He'd told her she wouldn't need a jacket for the climb, but she felt the cold more easily than he did and she wore one anyway. "Maybe I'd better take my jacket off," she said. "I guess you were right."

"Warm? That's why they call this mountain Little Furnace. It heats you right up."

"Is that really why?"

He laughed. "You're as gullible as Maggie. There are some hot springs over on Big Furnace, and that's probably how the mountains got their names. You're ready for a breather, aren't you?"

"I guess I am. Can you hear my heart? It's really thudding."

He reached for her wrist and felt her pulse. "You're not in shape."

"How could I be? I don't come up here every day."

They sat down among ferns. They were in a hollow full of tulip poplars—straight silver stems, big orange blossoms. "How much farther to the top?"

"We're about a quarter of the way."

"Are you kidding? We've been walking for an hour."

"About five minutes."

"More than that, it had to be. I'm not that feeble."

"Ten minutes maybe."

"The mountain doesn't look that big."

"Foreshortening. You can't really see it from the house."

"How high is it?"

"We've got a climb of about fifteen hundred feet."

"How long does it take you usually?"

"About half an hour, I guess."

"Do you ever stop?"

"At first I did. I had to. But you get used to it. It doesn't seem so big once you've been up and down a few times."

They stopped twice more on the way up, and when they reached the top they looked across the valley at Big Furnace, a long, heaped-up, forested ridge with other ridges radiating from it. It was all green, green in the spring infinity of shades, from the deep green of the hemlocks to the transparent greens of the leafing hardwoods, and in the hollows where the masses of shadows gathered, the air itself was a secretive green. To Anna it looked mammoth and wild. "It looks as if it should make a noise, doesn't it?"

"What noise?" Steadman asked.

"Don't you think of mountains, big mountains, as making a kind of eerie noise?"

Steadman made a chill whooshing like sound-effect wind.

"Sort of like that."

His face took on a teasing, demonic expression. "That's the invisible worm that howls in the night." More whooshing.

She laughed. "You're making fun of me, aren't you?"

"I'm just quoting Blake—a mountaintop needs a little poetry."

The top of Little Furnace was a nimble plateau with its own topography, its own streams and hollows and ridges. The mountain was five miles wide and twelve miles long, and nearly all of it belonged to the Virginia Game Commission. Just above their own land they'd passed the trees splashed with yellow that marked the boundary of the public land. Anna knew that at one time people had lived on the mountaintop, and she'd heard Steadman and Harry talk about the meadows up there, but she wasn't prepared for ruins. They passed roofless cabins with trees growing inside the walls; in the yards stood old wagons, anatomies now, wheels and spine and tongue; from stone cellars there was a glitter of jars; on the slopes orchard trees bloomed white and pink. They followed a track from one abandoned homestead to the next. In the woods Anna saw rotting rail fences, crooked veins of humus now, separating young woods from old. The fields that were still open were brushy, full of briars and vines, rusting machinery, inexplicable heaps of stone, the sprouting hulls of automobiles. "What happened up here? Didn't they have time to take anything with them? It looks as if they were all wiped out at once."

"Most of them were," Steadman said.

And he told her that many of them had died in the flu epidemic; in the graveyard up here the date on nearly every stone was 1918. People still lived on Little Furnace after that, but the farmers down in the valley started to buy up the mountain land for summer pasture. It was cooler up here, and the animals thrived. The families moved off the mountain, all but the most stubborn, and their places were occupied during the summer by the hands who came up to look after the stock. "Somebody loved these places once," he said. "They must have, to do all the work they did. And you can tell, just by the way the cabins sit and the way the fields lie, that they thought about making them beautiful."

They stopped in one of these places where a spring pulsed out from beneath a slab of limestone. "Far enough," Steadman said, unslinging the pack and putting down his gun. He cut armfuls of evergreen branches with his hatchet and they spread them out on the ground, spread the sleeping bags on top of them. "Our couch."

It was right out in the open. Anna said, "Won't something get us?"

She meant it as a joke, but when it got dark she did feel exposed. She sat close to the fire while Steadman fixed the steak, but her back was cold and she heard every rustle in the black brush. Steadman didn't pay any attention to the noises. He was briefing her about turkeys, but his hunting and fishing talk always bored her a little. It reminded her vaguely of sermons, the mixture of piety and esoteric detail. A turkey gobbling—how could that be awesome? Even the words, *turkey gobbling,* were comic. The only wild turkeys she'd ever seen were the ones he brought home, big black birds, overgrown crows. The toms gobbled only in the spring, she gathered, to attract the hens; the gobble was the mating call. Steadman spoke about these birds as if their powers of sight and hearing were supernatural. Duty Armstrong had told him that the only way to be still enough to fool a turkey was to be dead, and the only way to be hid enough was to be buried.

He fucked her when they got into the sleeping bags, which were zipped together. She was too conscious of where they were, of all the things bashing around in the dark, of the shell of the bags scratching on the boughs beneath, to feel much. And when he got off her, he said, "That was your basic minimal woodsman's fuck, the one they describe in the chapter on survival." He kissed her goodnight and told her he hoped she'd sleep. Hoots, barks, howls, shrieks —how could she sleep? "I think I hear the invisible worm," she said.

He listened, laughed.

She said, "Doesn't it sound kind of like a nuthouse up here? Like madmen?"

"It's probably best not think of them as people. After all, it would be a lot stranger if they were out there talking to each other."

Then he dropped off. Maybe she slept a little in fits, but it was a long night and she was awake when Steadman sat up. He sat up, squirmed out of the bag and put on his pants and boots, went down to the spring and splashed his face. It took him about two minutes to get ready to go. He ate an orange in the darkness while he was waiting for her. "Tie your laces," he said. His normal voice sounded loud and hard in the cold dark. She was shivering, and her stiff fingers blundered on the knot. He held a flashlight for her but turned it off when they walked up a ridge. Her eyes would get used to the dark, he said, but she kept stumbling and branches lashed across her face. It irked her that he wouldn't slow down and wouldn't use the light. At one point she could not even see him, stopped, listened, couldn't hear him. A call flew out of her: "Steadman?" "Right here." He wasn't ten steps away. "Quiet now. They'll be coming off the roosts before long."

They crashed through laurel. Steadman cut branches from it with his knife and made a blind for them at the edge of the thicket. They sat down, waited, but she couldn't get comfortable. The ground was damp, her feet were cold. Nothing happened. Steadman didn't move and she kept squirming. She yawned. Finally, here and there, a few birds began to sing, drowsily at first, but they perked up as the light increased. And the light was pale at first, and sinister; it looked as if it were coming from the earth, emanating from rocks and trees. It was all a silver gray, not really a color, but more like an absence of color, a suspension of color, and then there was a drugged expectant lull even in the song of birds—and then it happened. Maybe it didn't happen all at once, but Anna noticed it all at once. She was looking from the blind across a clearing, at dogwood and laurel on the opposite slope, and thinking how the flowers were like the connect-a-dot pages in kid's coloring books, when suddenly she saw the colors, the creamy white trumpets of dogwoods, lush pink clusters of redbud. She looked up; light was streaming over the ridge behind her and the sky was orange and saffron, high rifts of color in the blue. And when she looked down again there was light and auroral color everywhere: the great delicate expanse of green leaves, every green paired not with a shadow but the reverse of a shadow, a blond shimmer on the side the sun struck, the profuse blue sparkle of dew in the field in front of them, each drop containing its prismatic gleam, and flowers everywhere, stipples of yellow and violet and pink and white.

And over all this broke a noise, savage and brassy, unbelievably loud, that made her heart thump. She flinched and her heart thumped. That was just a fact: her heart thumped the way it did yesterday when she walked up the mountain, and she didn't have to feel her pulse to know it. The noise was repeated, raucous and thrilling. Then she thought, a turkey. That was a turkey gobbling.

Keawk, keawk, keawk. This call, right in her ear, made her flinch again. She'd forgotten about Steadman, but he was answering the gobbler. And she'd heard this call before when Steadman fooled around in the house with his caller, a flat U-shaped piece of rubber with a bit of balloon stretched in it. In the house it sounded ridiculous, a gimmick, a noisemaker—but out here she heard the lust in it, the lust and coyness. And right away the gobbler answered, that fierce call. Anna wanted this, whatever it was, to stop right now, but Steadman called again. His face looked so treacherous. He touched her and whispered. "He'll come now, don't move." He shifted his gun so that the muzzle poked through the laurel at the front of the blind. She waited, listened, watched, saw nothing. It's not coming, she thought. Then, suddenly again, and louder than before, it called so close that she balled her hands into fists and forced them against her thighs to keep them still. She heard the bird move in the leaves in the woods on the opposite side of the clearing. Steadman called again.

It sprang out of the woods, from where she didn't see, but it was suddenly there, huge and black. It was drawn up to its full height, brutal, and its extended heavy wings dragged the ground. The long neck was arched back into the body, the whole weight balanced to strike. And Steadman was beside her with the gun. The tail was raised and canted, opened, brandished; the feathers were not just black but had a coppery sheen; the head was an inflamed blue. Steadman didn't shoot. Anna heard a noise, *whump whump*, and thought it was her own heart at first, but it was this beast, maybe not its heart but something that sounded like it, and then another noise like the cracking of bones. She wanted Steadman to shoot, she wanted this to be over with, she wanted this thing not to exist. She could not stand this massive pause before death.

Steadman did not shoot. He didn't shoot and didn't shoot. Anna couldn't look at him. She looked at the rutting bird, and when Steadman still didn't shoot she didn't want him to any longer. The more she looked, the more she saw how the bird had puffed itself up—just feathers, after all. And in its pomp and swagger, its waddling vanity, it had begun to remind her of something—of the archbishop, she realized, the robed fat strutting archbishop.

It gobbled again. It was looking right at the blind and made a leap toward it and Anna flinched. The turkey saw the movement and panicked. It ducked and took off. It had to run several steps, flapping its wings, just a big black frightened turkey, before it could get itself airborne.

"Why didn't you shoot it? Oh Steadman, I'm so glad you didn't. All I did was move my hand—I couldn't help it. Is that why you didn't shoot it? Why were you waiting?"

"I was watching you," he said, and stood up in the blind.

"You were? Don't laugh at me, Steadman."

"I'm not laughing. I like to see you excited. I love you, Anna."

He was smiling at her. Anna went over what he'd just said, trying to get it right.

"What?" she asked.

She tried to stand up, but her legs had gone to sleep under her, they were wobbly and stinging, and she staggered in the laurel.

Seven

One May morning Steadman was finishing up the cabinets in the kitchen. Through the open window he could hear Anna and Maggie out in the garden, their companionable murmur. He glanced at them now and then in the rich black plot—Anna, who'd never owned a houseplant, was out of bed early now to run down to her garden to see what had happened overnight. She still didn't quite believe that all these seeds did what they were supposed to do. Before planting she'd made a map of her garden, marking off the territory of each vegetable; now, when she marked on it the dates of planting and germination, she regarded it, Steadman thought, with some wonder, as if that document were responsible for what was happening in the garden. This morning she and Maggie had the string and stakes out, planting beans; Otto was down there with them, pointing butterflies; the sun flashed on the silver barrette Anna used to pin back her hair.

"Morning, ma'am, morning, miss."

Steadman wasn't used to voices on this side of the creek, and when he looked out the window he saw the caller at the garden gate, a man in a white cap with a long orange bill. A goose! But the rest of him was in blue denim, and he had a cigar clamped in the corner of his mouth; his hands were in the pockets of pants held up by suspenders; the pants were so large that Steadman thought at once of those cartoons of men wearing barrels.

Anna was standing up straight now, and Maggie had hooked an arm around her thigh. "I'm afraid I've done give the girl a fright, busting in on you this way."

Steadman didn't catch what Anna said, but the man opened the gate and walked into the garden. His voice was certainly clear enough. "Here I come, disturbing the morning's work, just meddling, that's all I'm doing. This is my old home place, and I won't kid you—I been curious to see what a Steadman looks like."

Anna turned to Maggie, said something else inaudible to Steadman.

"Two of 'em's pretty, I can see that much. Excuse me, ma'am, but you and that child outshine any Argenstill that ever come to this gate. We was homely as rats, the women especially."

Anna reached down and gave Maggie's shirt a tug and held her forward to distract attention from herself.

"She looks like you, she's the picture of you. May I presume to ask what brought you and her to this place? You come plumb out of the world when you come here."

"Steadman," Anna replied, and looked up at the house.

He came out then, and when he got to the garden he said to the caller, "Did you sneak up here from the bridge?"

"No sneaking about it. I'm too old to sneak. It takes about all I can do to set one foot ahead of the other. Mind, I never have cared for that bridge. Been struck by lightning three times I know of, but my daddy never would take the hint, and Arlie was just as stubborn. If it was my bridge, which it ain't, I'd take a ax to it."

Anna said, "Mr. Argenstill was born here."

"Yes ma'am, on the ninth day of January in 18 and 95. I was the first born, Amos, named by my mama after her own daddy. She had us all A's—Amos, that's me, then the girls, Alice and Annabelle, then come the twins, Abraham and Alvin, and last was Arlie. He always was puny."

"I didn't know there were so many of you," Steadman said. "I've heard of you, but Mrs. Argenstill—"

"I reckon you mean Lulu. She never was overfond of Argenstills. She come from town, you know, and thought our ways was all backwards. She cleared Mama right off the place—she come over to Berry Hill to live with me and Toots—but she never did get rid of

Daddy till her died. But Lulu hung on all right and got the place herself. Daddy had done wrote me out of the will and Arlie in, so you needn't worry about me going to law about it. If you paid for it, and I hear Miss Lulu put the screws to you, it's yours legal."

Steadman said, "We could have paid more."

"Seems to me like I heard something about some real estate feller wandering about in the Gorge one rainy day. You don't know nothing about that, I reckon."

"He was probably just upset by some deal that fell through."

Amos was watching Steadman closely. In fact, the orange bill of the cap almost touched Steadman's nose. Steadman thought that Amos, with his jaw and his squint, looked something like Popeye. Amos backed off, smiled, flicked the ash off his cigar in a powdery explosion.

"It's time somebody other than a Argenstill took hold here."

"I'm not sure we've taken hold yet."

"I see you've got your fruit trees set out, and the missus looks like she's worked up the garden good."

Maggie sneezed.

"God bless you! This child got a cold?"

"Not much of one," Anna said.

"It does me good to see a child back here, indeed it does. Coming along the road just now it seemed like it was all going back to the wilderness—houses burned down, barns stove in, fields growed up. It used to be you could just about talk from one farm to the next, it was settled that thick. This place even had a name then, Panther Gap, and a store, and a post office, and a schoolhouse where I learned my letters. You'd never know it to see it now."

"It has been depopulated," Steadman said.

"De-which?"

"There used to be eight thousand people in Zion County. There aren't half that many now."

"I don't know the figures. All I know is the ones with good sense have done cleared out. Here am I, so it had to be the ornery ones that stayed."

"Do you have children?" Anna asked.

"Children, grandchildren, great-grandchildren, and if I live to a hundred I'll have great-greats. But you won't find none of them in

Zion County except on a visit. They got the idea they need to look after me and Toots. I never did farm for my sprats the way Arlie did for that boy of his. Just because I couldn't live out of the mountains and wasn't suited for no other way of life, that wasn't no reason to keep them back. I got two daughters who took up nursing, one son in the cement business in Waynesboro, and the least boy builds jet airplanes in the state of Washington."

And then, shyly, trying not to sound too inquisitive, Anna asked about the twins. "Those twins, your brothers—their names were Abraham and Alvin?"

"That's right."

"Were they fraternal or identical?"

"You mean did they look alike? Yes ma'am, right down to their toes. The only way you could tell 'em apart was that Alvin had a kind of pinched look, like he'd just bit into a lemon."

"Which one was the oldest?"

Amos smiled. "Oldest? That don't count for much when it ain't but a few minutes' difference."

"I don't know if she'd agree with you," Steadman said. "She's a twin too." He saw that his remark annoyed her.

"And which are you? First or last?"

"Last."

"Twins don't figure. Abraham—he was the last—him and Alvin could set out from the house different ways and meet up on the mountain like they set the time and place, which I know they never did do."

"Did they get along?"

"If you mean did they like one another, I couldn't say. I know they didn't get along with nobody else. And it didn't seem like they cared if they got along with each other, either. It was like they was yoked. Switch one and the other felt it, cut one and the other would bleed."

"I've heard—"

"You ain't heard that old story about the fox?"

"Is that what it is?"

"They say it's different things. Mama always said it was Alvin, but I never did hold with spirits. It was bad enough what happened to them two boys."

"What did happen?"

Amos pointed up the mountain. "It was a den up there with two foxes in it, a dog and a vixen, red foxes. The pelts was worth some money then, and Abraham and Alvin took a notion to kill them foxes and skin 'em out. They set out from the house one evening, and come dark we heard a rifle shot down to the house. That was Alvin, because it had done been settled between them that he was to kill the dog fox, which would be the first out of the den. Directly we heard the shotgun—Abraham. So the vixen must of come out of there too. In a little bit we heard the shotgun again, but nobody thought nothing of it till it got fast dark and they still wasn't down from there. Mama said, 'Amos, you better go look what's keeping those boys.' So I climbed up there with the lantern and come upon the foxes first, shot dead, both of them, and then upon Alvin, shot dead as either of them. He still had the rifle in his hand, and dang if it wasn't near about as long as he was stretched out there on the ground. He wasn't but twelve years old. And then I found the shotgun in the brush where Abraham had throwed it down. But Abraham couldn't have shot from up close because Alvin wasn't tore up that bad. It looked like to me Abraham come down after he shot to see what he hit, then dropped the gun and lit out over the mountain. We had the hole dug before he ever got back, but we waited on him two days before we ever put Alvin in it. Two days he hid up there somewhere. First thing Daddy said to him was, 'Cain. Your mother hung the wrong name on you. Come up here on the porch, boy, and get your mark.' And he did come up, and Daddy bloodied him good with the blunt end of a hand adz, which was the nearest thing to hand. All the tools were set out on the porch —he built the box right in the yard there. Knocked Abraham back down the steps, and he carried that mark to his own death. One year later to the day and he was in another box, and the last thing I saw before we closed it was that scar Daddy had set on his forehead."

"What happened to Abraham?"

"Horse kicked him in the head."

Amos was looking at the porch—a little ramshackle now, the roof supports in need of paint, the steps curling at the ends. He said, "Daddy was always building. He had just finished boarding up the house and adding on the back there."

Anna said, "Isn't there any explanation? Was it deliberate?"

"I never did know. I don't believe Abraham spoke a hundred words before he was in the ground"—nodding at the burial ground on the slope—"up there."

And then he said, "You haven't had any of those bad foxes, have you? Seems like it's something in the paper every week about 'em. Those rabbit foxes."

Steadman tried to hide his smile. *Rabbit foxes.* The county paper had reported several rabid foxes. "We haven't seen any," he said.

"This is the place for 'em, by golly, these old places where it's all brush. They get too dang thick and that's when they take the sickness. We used to keep all the varmints killed out."

Amos blinked, shook his head. "I've gabbled so I near forgot what I come for. If you got no stock to set out, what do you say to renting me pasture?"

Steadman said, "Will it make me rich?"

"I don't know about rich. I'd pay a fair price."

"What is a fair price?"

"Three dollars per head per month is about what we pay in these parts. It's more than enough grass to stand forty cows with calves."

"Some of these fences aren't much."

"I'd patch 'em. It wouldn't hurt none to get some manure on the sod."

"This is late, isn't it, to be looking for pasture?"

"You're right about that, but I been putting my cows out every summer over on Hoot Mountain. When I went over there this year they'd done rented to some young feller who set out a bunch of yammers."

"A bunch of what?"

"Yammers, you know, them shaggy brutes."

"Llamas," Anna said.

"I wouldn't be wanting the fields right here by the house if you're thinking you need some room about you."

"Shall we write up a contract?"

"Contract? I do my business by hand."

And so they shook on it.

Amos said, "I got a fence line to walk. Maybe you'd care to come? There won't be no misunderstanding if we agree from the start."

They set off, all of them following Amos, who talked steadily, first

about the high water of 19 and 12—"That's when them river jacks
got in the bottom, and where it used to be a cornfield it looked like
a quarry"—and about Arlie, who was never intended for a farmer.
"Scared of beasts, always was." A laugh. "Once he got hold of the
ornriest big bull in this country, and every now and then he'd pump
a load of birdshot into its back end, just to keep it down, you know.
That bull got so it recognized the gun and took to hiding from Arlie,
courting vengeance, till it caught him around the corner of the
granary and from what Lulu said, it just dug a hole with him." What
Arlie lacked, from his stock and family both, was respect. That boy
Charles had been as wild to get out from under Arlie as Amos had
been to get out from under his own father, they'd both took the same
route, the Arm Service. It didn't take Charles but about ten minutes
to get himself killed—he wasn't what you'd call quick. But Arlie was
took hard—"He'd set a high sight on the boy, after all, even if he
never showed it. Him and Daddy was about the same. To them a
ear wasn't something to talk to, it was a target for a blow." It was
lucky the pastures were right up against the mountain where the
limestone kept 'em sweet; Arlie hadn't limed, fertilized, or seeded
for thirty years, but still it was plenty of bluegrass and timothy
volunteering.

Volunteering, like all this talk—every rock, every rise, every tree
solicited a memory or an observation, and Steadman, who ordinarily
felt squire-like when he tramped about the place, had to recognize
a title different from his own. His tenancy was still in prospect; Amos
found his own tracks everywhere he looked. Here was a rock that
chewed up many a mower blade, these were posts he split and drove,
those big sugar trees he'd once tapped. The cabin that Steadman
proposed to move, Amos had occupied: "Had a falling out with
Daddy and went down there to set up house for myself. It used to
be a nigger cabin, you know, back in the slave days." Amos recommended leaving it where it stood. "A building's like a man, it'll last
till you go to fooling with it. Take me out of Zion County and set
me down in one of them sanaterrariums, I wouldn't be long for this
world." There was a well not far from the cabin; it was dug by hand,
Amos said, and he heaved a time or two on the rusty pump handle.
No water came, but he pushed aside one of the boards that covered
the well and dropped in a pebble. They waited—plink! "Make a

wish," he said to Maggie, and to Steadman, "If I was you I'd paint this pump red and leave it here for a relic, you know, an ointment."

Ointment?

Amos pointed out where the deer had rubbed bark from the trees, polishing the velvet from their antlers, and along the creek bank he found the spoor of the raccoon, the skunk, and the groundhog—for him, coon, polecat, and whistle pig. Before long they ought to be seeing fawns, "little suitcases," he called them. He asked Steadman, "You heard the turkeys carrying on up on the mountain? I reckon you have heard 'em."

"I've been among them once or twice."

"I heard you was a walker," Amos said. "They tell me you keep the game stirred up pretty good."

"Stir 'em up is about all I do."

"You caught all the trout out of the creek yet? It used to be some good ones run up here every spring."

"I've left a few for pets."

Amos put his face close to Steadman's again, just for a second, and then he said to Anna, "He walks, and he talks some too, don't he?"

Then, satisfied that a roll of barb wire would keep his Charolais and Angus from roaming, Amos took his leave. The cigar had gone out; he didn't bother to relight it. "I'll wait till I'm on the other side of the creek. Case I fall in, you know. No need to waste a match."

When he'd tipped his hat and started back toward the bridge, Steadman asked Anna, "An ointment?"

"An ornament," she said.

Eight

"The trail of the Vienna sausage," said Harry to Steadman, referring to the cans that outnumbered the spleenwort on the floor of the forest they were walking through.

"Like Pabst Blue Ribbon, they bloom for years," Steadman said.

They were going fishing, and they were on their way to the top of Big Furnace Mountain. They had driven as far as they could on a paved road that ran beside Jerkemtight Branch, past yellow signs that advertised TROUT, into a picnic area where the tables were bolted to concrete slabs and the yellow trash cans, stenciled with the name of their donors, the Izaak Walton League, were chained to trees so that sportsmen would not make off with them. At the end of the area a wooden sign noted the beginning of the Jerkemtight Trail. And after a few miles the trail really began to deserve its tonic name. They do not venture far into the woods who carry Pabst and Vienna sausages, or so it seemed; farther along the trail Steadman observed a better class of litter. The trail was narrower, shadier, steeper, the banks of the stream not so trampled, the blooms of rhododendron more numerous than those of aluminum. They took a detour up a dark hollow just to stand for a moment under virgin hemlocks; the light was sieved through the great trees, and on the floor of the hollow, deep in crackling brown hemlock needles, nothing grew.

After that ritual stop they began fishing. They started in a long flat pool where the water ran over a slate bed. Two fish were rising and they spooked them both. That, too, was more or less ritual, and Steadman remarked that having now given fair notice, they could proceed. Harry soon disappeared upstream. As a fisherman he was a marcher. He moved steadily, hardly stopping long enough to cast, never casting more than five or six times over the same pool. He scorned all wiles and deceptions. He marched straight up to a pool, offered his fly, and moved on if he had no takers. When asked to account for these tactics, he said that he refused to try to outsmart any fish—suppose he failed? He took the Darwinian position that by removing eager, dumb fish he was contributing to the improvement of the species.

Steadman, on the other hand, was a creeper. On a stream like the Jerkemtight, where the water was clear as vodka, he spent as much time on his knees as on his feet. Of course he loved to find a rising trout, but his specialty was the extraction of the dark sullen trout from under stumps, roots, fallen trees. Although he carried an expensive cane rod, he was no purist. He was more a junk artist. He would use worms, crickets, hellgrammites, salmon eggs, or whatever else he thought might entice the trout. If possible, he liked to dap a dry fly where a dry fly had no business, dap it and keep dapping it until the trout at the bottom of the hole, under the stump, beneath the roots, came blasting out of its lair like a trained porpoise. Harry called Steadman's methods vulgar, and on the frequent days when Steadman caught more and bigger fish than he did, he called them unspeakable.

So Steadman waited until Harry was out of sight upstream before he crept to the ferny edge of a pool. There he watched, and presently a trout did flick out into the glide where it fed in darts and splashes. A good hatch of caddis was coming off the stream, but Steadman didn't try to match it. He cast his tinsely bivisible fly over the trout and caught it.

That was how the morning went. The trout were all feeding and they'd take anything. It was Harry's kind of day. Steadman loved to see the fish in the water, the brilliant flash of orange, and like any fisherman he loved to feel the line come tight against that weight in the water, but he missed the jolt to the imagination that came when he crawled up to a dark hole and invoked a trout. When they rose out of nowhere, it was as if they rose out of imagination. These willing, visible trout were plainly the handiwork of a different agency. Not the Game Commission—they were responsible for the muddy-tasting rainbow trout in the lower part of the stream, stocked fish with pale stripes and backs like mottled linoleum. These wild brook trout had that gash of orange, bright spots of yellow and red, and succulent pink flesh. Steadman conked a few of them on the head and put them in his creel, and told himself that if he didn't kill them someone else would, probably some jerk with dynamite caps or a hot wire on a crank.

"How many?" Harry wanted to know when he reappeared.

"Four. I see you have a sagging creel."

"Look at these beauties." Harry dug his catch out of the moss he'd packed them in, six brookies, most of them eight or nine inches long, fat and chunky. He had one twelve-inch colossus. "This was the right day."

"I'm thinking of billing you for a guide's fee."

"You think I can't find my way up here?"

"I know you wouldn't be here unless you'd been urged by a member of the leisure class."

"Bill me, then," Harry said, "and I'll bill you for lunch."

He'd brought a creamy wurst that his parents had sent him, the black bread Diana baked, a slab of good smelly Appenzeller cheese. They'd put a few beers, not Pabst but Tuborg Gold, in the stream to cool, and they stretched out on the rocks, in the sun, to eat.

"So," Steadman said, "that brings your season's catch to ten."

"I can't keep up with your torrid pace."

"I'm not sure I can keep up with it either."

Steadman meant that the fishing would go off with the hot weather, but Harry said, "That happens over here. Going out more, enjoying it less."

"Is that the stage before going out less? That's the one you're in."

Harry nodded. "I had the idea when I came that there'd be hunting, fishing, books, music, sheep."

"And it all boils down to—sheep."

"They're as interesting as fish."

Harry was serious, and there was a lull before he said, "You saw what Silesia was like on the opening day of trout season. Everybody in the state of Virginia who owns a trout license and a Zepco was standing in the St. Margaret's trying to catch their money's worth of trout."

"There's nobody up here."

"On the trail of the Vienna sausage."

"What's the lesson?" Steadman asked. "Give up fishing because there are too many Zepcos? No more trout, no more wilderness, no more Hemingway. That's all utilized up."

"Something like that."

"But I love to shoot elephants. Don't you think it's wonderful when we shoot elephants? I wish we could always shoot elephants, don't you? Life would be tragic and happy if we could shoot elephants all the time."

"You asshole."

"I'm serious. I would love to go elephant hunting every day until I became a great white hunter, and the only elephants I wouldn't shoot would be the members of Babar's family."

"Who is Babar?"

"The king of the elephants. He's in Maggie's books. She wouldn't forgive me."

They ate wurst and black bread and drank Tuborg Gold on the banks of the Jerkemtight. It sometimes seemed to Steadman that it had been an accident of convenience that Harry was the one college friend he'd kept up with. While he was in Washington and Harry was in Zion County, he'd taken advantage of Harry's hospitality. There'd been a fiction that it would be returned in Washington—but Harry never went to Washington. He had dispensed with cities as he had dispensed with hunting and fishing, as frivolities. Human beings were also frivolities, at least as compared with sheep; Steadman sometimes suspected that Harry's manners, polite and formal, were used to mask an indifference toward bipeds. He never gossiped, was never censorious, and in any serious conversation he stated his opinion, often in one sentence, and neither modified it nor attempted to persuade others to it. He was always direct and even looked that way; he gave the impression that he had dispensed with peripheral vision. Yet he wasn't solemn and righteous; his humor took a sly, silly turn or else, with the sheep, became downright silly. The novelists he liked were Austen, Tolstoy, Trollope, and Evelyn Waugh; the only journalists he really admired were Hunter Thompson and a few baseball writers. He had an excellent library of classical music and a poster of Tammy Wynette in his workshop. Steadman knew that he wouldn't be in Zion County if Harry hadn't been there first; he knew that Harry had been generous with his help, time, tools; but Harry puzzled him. They seemed to be comfortable enough there on the stones by the stream, either speaking or not speaking, but Steadman was not used to laconic friendships, not, anyway, to the extent of the privacy which Harry respected. And so he was surprised when Harry asked point-blank, "Are you going to farm?"

His impulse was to make a wisecrack but he checked it and said, "Probably, sooner or later." Harry wasn't looking at him and he thought the conversation could end right there. "What's on your mind, Harry?"

"I think I want company," Harry said slowly. It was a confession, and it embarrassed Harry, who added, "I guess I have social urges after all." He tried to laugh at himself, but Steadman knew he didn't think much of his joke.

"I'm glad to help out when you need a hand, but that's not the kind of company you mean."

"No," Harry said. "It helps, but I expected you to have a few animals by now. I didn't know you were going to make a career of remodeling your house." That didn't quite come out as a joke, and Harry pushed on. "They're not going to farm down at Xanaduc—they're just playing around with those sheep and goats. And these old farmers around here, even people like Other, want to do everything by themselves. They're just trying to keep these old places from falling apart. There's a lot of momentum in a farm if you just keep patching and mending. What I'm saying, I guess, is that it gets to me sometimes to be doing this stuff alone over here. I can do it, but—"

He shrugged, and Steadman didn't know how to reply to this

extraordinary disclosure. He said, "Is this a proposal of marriage?" and he was greatly relieved when Harry laughed.

They talked more easily after that. Harry said, "Out here, in a place like this where nobody else is really farming, you start to feel like a fanatic."

"Aren't you a fanatic?"

"I probably am."

"You ought to be out in Kansas if you wanted to be in a community of fanatics."

"I'm not looking for a community. I'm just looking for one or two others. That would be enough to make it seem less personal. Christ, it's gotten so I even take the weather personally."

Steadman said, "I've put off thinking about farming because there are already too many things between me and the writing desk. There are trout, for example."

"Take up farming," Harry said. "Your first book can be called *The Romance of the Tractor.*"

"You'll have to dictate it to me."

And so they talked about writing and farming and lolled on the banks of the Jerkemtight.

Anna was in the garden with Maggie when she heard Diana shout, and she looked up in time to see the two dogs streaking after a groundhog. Otto jumped the garden fence and romped after them. "Wig! Thump! You come back!" The setters ignored her. Anna thought that if she were a dog she wouldn't mind Diana either. All three animals dove into the brush. Maggie looked over with big eyes, mugging. "It got away, didn't it?"

"Yep." Anna was glad it had. She liked this particular groundhog, which often sunned itself on the big walnut stump at the edge of the field.

Soon the dogs came ambling up to the garden fence with Diana behind them. She had a nice loose walk and she was puffing a little when she reached them. "Whew. That hill's steeper than it looks." She blew for a moment and then stooped down and picked up a handful of soil and let it fall through her fingers. "Gosh, this ground is nice and light. You're lucky—to have a garden that's been worked before, I mean. We turned over a garden the first year, the old one was just too far from the house, and it was awful. You just couldn't work it with all those great big clumps of sod in it."

"I don't know. This is my first garden. It still seems—kind of miraculous to me."

"It looks great. This is the time I like best, when all the seeds are up and everything's nice and neat, no weeds. About two weeks from now it'll turn into a jungle. Are you getting any peas yet?"

"A few."

"What're you doing?"

"Just thinning these carrots."

"Let me help you."

"I'm almost done," Anna said, "and I'm ready to knock off for a while. We don't get many visitors over here, do we, Mag? We shouldn't put them to work when they do come."

"If Harry and Steadman can take a day off to go fishing, we ought to be able to sit for a while. I'm really glad Steadman makes Harry take some time off, you know?" Then Diana jabbered for a while with Maggie, who strode about thumping with the hoe to show Diana how she worked.

"That's it," Anna said. "I've been in the garden long enough. If I don't stand up straight for a while, I'm going to have a back like a crook. Bent over, I mean, not like a criminal."

She felt stupid for adding that explanation—of course Diana knew what a crook was. But as much as she liked Diana she'd never got the knack of talking to her. Diana never thought that things had to be made interesting; to her they were absolutely fascinating in themselves. Ordinarily Anna was grateful for this, and grateful too that Diana was never confessional. Laurie, and especially Val, whom Anna had got to know a little, discussed their moods and emotions in such a way that Anna felt called upon to make similar revelations about herself. She did not make them and felt guilty that she didn't. Diana had plenty of moods and emotions but she didn't treat them as states or conditions that illuminated the truth of her life. They were more like some common bug or low-grade virus, like a mild cold she expected to get over soon.

As they went up to the house Diana was talking about the latest at Xanaduc: Rod and Stan had argued, again, and Rod had threatened to leave, again—over a TV. The Watergate hearings were on, and Rod said they had to watch them, and Stan said it was just politics. And there was another girl at Xanaduc too, Peggy, a friend of Laurie's—and maybe, Diana thought, Zep would finally find a partner. Anna took this in, even took in some of the details while she made banana smoothies in the blender. Banana peels, ice trays, milk cartons, the bag of sugar—the counter got wet and she spilled the sugar filling the jar, the sugar turned into glucose, the blender foamed over.

"What are *these?*" Diana asked suddenly.

"Mama's bugs," said Maggie.

"They're so *big.*"

Anna wished she had put them away. "They're just sketches I tried to do."

"Bugs."

"I guess they're not too pretty, but I got interested in them—I'd never really looked at bugs till I started working in the garden. And I don't really mind them, not the hard scaly ones anyway. The squishy ones, the slugs and larvae, I can't stand."

Diana looked through the sheets. Most of the sketches were about the size of a hand. "I'm glad the real things aren't this big."

"I just draw them that way because it's easier. I have a kind of magnifying glass, it's a sort of jar—you put the bug down in the bottom of it and it blows it up."

"They're too lifelike for me. I like your flowers better."

Anna would have liked to say that she thought the bugs, the beetles especially, were beautiful in their way, but she knew that her oversized drawings were monstrous. It was color, symmetry, and especially scale that made insects tolerable. They were grotesque when they were as big as rats.

Diana laughed. "What's this?"

Anna turned from the counter expecting to see a bug, but Diana was holding up a list. "Tie boots. Pick up hairbrush. Make bed. Do not leave clothes on floor."

"That's my self-improvement list. It was mostly a joke, but I've been making all kinds of lists lately. The trouble is I can never find them."

"I used to keep lists too, but now it's all so routine—" Diana laughed again. "I remember one time, one really bad time at the beginning, when I used to make a list and then copy it over, and make it all neat, you know. It made me feel like I was getting something done."

"That's about the way I feel. I think I waste as much time trying to be efficient as I used to waste because I'm so sloppy. And I'm still sloppy anyway." She waved at the counter.

"Listen, you and Steadman are doing great, I think. When I remember our first year over here, our first two years—it was just chaos."

And while she talked about how most things had become routine by now, and would for Anna too, Anna brought the banana smoothies to the table and watched Maggie go to work on hers. Glug glug glug. A stream ran from the corner of her mouth, rich and thick. She closed one eye and peered into the glass with great detachment and curiosity. Then she put her chin in her hand and looked at Diana with an expression of consummate boredom. Diana was saying now that she'd been to the doctor that morning.

"There's nothing wrong, is there?"

"Just a checkup."

"I ought to go soon. That's another thing I should put on my self-improvement list. The doctor. The dentist. I haven't been to the dentist since I got married. What doctor do you go to in Staunton?"

Diana gave her the name and described the man. Anna's attention slanted off; she thought about the IUD working its way up her like a corkscrew. She hated the thing but the pill made her sick and she'd been meaning to get a diaphragm.

Suddenly she realized she'd missed something. Diana was staring at her in a goofy way, her face all lit up. Diana, mercifully, repeated, "Yep, I'm preggers." She swallowed the word in a gulp.

"Diana, that's wonderful."

But Diana's elation was confused. "You're the only one I've told," she said, and tears started to run. She didn't try to hide her face but kept looking at Anna and trying to smile.

"What's the matter? That's good news, Diana, it's wonderful news." Anna left her chair and put her arm around Diana's broad shaking shoulders.

"I don't know why I'm sniffling over this. I guess I really am worried."

"About what?" Maggie asked.

"You have to keep my secret, okay?"

"What is it?"

"I have a baby inside me."

"Oh," said Maggie.

"I just had to tell somebody, and I can't tell Harry, not yet. I don't want him to have to go through it all again—if I have another miscarriage he'll know about it, but I don't want him to have to dread it too."

"How far are you?"

"About two months. There's a real heartbeat in there. God, that's spooky, isn't it? When you listen to that thing inside you? Anyway, this is just about the most dangerous time for somebody like me who's had two miscarriages before."

"But why can't you tell Harry?"

"I couldn't stand it if he was disappointed again." The tears were standing on Diana's lashes. "I think he wants children more than I do. He always acts very gruff, I know, and pretends he doesn't care, but sometimes, really, I feel like I was married to a king or shah or somebody, and I just have to produce an heir."

"Won't he guess?"

"I don't show yet, do I? I shouldn't, as big as I am. And I feel fine, woozy in the morning sometimes, but I never throw up."

"You'll have this one," Anna said. "You have to."

"I'm even pretending that I'm still on the pill. I have one of those cases, the kind with the days on it, and I flush one down the toilet every morning."

"Harry wouldn't check that."

"I don't think he would either, but you know what? Sometimes I'd just like to wait till I'm as big as a barn, just as long as I could, to see when he'd finally notice."

They talked more about babies and birth. Anna enjoyed, for a change, having information that Diana didn't have, and Maggie loved hearing how she'd come into the world.

Nine

Beep Beep Beeeeeep.

Kay was at the bridge.

Anna, in the garden, had been glancing at the road all afternoon but hadn't seen her arrive. Mid-June, real summer now, and most of the road was hidden from sight by the dense trees.

"I'll go down and help her bring up her things," she told Steadman, who was unloading logs from Duty Armstrong's big truck. Harry had come over to help them move the cabin, and they were stacking the logs where the studio was to stand, at the edge of Steadman's orchard. The little trees with their tufts of green looked like arrows someone had shot straight into the ground.

"Take the Blazer down if you want."

"She probably doesn't have much to carry."

Maggie was already on her way. With Otto she ran ahead of Anna, took a spill, hollered *Bingo* as Steadman had taught her, picked herself up, and kept going. By the time Anna reached the bridge Maggie was in the middle of it, swinging on it with Kay, making the cables groan. In the bright sun Kay looked pale, white, bleached. She was wearing shorts, a halter, sunglasses, sandals. Her hair had been cut short, just chopped off. And when she followed Maggie off the bridge, Anna saw that she had a raised white ragged scar on her forehead. It was notched like a saw blade and slanted from the part in her black hair to the space between her eyes.

"Pretty, huh?" said Kay. "Everybody notices it."

"What happened, Kay?"

"I was just telling Maggie—I walked through a sheet of plate glass, one of those sliding doors. Never saw it."

Anna knew, she wasn't sure how, that Kay was lying. The sensation was strange and painful; she realized that it was the first time she had doubted her sister.

"Well, you made it here all right."

"Yeah. This is some bridge. Okay, Rover, that's enough."

"Get down, Otto."

"Does he always go for the crotch? Or am I something special?"

"Steadman says he has a good nose," Anna said, and heard how absurd she sounded.

"Baby, you look great, nice and sleek. You've put on some weight, haven't you?"

"Have I? I guess I have. Everybody eats like a horse down here."

"You're getting muscles too."

Anna put her hand on her bare arm. "I've been doing a lot of work. Where are your things, Kay? Are they still in your car?"

They crossed the bridge and got Kay's suitcase out of the car— a small red rusting car with a bashed fender that Kay called the Cherry. On the way up to the house Anna chattered. She told Kay the cows she saw weren't theirs, and that the bridge really wasn't so bad, and that the place looked better in the spring, not so straggling and lush. She heard that she was apologizing.

"What's going on up there?"

"Steadman just moved those logs. There was a cabin down in the field there, but it was falling in, and he decided to move it closer to the house. It's going to be a studio."

"Who are those other guys?"

"They're neighbors. The one in overalls is Duty Armstrong— that's his truck. The other one's Harry Obenwald. He lives right across the creek."

But when they reached the men it was Steadman, not Anna, who introduced Kay. Duty made his quick bow, quick tip of the cap, and Harry—what got into him?—raised his hand and chirped Hi! in a fruity voice. Steadman said, "Kay is Anna's twin sister."

"Anybody'd know they were out of the same litter," Duty said.

"Nobody'll have any trouble telling us apart now," Kay said, tapping her forehead. "In case you didn't notice."

"I saw you got whacked," Steadman said.

"Walked through a sliding door. There's an old conflict between me and glass." She didn't try to sound funny. "But I don't look much like Baby anymore, do I? Everybody around here grows muscles. You look like a blacksmith."

"These logs are heavy."

"This old oak's about like pig iron," Duty said. Anna heard *abart lark p'garn* and wondered if Kay had made out a single syllable.

"Maybe it'll build me up if I stay here for a while. Don't look so worried, Steadman—just kidding."

They stood there and watched the men take down another log from the truck, and Anna saw that the weight of it made them bandy-legged. They tottered, took tiny blundering steps, looked as if they were competing with the whole magnetic force of the earth. Anna knew she should take Kay up to the house but she couldn't move.

Duty blew, spat. He grinned, showed those brown teeth. "Why, we could move these logs if they wasn't half so heavy."

"Don't let us slow you down," Kay said.

And Anna did move, following Kay, who said as soon as they were in the house, "Who is that fucking cracker? He's straight out of Dogpatch." Anna defended Duty but Kay didn't pay any attention to her. She was looking around the kitchen, taking it in. "What a cozy little nest. What's that weird-looking thing there?"

"That? That's a pie-safe. Steadman got it at an auction."

"A safe? You bake pies now, Baby?"

"That's not what we use it for."

"Rugs on the floor and everything. A real country kitchen, all spick-and-span. You've turned into quite the little homemaker, huh?"

Anna had spent the whole morning cleaning the house. "It looks a little better than it usually does. I tried to straighten up a little this morning—you know, company coming."

"Am I company?"

"I didn't mean it that way, Kay. I only meant—it was just an excuse to put things away. I'm not very good at that."

"You used not to be. Divine squalor, Baby."

"You should have seen this house when we moved in. There was nothing so divine about the squalor then." And she tried to make their efforts, all the scraping and sanding, the flies and mice, sound amusing to Kay, but none of it came out right. Kay sat at the table, smoked cigarettes, asked for a beer. After a bit Anna showed her the rest of the house and then took her out to the garden and tried to talk about the vegetables. Kay stretched out in the hammock while Anna and Maggie picked peas. Duty drove off, Harry left, and Steadman came into the garden and said he'd asked the Obenwalds to come to dinner—Harry had earned a meal. Anna wished he hadn't asked them. When Kay was in the shower and she had a moment alone with Steadman, she grabbed his arm. "Don't you be hard on her, Steadman. I think something's really wrong."

"I'll try not to be, but I'm not sure there's much I can do about it."

"What do you mean?" Anna asked, but she knew what he meant.

Before dinner, before the Obenwalds arrived, Kay lit a joint in the kitchen. She offered it to Steadman and Anna, who both declined. "Is that part of the virtuous country life?"

"I'm a gin-and-tonic junkie," Steadman said. "Do you want one?"

"I didn't know I was in the suburbs."

"You're not," he said. "Look out the window."

"At the cows?"

"This is the best time of day here," Steadman said, "when we get the shadow from the mountain. You can feel the temperature fall. We don't have sunsets—it's more like an encroachment the way the shadow reaches across the valley."

"I guess I'm in the way in here," Kay said, and slammed out the door.

Steadman looked at Anna and shrugged.

The Obenwalds arrived and Anna got stuck in the kitchen. Steadman was outside cooking a steak over the fire, but she had to cook the peas and the fancy potatoes he wanted and make the salad. She could hear them talking outside, Diana at the table out there asking Kay gawking questions about twins. "What's it like? Gosh, it must be weird. You and Anna look so much alike." Anna knew how Kay must feel. Now and then she heard her say a word or two—"Waitressing," she said when Diana asked her what she'd been doing for a job, and when Diana asked her about Washington, she said, "It sucks." Harry was talking to Steadman near the fire, and Maggie, with a red bow stuck in her hair at a crazy angle, was trying to help Anna. "Why are you putting that butter on your hand, Mama?"

"Because I burned my fucking hand on the pan, that's why."

Maggie stared at her, dark, fiery. "Don't get mad at me if you're clumsy."

Steadman came to the door. "You almost done in here? The meat's off the fire."

"Coming."

When Anna went outside carrying the food, she thought for a second that it couldn't be as bad as she supposed. The air was crisp, floods of dark shadows moved across the grass and faces, the little incandescent lights of fireflies had already begun to appear. She set the containers down on the table and said, "Don't hold back, Kay. These people are grabby."

Kay was still wearing the dark glasses, watching Steadman cut the beef. "It's nice and rosy," he said.

"I don't want any. I don't eat meat anymore."

"Oh really?" asked Diana. "Are you a vegetarian? I just don't know how people can give it up."

"It's not hard. You are what you eat and all that."

"Tomorrow," Steadman said, "when you wake up a large head of lettuce, Anna will transplant you immediately."

"I'd just as soon be lettuce as a cow's ass."

"Don't be misled by resemblances."

"You look more like a horse's ass," Harry said.

Kay said, "Have you guys ever come across this little thought: Bury an acorn and you get an oak. Bury a sheep, and—you get the idea."

"That sounds like Shaw," Steadman said. "He was the only vegetarian who had any wit."

"Come on," Anna pleaded. "Can't we talk about something else?"

It was dark now, and the kerosene lamps were lit on the table, and the crickets and peepers were chirping. "Listen," Steadman said, and when they had listened to the croaking he told them how Keats and his friends, in one of their sonnet-writing contests, took insects as their subject. And the first line of Keats's sonnet—"Don't kill us with suspense," Kay said. Steadman quoted like Tarzan: "The poetry of earth is never dead."

Anna stared down at the bow in Maggie's hair—poor Mag, expecting a party, and she got this. Anna cut up her meat for her.

Diana said, chewing, "The problem for me with being a vegetarian is that I just wouldn't know what to cook. What kinds of things do you eat?"

"There are plenty of things."

"That's not your problem, Di," Harry said. "Your problem is that you like to eat meat, and butter, and sweets—"

"And everything else," Diana said. "I know."

"All right, Diana," Steadman announced. "I want you to try to imagine real hardship. Imagine that you have to give up all but three tastes. The staple of your diet is going to be Cheerios or something else absolutely bland. What three tastes would you keep?"

"Agh! That's an awful question."

"Name three."

"Meat, I guess. I couldn't give up meat. And butter, I'd have to have butter and cream."

"Garlic," said Harry.

"Careful—what would put the garlic on? You have only two tastes left."

"Let's talk about something besides food," Anna said.

Kay said, "What about bread and water?"

"The prisoner's diet," said Steadman.

"I could live on bread and water longer than you'd live on garlic and butter."

Kay was sneering but Steadman laughed. "That's true."

"It is true. You're sitting here running all this shit about fancy food and you don't even stop to think you couldn't live on it."

Steadman kept smiling but Anna saw that temper pinched the corners of his mouth and eyes. "I'm just a slave to appetite."

"You know what happens to meat inside you—it putrefies and turns to shit."

Kay was so extreme that Steadman laughed. "And what happens to vegetarians?"

"They have nice little round turds like sheep," Harry said.

Diana asked earnestly, "Is it just that you don't like meat, Kay, or is it religious, you know, Buddhist or something?"

"Yeah, it's Buddhist or something," Kay mocked.

"Have you changed your politics too?" Steadman asked.

"What? You don't know shit about politics."

"Not your politics then, your principles."

"There's only only principle: no more fucking patriarchs. Out here you guys act like you're Solomon and Moses. You've got your houses and your lands and your animals and your women and your kids. Generations, and begetting—isn't that what all this country shit is about? What's the matter with you, Diana? Where are your little ones? Where's Mother's little helper?"

"I think I'm on Kay's side now," Harry said. "No kids, okay, Di? I can't afford to hire a hand."

"Is that what Diana is? The hand?"

Harry took Diana's hand—long, narrow, fine—and held it up beside his own. They were almost identical. "That's the lamb-puller, the one that goes into the lamb-bed to haul 'em out." He brought it to his lips and kissed it.

"This is really touching, you know."

God damn Kay, god damn her. Anna hated feeling strange and she hated crying, but she was about to start. She felt her legs tighten, felt the splintery edge of the bench drag against her calves as she stood up and slid along it, felt her burn when she clenched her fist. "Excuse me," she said, and tried to walk, not back to the house but down the slope into the darkness. Maybe they'd think she was going to pee but she didn't care, she had to get away from that table. The grass was wet with dew and soaked her boots, the moon was just past full, the field was silvered. What were tears anyway? Did they just sit there behind the eyes, waiting for sadness or anger to release them? And how could emotion open a duct or valve or whatever it was? She looked back where they were all sitting at the blurry table, huddled in the orange glow—those kerosene lamps—and felt the tears come hot and stinging while the rest of her was chilly. Her eyes were going to be puffy. She saw Steadman rise and come after her and thought of trying to get away from him, but she stood her ground and tried to calm herself. She didn't know what she'd do if he said one word about Kay.

She was standing near the darkness of a grove, and when he got near something rose and burst out of the brush. Rustling, crashing —and Anna saw the flickering white motion, the upraised tail of a bounding deer. But she had already pitched forward against Stead- man and he was holding her. The deer stopped, started again, snorted. "It sounds like a gorilla," she said, and she thought she was all right then.

"I thought you were down here alone."

"You flinched too," she said.

He hugged her.

She thought she was all right then and they walked back up to the table together for strawberries and cream. They talked about the moon, about dreams. Steadman told his dog dream. They were in Italy, in a pensione with thin walls, and so when he was a dog and about to bark in the middle of the night, he tried to suppress it out of respect for the other sleepers. He failed. He awoke sitting in the bed, baying.

"Baying?" Harry asked. "Or did you go woof woof? Arf arf? Alpo?"

"Woof woof, I think."

"What breed were you? Basset? Doberman? Poodle? I can't inter- pret this without more information."

"I was just a mutt."

"Were you happy as a dog?"

He said he was. And then Diana talked about her hair dreams— it just kept falling out—and Harry confessed that his recurrent dream was of Chinamen who arrived in hordes and did absolutely as they were told and simplified his chores. Steadman said that when he was putting in the bathroom he dreamed of checking into a motel —and leaving it seated on the toilet, which still had its sanitary band across the seat, riding it, for it was motorized, like the engine of a small train, pulling behind him the sink and the bathtub and heading for Zion County with these amenities in tow. They ate berries, drank coffee. Kay was silent. Maggie was sleepy now and curled against Anna, her weight increasing by the second with drowsiness. Anna could feel the dark head rolling against her ribs, the bow pricking her.

Diana and Harry got up to leave. "I've got to get back to milk Gertie before she panics," Diana said.

"Good dinner," Harry said.

They went down the slope, arms around each other, for a few steps bulky against the low stars. When they went below the edge, Anna heard Harry's voice say something in a burr, a sexy threat, then Diana's giggle.

"Well, here we are, just family," Kay said.

"It looks like this one is about through," Steadman said, picking Maggie up. "The sandman got you, didn't he?" He kissed her good-night and she clung to him.

"I'll clean up out here," he said. "You better get her to bed."

Anna saw that Kay felt ignored, but when Steadman gave her Maggie she carried her in, upstairs, undressed her. First the orange, green, and yellow sandals that Maggie had chosen for herself from the rack at K-Mart, then the denim shorts and cotton panties, then, sitting her up and balancing her, the sweater, and last, over the dreaming head, the *Virginia is for Lovers* T-shirt. Steadman had bought it for her and Maggie adored it because of the bright red heart. She was naked now and Anna smoothed back the hair from the forehead and dabbed at the corners of her mouth with a tissue. The sturdy little body was white and firm as the flesh of an apple, the arms and legs were brown and nicked. Anna spread Cutter's lotion over Maggie's hands and face to protect her from bites and nibbles while she slept. She gazed at Maggie, dreaming: had she been so once? She and Kay?

She put Maggie's nightgown on her and covered her with her quilt. Then she turned the light out, and in the darkness she stood and waited to hear the breathing. It came firm and steady.

The house in Washington, the tall windows, the light between the slats of the blinds: Anna's room. She was dressed for school in the uniform, gray sweater buttoned at the neck, gray pleated skirt, knee socks. She felt very correct and neat, as neat as the nuns, and she walked solemnly down the stairs. Dark steps, dark polished wood, square landing, high railing. Her satchel, leather with pockets and buckles, was in its place on the floor in the hall beside the grandfather clock. She tried to lift it but couldn't. She couldn't drag it or turn it over or even open it to see what had been placed inside. She ran upstairs, her feet loud on the steps now, calling for Kay to help her, and pulled the rug aside and lifted the boards of the floor. Kay was there in bloody pieces, arms and legs and chunks. Anna kept pulling them out, trying to fit them, screamed when she saw the stains on her hands, skirt, socks.

So she'd slept enough to dream at least, and when she woke from that nightmare she found that her period had begun. There was actual blood on her thighs. When she pulled back the covers she saw a stain on the sheet, for the bedroom, moonlight reflected on the white walls, was not dark. She went to the bathroom, put in a Tampax, brought back a towel to put down over the stain. Steadman stirred, flung an arm over her.

Not long after dawn Maggie woke and came into their room, as she usually did, and snuggled in the bed with them. The windows faced east, caught the sun, let in shafts of light that had edges like incisions, made openings in the chiller air of the bedroom. Steadman turned; Anna felt his stiff penis, Maggie's heel, against her thigh, stomach. "Your whiskers are scratchy," Maggie said, stroking his cheek and chin. Steadman put his arm across both of them, his hand on Anna's breast. "Am I the last one up?"

"You always are," Maggie said.

"But I'm the first one out of bed."

"I don't like to get up first."

"Neither does your mama. Maybe we'd better tickle her."

"Don't," Anna said.

Steadman did tickle Maggie for a second, gave her a kiss, squeezed Anna's breast, got out of bed with his penis half-hard and kind of wallowing in the air as he got into his clothes. It took him only a moment to dress, piss, brush his teeth, go downstairs, where they heard him open the door to let out Otto, heard the first low snarls of the radio, the bumping around as Steadman fixed himself breakfast.

"I guess we better get up too," Anna said.

Right after breakfast Steadman left to haul rocks for the studio. Anna and Maggie cleaned up the kitchen and waited for Kay, who didn't come down till nine. "Baby, I slept like the dead," she said. "Maybe there really is something in the mountain air. I can't remember the last good night's sleep I had."

Anna hesitated, then said, "It's helped me a little, I guess. But I'm still—restless."

"I was just knocked out. I don't even remember hitting the pillow. How'd I get here, Baby?"

Anna supposed that this was an apology. Kay had coffee; she said they'd probably inherited their insomnia from their mother. "Maybe that's why sleeping pills never worked for me," Anna said. "I probably have some genetic immunity. I wish I was immune to all the side effects too." They talked about their mother and father, about Papi, their grandfather; Anna said that after all she did miss them and wanted to see them. "I haven't seen any of them since last fall— everything starts to seem so remote when you live out here. It's only four hours to Washington, but sometimes I feel like I'm on a different continent."

"You were always on a different continent, Baby."

Anna laughed. "You know what I mean. I was afraid of this place when I came. It seemed kind of . . ."

"Primitive," Kay completed her sentence.

"And it was so different from any place I'd ever lived. Anyway, when I think of Washington now I can hardly believe I lived there once. I'm afraid of it now. All I can think about is muggers."

"This place seems pretty safe," Kay said, "the house does anyway. Even Mama would feel safe in here."

They laughed at the idea of their mother in Zion County. Kay was wearing her dark glasses, and Anna still wasn't entirely comfortable with her; everything, even her laughter, was too bright and skittery. Maggie reminded Anna that she'd been promised a swim.

"That sounds good to me," Kay said.

And so Anna put a few towels in a tote bag with Maggie's toys, and changed Maggie into the blue swimsuit with the front shaped like a yellow heart, and tried to persuade her that the walk to the Lime Pool was rough enough to call for sneakers instead of sandals. "She gets attached to things," she said to Kay, "and you can see how every little trip becomes an expedition." Then Maggie led the way out of the house and through the field in grass to her waist, stopped and waited to take Anna's hand when she reached the rocky gully, a passage crowded by trees, that led to the creek.

"I can see why you were afraid of this place, Baby. Are there any creepy things in there? Snakes, for example?"

"I think about snakes too, but I haven't seen any yet. Let's just walk through here fast."

They reached the creek in a few minutes. "Yours?" asked Kay. "Your private swimming hole? This is terrific." They spread the towels on the gravel bank and Kay peeled off her shorts and top, stepped out of her sandals. "It's okay, isn't it? There aren't any little boys hiding up in the woods, are there? Are you coming in, Baby?"

"I think I'll wait a few minutes. I like to get heated up first."

Kay stepped into the water—"Oh Baby, it's freezing"—but walked right in till it was up to her ribs and then she plunged. She swam and splashed up to the head of the pool, drifted back with the green current. "That wakes you right up. It makes your head tingle it's so cold. But it feels wonderful, you know? I love the way water pushes against you—it makes you remember you have a body. It's definite. Think of a fish, Baby, with water around it all the time—I wouldn't mind being a fish. In all this air I just dissolve."

She put on her sunglasses and sat down on her towel. Her teeth chattered. "That's as long as I can stay in. I'm just too skinny for these temperatures." She put her own pale arm beside Anna's. "Look at you, Baby, look how dark you are. You'd make a fine fish. Hey look, the hairs on your arm are sort of gold, and mine are still black. We really got cursed, didn't we? I still remember the first time I saw Papa with his shirt off—he looked like an ape with all that fur. Do you remember how we used to try to keep anybody from knowing about our pubes? How old were we? It seems like we couldn't have been more than seven."

"I think we were a little older than that."

"But we sprouted before anybody else. Sometimes I think my snatch is still spreading—I look at it and think it's going to be up to my navel soon." Kay was on her back, holding herself up with her elbows, looking at the patch of black hair that rose at the bottom of her sunken belly. The drops of water sparkled in it. Anna saw Maggie crouched beside the water, watching, listening.

"What's with you, Baby? Modest?"

Anna hadn't taken off her clothes. "I'm on the rag," she said so Maggie wouldn't hear. But she did pull her shirt over her head and in a moment she stood up and unbuttoned her khaki shorts and stepped out of them and her panties together.

"Where'd you get those shorts? They look like they'd fit Steadman."

"They are a little roomy."

"Baby, you really look great. I can't get over it, you know? I expect you to look like me, I expect to see myself when I look at you —but you're turning into centerfold material." And then Kay said, "I guess I'd better shut up if I'm going to make you hunch up that way."

"It does make me self-conscious," Anna said. "I'm not very—"

"In-body," Kay said.

"I don't think I've ever been. I had a dream last night, and I wasn't even in it, my body wasn't—I was nothing but clothes walking downstairs. I had on that convent uniform."

"That thing. I hated that."

"I didn't mind it. It made me feel nice and anonymous. I guess I never was one to assert myself."

"What was I doing in this dream, Baby?"

"You weren't in it."

"Come on, Baby. You never could lie. What happened in this dream?"

"I had to get you to help me carry my books. Remember those book satchels we had, the ones with all the flaps and pockets on them? Mine felt like it was full of lead—of pig iron."

Kay lay back, gratified. *"Pig arn.* Baby the cracker. Is that so terrible that you couldn't tell me? You don't need help anymore?"

She didn't seem to expect an answer. She lay back in the sun and spread her hands on her belly—her fingers were as chewed as Anna's —and said, "The sun pushes too, doesn't it? It's almost as good as water, the way it identifies you." They were silent for a few minutes. Maggie began to throw stones into the creek. Anna watched how Maggie squatted, how the backs of the calves and thighs met, how the skin stretched over her knees. She sorted through the stones, looking for ones that fit her hand. She knew when they were just right. She laughed at the splash, the water, the stone. Anna thought she'd better speak out now.

"I don't think I'm so passive anymore."

"Huh?"

"I don't think I'm as passive as I was, Kay."

Kay sat up. "What's this? A little rebellion?"

"No, not that. . . . I just have more to do over here, more things of my own. . . . Maybe I can't explain."

"So Baby's a big grown-up now?"

Anna tried to smile. "Sometimes I feel like I'm impersonating a grown-up. But I do have things, Kay—the garden, and Maggie, and I've been drawing a little, and I've made some friends over here. I guess it doesn't sound like much."

"It sounds so precious, Baby."

"Don't make fun of me."

"Your precious little girl, and your precious little garden, and your precious little house, and your precious little hubby—I'd better start calling you Mrs. Steadman, I guess. No more Baby."

Kay stood up and started a taunting chant, swaying in front of Anna. "No more Baby, Baby all gone, bye-bye Baby, bye-bye Baby—"

And she screamed. Anna, who had looked down, heard that the scream had nothing to do with the taunting. It was critical. She sprang up, threw a towel over the red jaws and purple gums, and pushed Kay into the water, grabbed Maggie and ran into the current, trying to keep her feet on the slippery rocks, Kay holding to her. When they stopped in the shallows on the other side, she looked back and saw the fox all hunched up and puffing. Kay was wailing. Anna's foot stang. The water was running pink around it but she must have cut it in the creek. She'd know if she'd been bitten. Kay's arms were forked across her naked body and her sunglasses were still on. The fox limped stiffly into the woods.

Ten

"It had to be rabid," Steadman said. "No healthy fox would have approached you." Approached—from what Anna had said he couldn't tell whether it had merely approached or whether it had attacked. Anna's account was vague, and she got annoyed when he tried to pin her down with questions. She got annoyed, but he couldn't stop grilling her; he was, and he knew it, punishing her for her superstition. He was sure that Anna refused to discuss the fox because she regarded it as a personal scourge. When he tried to joke that she was probably lucky, that she must be immune now, that the odds on being attacked by a rabid fox must be about like the odds on being struck by lightning, and lightning doesn't strike in the same place twice, she reminded him that Amos had said that the swinging bridge had been hit three times—and so he knew that in her mind the fox was associated with those fated Argenstill twins. Carrying on with a show of scientific detachment, he borrowed the Obenwalds' Merck Manual, the veterinary edition, to bone up on rabies. He also cut and peeled ash limbs for all of them, fox staffs, a big one for himself, a medium-sized one for Anna, and—trying to get a laugh out of her, treating her like Goldilocks—one for Maggie that was *just right.*

"We have to take our chances out there," he said, and he continued to work outside, laying stones for the foundation of the studio. Anna had become housebound. She did go as far as the garden, which was fenced, but that was all. Maybe, if Kay hadn't been there, Steadman could have admitted to her that the fox appalled him too. Its nature perverted by disease, the fox became a vicious mutation, and the woods looked ominous to him.

But Kay was there, and Anna had lapsed into an apprehensive trance, and he almost wished for the appearance of other foxes—to show Anna that she had not been singled out and cursed. She was simply helpless. Visitors always disconcerted her—she just dropped whatever she was doing—but Kay had immobilized her. Almost the only thing she'd done since Kay arrived was bake bread—and she left the kitchen in a blizzard of flour, left dough to harden on the board and in the bowls. Steadman cleaned up after her. He felt like shaking Anna or slapping her, anything to make her less comatose. The way she hovered through the house reminded Steadman of a big dazed fly. Her only expressive gesture was a cringe. She was in some kind of attendance on Kay, who spent hours in the front room reading and listening to records, the same records over and over again, Dylan, Hendrix, Joplin, the Doors, the Stones, the Dead. She played them so loud that he could hear them where he worked, a hundred yards from the house. At dinner, the only meal they all ate together, she made an effort not to provoke Steadman. She referred to Anna and to herself as Prisoners of the Fox. It was clear that she did not want Anna released from that captivity.

Sometimes Steadman felt a dismayed longing to help Anna, just to be able to comfort her, and he did try, in his way. At night, in bed, he put his hands on her as gently as he could. "What would I do if you had to take the shots? You'd be so sore I couldn't touch you—hands off for weeks." It didn't work. Anna let him touch her but he might as well have been fondling a potato. Even though she was having her period he fucked her—mashed potatoes. They fucked loudly enough for Kay to hear them. It only made it worse.

They could not talk about Kay, for Anna would hear no criticism of her. Steadman didn't really criticize, but when he said, "Kay is so down," Anna took it as criticism. It was true, Kay was down, but he was not to say so. Kay was down, but Steadman couldn't see, as Anna seemed to see, that there was any cause for dread. To him the only apparent difference in Kay was that she was no longer, as she had always been, considerate and protective of Anna. Steadman had once made the mistake of trying to warn Anna that Kay could be treacherous as well, but Anna contradicted him flatly: "You don't know her." He did know her, he thought, knew her as everyone but Anna knew her. She was not only considerate and protective of Anna, she was also possessive, calculating, and manipulative. She knew exactly how to make Anna depend on her. She knew exactly how to keep Anna from letting anyone get close to her. Anna had never had friends of her own until she came to Zion County.

It did not really puzzle Steadman that Anna, whose intuitions about people were almost always correct, even when they verged toward the uncanny, should be so deceived about Kay. He did not underestimate Kay, for she had diagnosed his weaknesses and played on them with virtuoso cunning. From the beginning she had understood what Steadman hardly understood himself, that his solemn feelings toward Anna were a little topheavy, and that he, as well as Anna, found it difficult to live up to them. "Doesn't Baby just make you want to rape her sometimes?" She cornered him and asked him that, and other things like that, when he was first seeing Anna—and then laughed at him because she knew he could admit nothing. She knew also that he could not repeat her questions, let alone the aberrant violence he occasionally felt, to Anna. That violence had no place in their romance. It did have a place in his emotions toward Kay—and Kay knew that too. She made sure that Steadman heard all about the men she took up with. "Jealous?" she'd ask him. "Drives you wild, doesn't it?" Steadman could only try to carry it off as a joke.

He had not been able to avoid seeing a lot of Kay, who lived with Anna in Washington. Her greeting to him in those days was "Up against the wall, motherfucker." Because he worked for Congressman Biggs he was, in Kay's view, one of the warmongers responsible for Vietnam. Yet Kay, after a period of fierce opposition to the war, no longer had anything to do with politics. She regarded all radical leaders as runty little sawed-off Nixons. That was her pattern: to take up things with a passion, to drop them in disgust or indifference. She'd begun college at Smith, where she lasted for a year—till she got sick of knee socks, she said—and ended up taking extension courses at American University. Many of the courses were in literature, and she went through periods when she read every word written by a certain writer, by Beckett or Plath or Tutuola or Calvino, and then she seemed to lose interest. She went to California once, wrote ecstatic letters for a few weeks; a few weeks later she came home with loathing for Lotus Land. Her men were usually dopes—"cuties," she called them—and she usually got rid of them in a hurry. Kay was restless and reckless and it showed in her face, her body, her movements. Steadman had once compared her to a crowbar—not, of course, in Anna's hearing. He used to fantasize that Kay engineered a switch so that she, instead of Anna, ended up in bed with him—and he believed that she was capable of it. The only point of this fantasy seemed to be to allow him to indulge his lust under a pretense of innocence. He could never, even in the dark, have mistaken Kay for Anna.

Despite his jealousy of Kay—for he too wanted Anna to himself —and despite his distrust of her, despite his disapproval and desire, he couldn't help recognizing that it did Anna good to see her. Especially after they'd married, when Anna felt so huge and unsightly in her pregnancy, he began to get used to Kay and even to be grateful for her kindness to Anna. He could always tell when he came home from work whether Anna had seen Kay that day—she was more vocal, more affectionate, more lively. He thought that Kay probably had her own sinister designs in treating Anna as she did, and he knew that there was still an intimacy between the sisters from which he was excluded, but he became more or less reconciled to it. And he didn't often have to deal with Kay, for she visited Anna during the day and cleared out before he got home. When they did see each other, they still flirted but in a different way now. Kay pretended to scold, a caricature of a mother-in-law. "You better be nice to Baby, and you better be faithful too. Don't you run around on her while she's pregnant." Steadman would cross his heart and promise. "No floozies, understand? You've got obligations." And he'd say, "I don't know any floozies—except you." They carried on that way in front of Anna, and it seemed harmless enough.

It was, in any case, the best he could do, and as Anna's term drew near, it was Kay who was excluded. When Steadman felt the stirring child inside his wife, when he went to the breathing classes with her —the huffing and puffing, Anna called it—he believed that they were entering together the most profound of intimacies. And when he sat beside her during her long hard labor, and realized that Anna had a strength and courage that had nothing to do with him, he felt a terrible humility. Maggie's birth was not the triumph of love, as he'd expected. What he learned in the labor room was that they were all on their own.

Two nights after Maggie was born, he and Kay were at the hospital when visiting hours ended. Steadman drove her home. She had a bottle of Southern Comfort in her apartment. She asked him in. Steadman, boozy and giddy, sat on the couch with her. They could hardly help talking about babies and marriages. He knew that Kay was flattering him when she told him that he was a good husband. She was candid and funny about some of her cuties and seemed to be comparing him, favorably, to them. When she said she envied Anna, he knew that he was capable of fucking her. Capable, that night, with Anna still in the hospital. "I don't think Baby and I have ever fucked the same guy, but I can't help being curious, you know? When you're as much alike as we are, you have to wonder if you're alike in that way too." It seemed to Steadman that they talked for hours. At last Kay took his hand and slipped it under her panties— he let her put it there—and said, "All this talking has got me so fucking wet I'm about to slide off the couch."

He withdrew his hand.

"Come on, Steadman," Kay said, and put her hand on his fly. "There are things going on there too."

"We'd better not, Kay."

"Don't tell me we'd regret it tomorrow."

"We would."

"What's all this been about, then? You've had a hard-on for an hour."

Steadman got up. "I'm sorry. I shouldn't have got into this."

"We've been in it for a while."

"I'm sorry, Kay."

"Are you apologizing for not fucking me?"

He didn't know what he was apologizing for.

Kay said, "Well, kiss me at least. Kiss me like you kiss Baby."

She stood up and he did kiss her. He kissed her open mouth and pressed her tight against him.

And when he left he knew that if he could have believed for a moment that her desire was just desire, he would have fucked her. During that whole time he'd been sure that Kay was scheming. Even that kiss, passionate for him, was something else for Kay; when it was over she patted his fly once more and grinned at what she felt. Maybe it was as simple as a wish to inflict unhappiness—but Steadman thought it was more complicated than that. He didn't know what Kay was up to, and didn't think she knew herself.

After that they did not flirt. Steadman soon realized that he saw less of Kay, realized next that Anna saw less of her too. Steadman thought that she was probably jealous of Maggie. She did stop by now and then, and it was apparent, even to Anna, that she didn't know what to do with herself. She had a succession of menial jobs —the only one she seemed to like was on the night shift in a factory where she wound armatures by hand; she didn't know what the armatures were used for—and tried to make enough money to keep herself in pills. "I wish she wasn't speeding so much," Anna said, but that was as near as she came to judging Kay.

Neither Steadman nor Anna had seen Kay since coming to Zion County, not since that visit in Charlottesville, when she was her old insinuating self. That wouldn't work here, Steadman thought. He did not believe that Kay could come between him and Anna now. He had even been glad that Kay was coming, glad for Anna, who couldn't disguise her anticipation. But now that Kay was in their house, now that they'd seen that damn fox, now that Anna was addled and estranged, he just wanted Kay gone.

He laid stones in the hole Duty had scraped with the blade of the bulldozer. Zep, who was always willing to hire out, came to help him. Despite his size Zep wasn't all blubber, and he was a cheerful worker, more than cheerful, he was an enthusiast. Because of the fox Zep had armed himself with a holster and pistol—a cap pistol. He fired random fusillades toward the woods. He mixed mortar and beefed about Xanaduc. Stan, who was rich, was doing what Zep called a St. Francis number, making friends with the sun, the moon, and the tweety birds. He was also into self-denial, certain forms of it anyway. He was on a diet of yogurt and brown rice, and he'd been going barefoot since March to harden his feet. "If he's so fucking guilty about having money why is he such a fucking Scrooge?" But he was not tight when it came to dope or to toys for himself. He had just bought a Nikon and a Hasselblad, and all kinds of expensive darkroom fixtures were still in crates on the Xanaduc porch.

Zep got along well enough with Rod, mostly, it seemed to Steadman, because they had a common gripe against Stan. Rod's ideology was as tiresome to Zep as it was to Steadman, whom Rod had tried to enlighten. His demonstration days, when he'd been gassed and arrested a few times, were vivid in Rod's memory, but the Movement, he said, had gone to earth. He had laid his good-neighbor rap on Steadman, who listened politely before offering Rod a thought of Auden's: "We are all on this earth to help others, but God only knows what the others are here for." That stopped Rod for a second, but he rallied: "What elitist bullshit." The conversation took a nasty turn, and Steadman eventually said that the only obligation neighbors had was not to bore the ass off one another with their dogmas. Since then Steadman had noticed some friction between him and Rod, also between him and Val. As for Laurie, he did not understand her devotion to Stan. Stan was handsome, even beatific in his ascetic phase, and according to report very rich, but as far as Steadman could tell he was harebrained and moody, given to outbursts of bitterness as well as piety. Laurie seemed too smart to put up with him.

The big news at Xanaduc, as far as Zep was concerned, was the arrival of a woman named Peggy O'Day. Steadman hadn't seen her yet, but he'd heard plenty about her among the stones. Suddenly, Zep said, all those months of Portnoy's Complaint were going to pay off. He'd kept his hog in champion shape. And Peggy—wow! Dynamite! What a beaver! She'd noticed his hog too. They took afternoon swims down at Xanaduc, and this Peggy was an eyeballer. Steadman was glad she was there, for Zep usually had to be fed after a day's work and topped up with beer—but he beat it at four o'clock to make the most of the afternoon dip.

It was Zep who relayed the invitation to the barn dismantling. The idea seemed to be Rod's: tear down the old sagging barn and use the materials to put up a kind of crafts factory with kiln, looms, forges, pottery wheels. The day was to be festive, work followed by a feed and a session in the Feelgood Lounge. That Saturday Steadman, with Anna and Maggie and Kay, went to Xanaduc.

"What a great room," Kay said in the kitchen—so she had decided to please. And it was a good big kitchen, with bunches of drying flowers and herbs hanging from the beams, with plants crowding the windows. The open shelves were ranked with glazed stoneware and canning jars that bulged green and yellow and bright sugary red. The room was filled with the smell of fresh bread.

"Yeah," said Laurie, who was picking the stems off strawberries. "We didn't do much with the rest of the house, but we figured we ought to do the kitchen up right."

"Those are wild strawberries, aren't they?" Anna asked.

"Yeah."

"Where'd you ever find so many? I went with Maggie one whole day and we found eight." Anna, putting herself down.

Laurie introduced them to Peggy, who was sitting at the table with her and who wasn't the hussy Steadman had come to expect. She had red hair and freckles, small faint freckles under the delicate sheen of her complexion. The bib of her overalls was gaily embroidered with flowers and bees. She smiled—perfect white teeth—and said *Ha-wa-ya.* It was the first southern accent he'd heard in a while. She wasn't a hussy. She was a gaudy confection. Steadman went outside to join the men.

Harry and Zep were squatting in the shade of a walnut tree with the mechanism of a chain saw spread out in front of them. It looked as if it had crashed there from an altitude of several thousand feet. "Fuckin A," Zep said, "I was just trying to rewind the starter cord." Harry deftly reassembled it. Zep shook his head. "You krauts. How come you and the Japs know so much about machines? Machines and cameras."

"I'm just a farmer," Harry said. "If you can fix a baler, you can fix anything."

Rod and Stan and another man sauntered up from the barn. Rod, with his black hair and bristly beard, looked overdressed in the heat. Stan was wearing nothing but a pair of cut-offs held up with baling twine and, around his neck, the new Nikon. The other man was introduced as a visitor from Philly; he was wearing Earth shoes. Stan said, "Any more foxes down your way?"

"Just the one," Steadman answered.

"What a bummer that is."

"They're going to get the state trapper in here to gas the bastards in their dens," Zep said.

"It won't do any good," said Stan. "They should just let it run its course. It's just a natural correction, a natural thinning out of the population."

Rod said, "It's all PR. It makes people feel better if they think something's being done."

The screen door banged; Anna and Kay came out of the house. "Hello, Anna. Hello, Anna." To charm them Rod began singing the Doublemint jingle.

"Hey-a fox-bait," called Zep to the twins.

There were introductions, more talk of foxes. Kay described how they'd been attacked, making much of how they'd got home naked. Zep kept saying *Yip yip yip,* which was supposed to be the call of the rabid fox. By now they were all under the shade of the walnut tree, and a few reefers were passed—"Better toke up now before Duty comes." He was expected with his bulldozer to winch off the roof. Steadman noticed that Peggy was short and not exactly plump, certainly not chunky, but robust. She did have a lickerish eye, and she kept moistening her upper lip with her tongue. A few other barn wreckers from Barger's Mill and elsewhere joined them. Whether or not they could smoke dope in front of Duty was discussed as a social and ethical and legal problem. Maggie sat in Steadman's lap. "Don't you think she's pretty?" she whispered to him, meaning Peggy. Her tastes ran to glitter and tinsel, the gaudy and garish. Circus performers were her standard of beauty.

Kay, evidently feeling the dope, announced, "That barn is one huge mother."

"And growing every minute," said Rod.

"What time was Duty supposed to get here?" Harry wanted to know.

"He said one o'clock."

"That means two. Duty doesn't go on daylight savings with everybody else."

"Duty? Is this the guy I saw, Baby? The one with the tobacco and teeth? What's he going to do?"

"Pull the roof off with his winch."

The word *winch* struck Kay as hilariously funny. While she

laughed a technical discussion got started about whether or not the timbers would snap when the roof came off. Steadman and Maggie were experimenting with red ants to see how far they would climb up a stick before deciding that vertical was the wrong direction. Kay, in her sunglasses, was ripping along now; it was mostly for her sake that Rod described the Pentagon, as the crafts factory was to be called. It was going to be five-sided, it was going to be a fucking landmark, it was going to have stained glass, rafts of the shit. Stan, behind the black snout of the Nikon, kept snapping pictures. Zep had squirmed his way to Peggy's side, but honestly Steadman wondered sometimes about Zep; he was trying to set her hair on fire. It was plaited in a thick braid that reached almost down to the ground as she sat. It must have suggested a fuse to Zep. Anyway, his hand was behind her and he was trying to strike a match. It took several efforts to ignite her, and then of course Zep bellowed the alarm, and he dipped the pigtail into a bucket of water that he'd provided. Much commotion. And maybe Zep knew how to win Peggy after all, for she seemed to think that it was a merry prank.

Duty finally did come. He seemed a little flustered by the number of welcomers who came out to the truck. He dipped into the bib pocket of his overalls to pull out a fist-sized watch. "I said one o'clock, didn't I? I hate for anybody to have to wait on me. I got three minutes before one."

"That's your time."

"Yes sir, slow time I call it, not this daylight time. I never go by it. I stick to the one time. It don't change. It just stays what it is."

"You're right." Rod grinned. "Next thing you know they'll have us on the same time as Tokyo, going to bed with the Japanese."

"I don't know about that," Duty said. "I don't know how they do over there. I believe I told you one o'clock."

"No hurry."

But Duty was in a hurry. He didn't like being watched, didn't like being detained, didn't want to spit in front of all those people. He kept working the plug of tobacco from side to side. When finally he did spit, a few black gouts dribbled down his chin. "I ain't been chewing but twenty-five years," he said. "I expect to get the hang of it soon."

Then he got busy. He unloaded the little yellow bulldozer, stationed it before the barn, unwound the winch cable, stood there with the hook in his hands. "Where you want me to grab it?"

They converged on the barn, all but Stan, who climbed up the slope above the bulldozer in order to have a better vantage with the camera. "Now, I'm not the boss," Duty was saying as he disappeared into the barn pulling the cable. Harry stood on the wooden ramp that led up to the entrance. "It'll ruin every mortise and tenon if you pull that plate."

They decided to saw the plate loose, and Duty scampered up to the walnut tree to fetch the chain saw. In a moment it started with a roar and Maggie put her hands over ears like the monkey who hears no evil. "What's going on?" Kay said. "When's the show start?"

It took a while, but soon the plate was free, Duty trotted out to the bulldozer, the group moved back. He threw a lever and the cable tightened, there were sounds of cracking and groaning, the whole near plane of the roof began to move, boards snapped and shot through the air, the top of the barn just opened up and roared.

"That's how I feel at the dentist's," Kay said.

Duty said, "It can't hurt to let the sun shine in." He dragged the roof, what part of it held together to be dragged, away from the entrance. Now the work began, the men hauling the boards and timbers free, the women cleaning and stacking them. The walls of the barn were still standing, and Steadman was inside loosening the boards with a crowbar—a prize bar, Duty called it. Duty was taking down some of the big timbers with the chain saw. Through one of the vertical apertures in the wall Steadman noticed that people were running. One of them was Anna, lugging Maggie. She was followed by Kay, who'd lost one of her sandals. Behind her—not so much behind as after, for Steadman's vision was limited by the aperture, and the runners appeared singly—came Val, Peggy, Zep. Steadman couldn't hear anything except the chain saw. He stepped to the entrance of the barn for a look.

Everybody had reached the house, but Steadman heard somebody —maybe Harry, who was up on the slope with Stan—yell *fox*. Duty came to the entrance and stood there with Steadman. The saw was idling in his hand.

Steadman saw the fox. It made a noise, hoarse and rasping, more like choking than barking. It wasn't much bigger than a cat. The grass had been high enough to conceal it, but now it was on the worn track in front of the barn. Its coat was not the lustrous red it should have been, its tail dragged the ground. There were bare sores on its shoulders and flanks where it must have chewed itself. Its back was slightly arched and its gait was unsteady. It did not appear to have any particular destination, did not appear to have seen them in the entrance of the barn, but it must have heard the saw. It stopped anyway and cocked its ears. In one sinuous motion the tail rose and filled.

It was too lame to run. It stumbled as it crossed the few yards of ground in front of the ramp, stumbled again on the boards of the ramp. Steadman had raised the bar to bash it, but the noise of the saw when Duty pulled the trigger, either the noise or the sudden blurred speed of the chain, made it veer off. Its fur bristled now, and it was capable of a leap. Its aim was exact. The bar of the saw bisected the ridge of its snout. The teeth of the saw chattered on the bone. Gore and blood splashed up, but the fox stayed on its feet with its face hanging in shreds from its eyes. Duty moved one step and decapitated it. The head rolled down the ramp slowly, bumping against the uneven planks, and the blood flowing after it spread out in lines in the cracks between the planks.

Duty said, "That's one way to kill a fox, but it's a right messy way. I prefer to trap them."

Then he said politely, "I didn't mean to hog all the glory."

Eleven

Duty gathered up the remains of the fox with a pitchfork and took them, in a cardboard box, off into the woods to bury them. He cut the grave with the blade of the bulldozer. "You don't want no dog to dig it up and chew on it," he said. "It's enough poison in it to kill us all."

Steadman went around the house to the garden to rinse off all the blood that had splattered onto him. He was squirting his hands and arms with the hose when Anna came after him. Her arms were folded, shoulders hiked up. She stopped a few steps away and didn't look at him. "I'm taking Maggie home now."

Steadman let the water play on the ground. "Why? We've had our scare now."

"You weren't scared," she said.

"Look, Anna." He held out his trembling, twitching hand. His body shook each time he breathed; his breath made a sharp noise on his teeth and in his nostrils each time he inhaled.

She did look briefly. "I'm sorry, Steadman. I have to go."

"Everybody was afraid of it, Anna. There was nothing anybody could do about it. The goddamn fox is dead. It's over now. Forget about it."

"All right."

"Don't say 'all right' like that. Anna, the fox wasn't looking for you."

"I'm not going because of that," she whispered.

Steadman could hardly control his voice then. "So why are you going? What's the matter with you? What's wrong with you? Why is everything worse for you than for anybody else?"

She looked at him so helplessly that he swore. "Go ahead then. Get the fuck out of here."

She went, and his whole body jerked in spasms. Just adrenalin, he thought, late as usual. For a few minutes he thought he was going to sob. He was still holding the hose; he trained it so that the spray of water hit him right between the eyes.

When he went back to the barn Anna told him that she was going to get a ride with Duty so that she could leave him the Blazer. She touched his arm and looked at him with that cringing expression. There were people around them. *Yip yip yip,* Zep was barking. She removed her hand.

After Duty left Stan brought out the special reserve of dope. As they continued work, tremulous laughter broke out here and there. Steadman, on the other end of a beam from Zep, carrying it out of the barn, felt it bump against his belly. Zep was grinning. Steadman bumped back and grinned. They bumped the beam back and forth and started laughing. It occurred to Steadman that he was stoned. He kept working. People began pretending to swim through the air. Soon they were on their way to the creek, swimming through the fields. *Yip yip yip.* When Steadman undressed he saw that the big beam had left little scratches like a cat, and small delicate bruises. He was grinning at this violet damage to his belly. He saw Peggy watching him. She had large pink nipples and her bush was round and red. He felt his cock bumping between his legs like a punching bag somebody had begun drowsily to tap. Peggy was watching it. In a show of modesty Steadman hid himself with his hands and thigh. "No hands!" Zep said. "Look, no hands!" People watched him as he watched himself get a hard-on. It rose slowly and swayed like a cobra being charmed into the air. Then Zep sucked his big belly in and tried to balance it, as he might balance a broomstick, moving backwards, forwards, sideways under it to keep it upright. People began to laugh. Zep darted at Peggy, who escaped easily, splashing into the creek. Then laughter was general, and everywhere men chased women, and women fled into the creek. It felt like a moment of sheer play, but it was only a moment, and it ended as soon as they bumped into each other in the water, as soon as they made contact, paired off, showed preferences. They drifted and paddled, alone, in couples. Gusts of exhilaration kept rippling, laughs, outbursts, even when people began to leave the water, shy again. They straggled back through the fields. Some of them stopped at the bluff where a high rope swing was rigged up and they took great whooping tours through the air.

Back at the house there were more reefers, music now, but it was over. Zep was noisy, baffled, trying to prolong it. Steadman drank a beer and talked to Harry and Diana. "What happened?" he said. And Diana: "Wasn't that wild? I never thought I'd be at an orgy." "It was only a semi-orgy," Harry said, grinning.

Yet Steadman was aware of some disappointment when he sat down to eat, even of animosity toward Peggy who took the place beside him at the long table. He had put himself at the opposite end of the table from Kay, and Peggy had stepped over the bench, bumped a breast on his shoulder as she sat down. She'd taken her hair loose and brushed it; it looked like the pampered flank of an Irish setter. "I haven't had a chance to pick your brains," she said. "I hear you're a writer."

Pick your brains. That southern accent.

"They're a little unsettled right now," he said. He filled his plate from the containers that were as big as tubs. Ratatouille, cheese soufflé, bread, butter, salad.

"Mine too. That was potent stuff, wasn't it?"

They were squeezed together on the bench, hip to hip. He popped a can of beer. "It was a pretty typical post-fox reaction."

She had small, neat hands, freckled on the back, not a vein showing. "Really? Is that what always happens?"

Zep said, "He's a writer and lost his cherry too. He's published. Make the fucker talk about it. You talk, Steadman, or I'll tell her what your initials stand for."

"I just say I write to keep him company," Steadman said. "I have a novel which I don't write so that Zep and I will have a subject of conversation."

"A writing block," Peggy said.

"It's more like a life block. This novel I'm not writing gets in the way of my life, not the other way around."

She laughed. "That's an interesting way to put it."

"Fuckin A," said Steadman.

"Fuckin A," said Zep.

"Zep and I are going to collaborate on a book as soon as we're done not writing the ones we're not writing now. It's going to be called *The Sensuous Personality*. I'm going to not-write most of it, but Zep and I have a wonderful working relationship."

"What's the plot?"

"There's no plot. It's a how-to book. Zep's going to not-write the first chapter, on getting attention. Every sensuous personality has to be able to get attention—by setting people's hair on fire, for example."

"It works, it works," Zep said.

"Did you lose a lot of hair?"

"It was just singed a little. You can't even tell, can you?"

He couldn't. Zep tried to get Peggy to laugh again about her hair. Steadman ate without appetite. He turned and talked for a minute to the man on his other side, who said he'd just moved to a place not far from Barger's Mill. He was from Florida, and the subject of oranges came up. He told Steadman that while oranges were orange, orange juice was yellow. Steadman was stumped. He got the impression that his neighbor felt he'd put him down. "I'm into composition," the man said, "you know, music. I really get off on lyrics."

"Birds do it, bees do it, even educated fleas do it," Steadman said, giving the rhyme its lilt. The man was blank. "I'm a Cole Porter fan," Steadman said.

"Oh."

He let it drop. Down at the far end of the table Kay was holding forth. She and Rod seemed to be hitting it off, and Val was watching closely.

Peggy said, "Your daughter's fantastic. She's so verbal."

"You got her to talk to you? That's something. She's not always forthcoming with strangers."

"I've worked some with children. I had a job, just part-time, in a day care center, but I really liked it. Where children are, there is the golden age."

Steadman knew that she was quoting, even that her irony was aimed at herself, but he said rudely, "Let me guess: your favorite book is *The Prophet.*"

"That's real close," said Peggy in a lush drawl, "but actually I like the *Kama Sutra* a little better. I mean, it's so much more relevant." She laughed then at Steadman, who knew his cheeks were tingling. "What's the matter?" she asked. "My personality too sensuous for you?"

"You want to not-write a chapter of our book?" he asked.

"Which chapter?"

"Which chapter?" Zep roared. "You know which one—but you got to audition for it. Meet me tonight on the casting couch."

Zep was so loud that everyone at the table heard him. Peggy declined to reply. Steadman, feeling both angry and silly for letting himself get drawn into such an exchange, tried to get out of it with banalities. He asked Peggy what brought her to Zion County.

She and Laurie had been in the same sorority at Hollins. Peggy had just graduated and she was making a trip in the car, an Opel sports car, that her father had given her. From Atlanta she'd driven first to the Smokies and then up the Skyline Drive. She liked the mountains, liked driving the mountain roads—it made her feel daring, she said, smiling. Her father had a Cadillac franchise and thought Johnny Carson was a genius. Steadman agreed. Her parents were divorced; her mother was now married to a banker with kidney stones. In the fall Peggy was going to Columbia Law School. She thought she was probably their token belle. But she wasn't a belle, and she knew it; her flutters and expressions, the deepening of the accent—"so *day-ring*"—made a joke of that whole set of manners. And complaisant as she was on the surface, she had her quick, private, calculated amusements too; as she fended off Zep's interruptions, Steadman thought he was invited to share these. When she said she liked the country life-style, she added that she wasn't cut out for it. "I don't have a creative bone in my body," she said, and held up her fleshy arm. When she listed the things she did not do—hook rugs, throw pots, tie hammocks—he couldn't miss the dig. "What do you do well?" he asked. Three things: she could drive, she could think logically . . . she didn't name the third. She didn't have to. She didn't pretend to be innocent then, and he didn't pretend to be dense. He supposed he'd asked for it. She said that she was tired of looking young—those freckles. She was twenty-two and she was taken for twelve. There were anecdotes about having her ID checked—and of course Zep whooped about checking her IUD. "I'm an amateur gynecologist," he said.

When dinner was over Steadman slipped out of the house for a walk in the air—and hoped, damn him, that Peggy would follow. Harry and Diana had already left Xanaduc and he almost went with them, leaving the Blazer for Kay—but he stayed. Kay and most of the others had gone into the Feelgood Lounge. The man from Philly had brought down a drug called angel dust. Walking through the fields, Steadman looked for foxes—a waning moon was just rising —even though he realized he would never see them in the high grass. He made his way down to the swing. He supposed that Anna would hear from Kay about his flirtation, and in a moment of bitterness he thought those two had driven him to it—he didn't even much like this damn Peggy. She was too short and chesty, a redheaded fireplug who talked about growing—growing, which meant zooming around in a car and getting laid—and choosing life-styles and picking brains. But this self-deceit did not work. The fact was that he'd like to fuck Peggy. He was pretty sure that she'd like to fuck him.

The swing was Zep's best idea. It hung from a tall hickory that leaned over a gravelly bluff, and when Steadman took the stout stick at the end of the long rope and made a running takeoff along the brow of the hill he flew out, out, out in a a great loop thirty feet above the ground. He sailed twice, three times, out into the starry night toward the dark bulk of Big Furnace above the speeding silver ground, and the third time he climbed back up the bluff Peggy was coming toward him through the field.

"I thought I might find you down here."

"Trying to clear the pipes."

"I had to sneak away from Zep."

"No angel dust for you?"

"I don't much like hard drugs."

"Just fresh air."

He still had the swing in his hand. He said, "You want a ride?"

"I tried it once this afternoon and hit on my bottom."

"That's the next best place if you miss your feet."

"I'm still a little stiff. We all got our bruises today."

She was referring to his belly. He turned the swing loose and let it drift, slack, over the bluff. "How do I get away from you?" he said.

"Is that what you're trying to do?"

After a while, when the moment that he might have kissed her had passed, he said, "I guess I am."

She knew it had passed too. In the moonlight he saw her teeth glint; she was smiling.

And then, that settled, they sat down on the edge of the bluff where the ground was open and dry, and in a few minutes Steadman found himself confiding in her. He talked, seriously now, about his book, and about Watts, about how he'd come to Zion County—seriously, but trying to amuse her too, conscious of the way he was presenting himself, wanting her to like him. He talked about Maggie, even about Anna. "She seemed bashful," Peggy said, and Steadman knew he was lying when he praised Anna, not lying because he praised her but because his praise was so stingy. He praised Anna but described her so that Peggy laughed at her struggles here in the mountains. He did not think Peggy heard how much he loved Anna. He thought of Anna in their house, alone in their bed, not sleeping yet—and kept talking to Peggy. When she mentioned Kay and asked how he'd known which of them he liked, he said, "I liked the one who didn't keep calling me motherfucker."

So he was confiding but not quite candid, and they stayed there on the bluff for a long while. "I'm getting cold," Peggy said. He got to his feet and replied, "The nights are always cold here." He took her hand and helped her up.

"I'm glad we talked."

"So am I," he said, and they walked back through the fields to the house.

The moment they entered the kitchen Val said to him, "Where the fuck have you been? We've been looking all over for you."

"What's the matter?"

"Kay freaked, man, she fucking freaked. She just wasted the goddamn stereo. One minute she was flying and then, fuck, I don't know, she just freaked."

Val was shrill and angry and frightened. The innards of a percolator were in her hands, and coffee was strewn on the table.

"Where is she?"

"Where the fuck have you been anyway? We've been trying to talk her down for an hour."

Steadman went to the Feelgood Lounge. All the lights were on. Kay was seated on a straight chair in the middle of the room and her jaw, her whole throat, was shaking convulsively. Laurie and Rod were both kneeling on the floor beside her. Steadman had been thinking that Anna should be called, but there was something so deranged in Kay's expression that he knew at once he did not want Anna to see it. Kay appeared to be trying to speak but no sound issued from her mouth. A pillowcase, soaked through with blood, was wrapped around one of her hands.

"She's not so bad now," Stan said.

"What happened?"

"She went after Rod. Jesus, I don't know, I think she would have killed him. She was out of her head for a while."

"Have you called a doctor?"

"No, shit, she's just bummed out. We don't want a doctor for this."

Then she screamed. No words, just a single anguished pitch. Steadman thought he had caused it. She had seen him and she was trying to stand. She was kicking at Laurie but looking at him, and her face expressed such fury and hatred that he did not move. Then she began to struggle with Rod and the chair was knocked halfway across the room. One hand was loose, the bandage unwinding, and her hooked fingers were on Rod's eye. He hit her hard. Then Steadman caught her, holding her from behind. She tried to butt his face with her head and kicked his shins with her bare heels. "Put her on the fucking bed again," somebody said, and he carried her there. Rod got hold of her feet and they lifted her up and set her down on her back. Steadman was trying to hold her shoulders but her legs got loose and she got them under his arm and kicked his face, and then her legs were above her, she was standing on her shoulders and trying to turn her head back under, and he was afraid she'd break her neck. He let go of her arms. Then she was standing over him on the bed and there was still that scream of anguish. He seized her legs and her body was down his back. She was hitting him. He tried to put her back on the bed and realized Rod was still there, grabbing at her legs again. For a moment she was between them completely in the air, thrashing. Then Rod got her legs down on the bed and sat across them and Steadman straddled her waist, knees on either side of her, hands on her upper arms. She now tried to butt him with her face. Her mouth was shut tight and he realized she was silent now. He hadn't heard when she stopped screaming. He thought it had continued. Her halter had come loose and her breasts were bare and bloody and bright red drops of blood kept appearing on her. His nose was bleeding, he realized, and he could taste blood in his mouth. Her face was full of such pain. He saw the scar on her forehead then, and he realized that he was holding Kay, not Anna.

He didn't know how long he stayed over her. Laurie wiped his face a little with a warm damp cloth; she wiped around his eyes too and he thought he must have been crying. She wiped Kay off and talked to her. "I don't think she cut herself again," she said to Steadman. "That blood must all be from her hand." Kay would close her eyes and subside for a while and then struggle again, silently now, completely silent, trying to twist and break free, her face clenched and sweaty. At some point, still silent, she began to cry, and Steadman watched the tears rise from beneath the closed eyelids and run back across her temples. He could feel the strength go out of her body then, and she whispered, "Let me go now, Steadman."

Still he was afraid to move.

"Oh please let me go," she said, looking at him then.

He got off her and she turned, shaking, toward the wall.

There were a few people in the room. Laurie said, "Why don't all of you get out of here now and let her sleep, if she can."

Steadman drank a cup of coffee in the kitchen. The muscles of his arms ached from holding Kay; he could scarcely keep his hand closed around the mug. People talked about bad trips, about this angel dust. Several of them had done it that night. The man who'd brought it said, "She told me she'd done it a bunch of times. Shit, I had no idea." They all thought it would be over now. Steadman didn't know whether to believe them.

"She's out," Laurie said when she came into the kitchen.

"You think she's all right?"

"Yeah, I think so. Let her sleep it off."

Before he left Steadman looked at Kay again. Laurie had left a lamp on in the room and covered her with a blanket. Her arms were outside the blanket, stretched straight at her sides. Her face was turned up to the ceiling. He didn't go near but stood at the door, listening: Kay was breathing evenly, lightly, asleep.

Steadman turned off the lights when he got home, and as he blundered up the dark stairs he heard Maggie groan and move in her bed. The only light now was from her room. Her door was ajar, and the blue glow of the nightlight stood in the crack. Steadman stopped in the hall; she groaned again. He opened the door enough to admit himself. Maggie was out of her covers, huddled face down, head in the corner of the wall. Dream-infested, not fully awake, she heard him and, turning, recognized him. She held out her arms to him. Steadman lifted her up. She was warm and damp. Her nightie slid up to her waist and her thighs tightened on his flanks. She pressed her head into the hollow of his throat. Steadman, smelling her hair, his chest shielded by the length of her body, half-sang and half-hummed.

Hush, little baby, don't say a word,
Daddy's going to buy you a mockingbird.

"Daddy."

"Hush sweetie. Don't wake up. Shhh."

And if that mockingbird don't sing,
Daddy's going to buy you a diamond ring.

"Daddy."

"Hush, sleepyhead."

"Daddy."

"Shh. Sleep now."

She had to speak. She said, drawing back so that she could look at him, "There was a picture in my mind of a fox."

A picture in her mind, her dream. "A pretty one, I hope."

"No." Her arms and back stiffened as she sought wakefulness, where she filled her eyes with the sight of him. "I was scared."

"Not any more. No more fox. Go to sleep, my girl."

How he clung to her. He sang again, and as he sang her body crumpled with sleep. When her head wobbled on his shoulder, he returned her to her bed. He straightened her nightie and sheets and pushed the hair back from her brow. In the blue light he watched the last signs of wakefulness cross beneath the clear screen of her face. He kissed her.

In his bedroom he undressed without a light. Anna was awake, he knew, but they did not touch when he got on the bed.

"Steadman? Did Kay come home with you?"

"No. She stayed there."

Anna had the sheets and quilt pulled over her in a heap. He didn't try to get under them. "Why? Did something happen to her?"

"Yes."

"What happened? Tell me, Steadman."

Anna was sitting up now, her shape outlined against a window. "Why are you acting this way? Did you do something to her? Is she hurt?"

"She cut her hand, that's all. I didn't do a goddamn thing to her."

"What happened to her hand?"

"She wrecked the stereo."

"Why?"

"Why? How the fuck should I know?"

"Did she do any drugs?"

"What do you think?"

"I was afraid something terrible was going to happen."

"Something terrible—shit. You don't even know what happened."

"Please, Steadman, don't talk to me like that. It scares me."
He saw her hand coming toward him. The instant it touched him
he was off the bed. He was aware of not wanting to shout, not
wanting to wake Maggie. He walked around the room, around the
bed. He couldn't look at Anna.

"It scares me, it scares me. What doesn't scare you? You're a coward,
Anna."

"Steadman."

"You're scared of everything. You're nothing but a goddamn
coward."

"I knew something terrible was going to happen there."

"Something terrible—you fucking baby. The things you're afraid of
aren't even the real things. You don't stick around for the real
things. You're home in bed with your head under the fucking covers
when they happen. Don't you cry, goddamn you."

"Please don't call me baby, Steadman. Please don't."

She was kneeling on the bed, naked, her arms extended to him.

"You fucking pathetic baby."

"If you knew how much I loved you, oh Steadman, you couldn't
hate me, you couldn't."

She was sobbing. Her arms were still raised and reaching for him,
but her head was lowered and her hair covered her face. A naked
woman, reaching for him and sobbing. Her empty hands were opening and closing in the air. She reached so far that she lost her balance
and tottered at the edge of the bed. He caught her. She drew him
in. Something gave way. He was whimpering, and then, trying to
laugh, wiping her wet face, he was saying, "We're in full flood
tonight, aren't we?" On the bed, cleaving to her. Anna, almost
laughing. "Hey, wait a minute. Let me pull the Tampax out." She
dropped it on the floor. They made love and then Anna reached
down and took his penis in her hand. It was bloody in the moonlit
room. "Steadman, look what I've done to you. "God, what a mess,"
Anna said. They both smiled.

They cleaned up together and lay in each other's arms.

The phone in the bedroom. Anna was on her feet quickly, stood
on the sides of them because the planks of the floor were cold.

"Yes," was all she said. She listened with her back to Steadman and when she lowered her head the chain of her vertebrae drew tight.

It was early. The sunlight reached all the way to the bed. There was a mist over the creek, birds sang, the Obenwalds' rooster crowed. Anna said, "Do you want to talk to him?"

She hung up the phone and faced him. "Your grandpappy's dead."

She came back to the bed, her movements furtive and chaste. She bent inward and kept her limbs in front of her, and after she pulled the quilt up to her chin she lay on her side facing him, not touching. The quilt, brown and blue, was filled with the prominence of her body. Beneath it she was clenched. Her arms were shoved down alongside her body, her hands closed together and closed between her thighs. "He died last night. Another heart attack."

"Who was that on the phone?"

"Your mother."

Steadman said, "Hold on to me, Anna."

Breakfast in the kitchen, the shady part of the house. The air was cool, delicate. Anna was wearing her nobby robe and her hair was pulled back and fastened, her neck and cheeks and temples exposed and still clouded. They were dappled with vague shapes that appeared as continents on a globe.

"How come you're making breakfast, Mama?"

She gave Maggie the first plate of buckwheat cakes, two of them adrift in butter and thick black syrup. Maggie concentrated on the plate, tried to keep it level as she carried it back to the table, but when she raised it to set it down at her place the syrup ran to the lip of the plate and over. "Oh well," she said, "I'm just too little to do that." She got a paper towel from Anna, smeared the syrup that had spilled, threw the towel in the trash can, wiped her hands on her shirt. "All cleaned up." She climbed into her chair, and kneeling in it began to skim up the syrup.

Steadman said, "I'm going to have to go away today."

"Where?" Intent on her syrup Maggie glanced up, a flicker of dark eyes.

"To Bristol."

"Oh."

Anna brought Steadman his plate and, standing behind him, put her hands on his shoulders. There was a hush in the room. Maggie looked up, her tongue sweeping to catch the syrup flowing on her cheeks and chin.

"Watts died yesterday."

A trickle of syrup got beyond the reach of her tongue and she bent her head, trying to gather it in. She lifted her chin to slow the trickle and she peered down over her cheek. She placed her spoon carefully on her plate, she rubbed her finger along her chin, she held it up, she licked the syrup off.

"He was old," she said.

Twelve

Anna sat alone at the kitchen table, her finger on her pulse. Her heart was chattering—too much coffee, probably. She was thinking she ought to give it up, thinking of her own grandfather, Papi, and the way he knocked back his little cups of espresso in a gulp, and then exclaimed, thumped his chest, blew and sputtered as if he'd just plunged into cold water. Grandfathers: how was it they became so definite? Papi and Watts were—like trees, she thought, remembering the wooden sound that came from Papi's mouth when he was excited or impressed. He shaped his mouth into an amazed *O* and rapped his head with a fist, and the sound that came out of him was like the deep reverberation when Steadman whacked a big hollow tree. Papi, Watts. In her memories, ordinary, random, Watts always seemed to be close up, his face shoved right into hers. The forehead with the long lines that bent at the ends and slanted across his temples, the blue eyes, the long upper lip that raised when he smiled, the gold in the teeth, the big jaw. "The gypsy," she once overheard him call her, and she was always uncomfortable when he poked his face at her—and yet she was affectionate now, and grateful, for he'd made her feel definite too, not obscure and muddled as she usually felt. He'd pushed at her with his big hands, as if she was a pillow that had to be bolstered up. Watts hacked at everybody in that way, everybody but Steadman; he was gentle when he touched Steadman, just tapped his chin or cheek, to make Steadman turn and look at him.

Coffee, and orange peel on the table, the plates filmed with syrup. Overhead Steadman's footsteps, and Maggie's, the patter as they moved back and forth together, their burred voices. Her heart was chattering like a telegraph key.

She took her hand from her pulse when he came downstairs. She didn't want him to catch her trying to decode that garbled message, and she had resolved not to cry. "Steadman"—his name flew out of her, he looked so tender and bewildered, so fragile in the town clothes he'd put on. He had a suitcase in his hand, and he'd shaved, and his hair was wet and combed.

"I'd better be on my way."

Anna stood up. They'd agreed that it would be best if she stayed here with Maggie—no point taking her to the funeral. "You know I'd go with you," she said. "You know that, don't you?"

When they embraced he whispered that he loved her.

She couldn't help herself. "I'm sorry I'm so teary." Her hands were on his shoulders, then under his chin; she realized that she was turning his face toward her just as Watts had.

And when he was gone, and she was cleaning up the breakfast things, she and Maggie discussed crying and funerals. She was at the sink, Maggie at the table, very thoughtful. Of course things were always dying in the grisly stories in her books, but for the princesses there was always the chance of resurrection, the lover's kiss. Maggie knew this was different. "Like Zack," she finally said, remembering Steadman's pointer, which they had buried. "That's right." Musing, Maggie said presently, "They put people in boxes when they bury them so their clothes won't get dirty." Then, a bit later—as Anna should probably have guessed, for Maggie had learned from Hope Byrd that God must always be accounted for—"They put flowers on the place so God will know where it is when he comes to get them."

Anna wondered if she should try to explain—what? Her fears and intimations? They were all that seemed to remain of those years with the nuns, they and a sense of the solemn holiness of Sunday morning —but that had to do with fasting to receive Communion, and dressing up, and with her father, who never went anywhere with them except to church. On Sunday morning, dressed like Kay, and with her whole family around her, the Host inside her, she had felt perfect. How old was she then? And when had she stopped believing?

When was Kay going to show up? And what could she say to her?

"I guess I'd better get dressed," she said to Maggie. The dishes were done and she had to get dressed, she had to make something of this day, this Sunday. She couldn't take Maggie for a picnic at the creek—those foxes. As she got into her usual outfit—the ankle-high boots, which she laced tight and tied, the baggy khaki shorts, the sleeveless knit top, also roomy—she heard Maggie in her room, playing with her dolls and animals, running, natch, a funeral of her own. A rain of commands and scoldings fell upon the mourners. Was that how she and Steadman sounded to Maggie? It must be.

She had to get going. Late starts always threw her. She'd once been able to lie in bed all morning, awake usually, or in that ambiguous state in which the illusions of sleep impinge upon wakefulness, but now she was frantic if the morning slipped by her, especially these summer mornings. It was only June, but the days were already hot and she liked to do her work in the garden early, when the plants were still upright with dew, before the sun got over Big Furnace and started to wilt them. This morning she was already too late. The bedroom was beginning to warm up. Standing in the window, the sun full on her, she felt too discouraged to do much of anything. The light was gauzy. The stones Steadman had been laying in the gash of clay—under the topsoil Duty had sheared off the ground was a dry orange—were stained with mortar, powdery, chalky. The trees looked limp, floppy, flaccid, and the fields—she could hardly look at them. Amos's cows kept the grass chewed close but they didn't touch the thistle or the gross mulleins which were shooting up their coarse stalks and pale bloated leaves. The cows were lolling in the shade, under the trees near the creek, where they'd beaten down the bank in a runway green with shit. She wondered if Amos would come by—he often did come on Sundays to check the cattle, and often brought his wife, who wore aprons and bonnets.

There was a cow in the garden, a big blue Charolais.

It sank in slowly that she was going to have to get it out of there by herself.

She told Maggie she'd be back in a minute. She picked up her fox staff outside the kitchen door and carried it down to the garden. The cow was standing in the beans with stalks hanging from its mouth like spaghetti, looking at her, munching. It could have been somebody else who hit it with the stick except for the shock she felt in her hands. The cow twitched its hide and moseyed through the cucumbers and squash. It walked into the corner of the garden fence, too stupid to remember where the gate was. She tapped it and pointed with the stick, but suddenly it lowered its shoulders and hunched its head back into them, and her own fury aroused just as suddenly, she slammed it as hard as she could across the only part of it that looked sensitive, the wrinkled fleshy lip. She knew it hurt by the vibration that traveled back up her arm. The cow took off bellowing. It found the gate and knocked the post loose as it passed through. Anna followed it down the slope to where the pasture fence had been mashed down. It jumped over it, surprisingly nimble. Anna pulled up the wire and propped it with her staff.

Then she waited. She'd heard the door slam and seen the red Xanaduc truck moving away from the ford. Kay was coming up the path from the bridge, under trees and then out into the open field where Anna was standing. Shorts, halter, barefoot, a bandaged hand. No sunglasses. "What's up, Baby? Tending the cows?"

She was breezy, jaunty. Anna knew Kay wouldn't mention last night. "What happened to your hand?" she asked.

"Had an accident changing a record."

"Steadman told me about it."

"Has he been telling tales?"

"They didn't sound like tales."

"What the fuck, Baby, have a heart. I'm the one that got wrecked, not you."

And Anna did feel uncharitable. Kay looked so pale, and that scar was a puffy white ridge, and her lips were bloodless, blue. Then she winked at Anna, that quick flash of her eyelid, the old signal of their unity. Anna looked away. "I'm sorry, Kay. I'm upset this morning. A cow just got into the garden and Steadman's grandfather died last night."

"The old hillbilly Steadman was always talking about?"

"Yes."

"Poor Steadman—poor Baby."
Kay hugged her.

Later that morning Harry came over with his pliers and stretchers and a roll of barb wire and patched the fence, and Anna went out to the garden to do what she could about the cow's blundering damage. It had chomped on a few stalks of corn and beans, but mostly it had flattened things—lettuce, peas, tomatoes. Two of the teepees Anna had rigged up to train the tomatoes on had been knocked over, and the vines were trampled. She and Maggie played doctor; they actually put splints and bandages on the broken vines. Kay, who'd come out to help, said that she was out of her depth when it came to bandages. But she stretched out near them—"You keep an eye out for foxes"—and stripped. "That's the one thing I'll say for this place—you don't need a lot of clothes."

And while they talked—about the smell of tomatoes, and the queer yellow stain they left on the hands, about tans and clothes—Anna felt herself giving in. The intimacy wasn't the same as it once had been, couldn't be the same, but still the conversation was effortless. She didn't have to edit. With Laurie, even with Diana, Anna always felt as if her perceptions and emotions were pitched wrong, but here in the garden, in the sun, on subjects that were mostly indifferent, Anna heard herself running on, and she was glad that Kay was there.

After one lull Kay asked, "Do you still get colors?"

Anna paused. "Sometimes. Now and then."

"I've had a lot of them lately. They come in bunches—for months nothing, and then they're back again. The other day I picked up this old *Life* magazine and read this thing by an astronaut—that'll tell you where I'm at, Baby, reading articles in *Life* magazine written by astronauts. But this guy was talking about the colors he saw out there, these fabulous colors he couldn't describe, and I thought if this nerd saw them, maybe they're really out there somewhere. Maybe we didn't make them up."

"I don't know, Kay. I don't think we were the only ones who ever saw them."

"Who besides us and Gauguin?"

"Plenty of others, probably. Gauguin isn't exactly an unknown."

"But it was our language, Baby. We saw the same things."

"It seemed that way."

"Not any more?"

"I don't know. Mostly I notice light these days—not colors really, but the way light hits things, the shapes it makes. That's been going on for a long time."

"And you draw bugs."

"You've seen the bugs?"

"I found a whole stack of them."

"They're just flat. I don't know how to draw this light."

"No colors?"

What did Kay want? Anna could remember the colors, expressive, deep, exquisite. At one time she'd seen them everywhere, rays and mantles of color, and believed Kay had seen the same. Colors were the vocabulary of that language they had shared. The colors had existed in their eyes, in their imaginations, in their emotions. Anna had never been able to paint them, and they were no longer so present to her eye; she felt them most strongly when she looked, as she often did, at the plates in art books. Gauguin, Van Gogh—those were the two whose colors were most like memories for her.

"I think they're beyond me now," she said, and she was relieved when Kay, pale, glistening, spread on a towel, didn't seem to mind.

"Yeah, I guess we're older. It ain't much fun, is it? The colors seemed so private."

"I think maybe they stunted us," Anna said.

"How do you mean?"

Maggie said, "Mama, I'm getting hot."

Anna touched her pulse—chattering again. "You know, we never tried to talk that much, not to anybody else. And then we had Papa and Papi talking to us in Italian—I'm still trying to get used to ordinary language."

"What's so great about ordinary language?"

"It has more to do with—reality."

Kay laughed at her. "Christ, Baby, you're really something. Baby's holiday in reality."

Anna made an effort and laughed too. "It does sound silly, doesn't it? But I like to hear these people out here talk about things—they're so accurate and so definite. They know the names of all the things around them. It's not just vague to them—anyway, I've been trying to learn my birds and flowers."

"And bugs."

"And bugs."

"And you plant your garden and raise your beans and tomatoes and keep your house and raise your kid and look after hubby. I get the idea. Reality."

"Don't take it wrong, Kay."

"I want to go inside, Mama," Maggie said.

"I'm talking to Kay now."

"I'm just jealous of you, Baby." Kay had turned on her side so that Anna could see the sadness in her face. "You're happy, aren't you?"

"I guess so." It made her feel guilty to say it. "Right now, anyway."

"You're in love with Steadman, aren't you?"

"Yes," she said, in confusion.

There were tears in Kay's eyes. "I haven't been in love for a long time."

Anna knew that she meant that she had never been in love—not since she was in love with Anna. And that's what it had come to, the colors and all the rest of it, though Anna had never thought of it as love: it had been given to them with their bodies. And when she looked at Kay now, pale, separate, white on the green grass at the border of the turned black ground, she remembered how Kay had once been her only visible self, the body she could see, more her body than her own. Most of her life she had known what she looked like only by looking at Kay.

"You will be," Anna mumbled.

Kay turned onto her front again. "It's so strange to see you, Baby. It's as if we had never been children."

"That's not so, Kay. I remember all of it."

"But it's different now, isn't it? Oh shit." And then her back shook.

Glittering at her through the tomato vines Anna saw her daughter's eyes. "I'm not going to stay here anymore," Maggie said.

It was Anna's fault that Kay got a sunburn. Kay fell asleep out in the garden. When Anna brought her inside, Maggie lay down for a nap. Anna lay down and dozed off too. She thought of Kay out there alone the instant she woke up, and was on her way to her when she saw a bonnet and a white cap bobbing down the slope. Kay was asleep—so Amos and his wife must have been scandalized, or amused. They probably thought she was Anna.

Kay had got a merciless scorching. She wasn't pale any longer but pink, and that band of her ass that was usually covered by a bathing suit looked incandescent and volatile. Later that evening it turned purplish. Kay couldn't put her shorts back on. She couldn't even stand to have the tail of the flannel shirt she borrowed from Anna hang down over her blister, and so she walked around the house with it knotted at her waist. The temptation was too much for Maggie. Anna saw her watching Kay, waiting for her chance, her shoulders, her whole body, moving just the way the cats' did when they got ready to pounce, her eyes focusing down on her target, her jaw undershot—and then she sprang. She looked demented. She looked a little like Dracula, teeth bared and hands made into claws. She had fingernails and she hooked Kay with all of them, a hand on each cheek. That too was probably Anna's fault, for she'd seen it coming in time to stop it.

"The devil made her do it," she said to Kay after she put Maggie to bed. Kay was sprawled, legs spread, on the couch in the front room, a big creamy couch that Steadman had picked out in a fancy shop in Washington. The only chair in the dingy unpainted room—there was a Finnish rug on the floor, shelves of books, the KLH—was a rocker. Anna sat down in it.

"She's getting to be quite a person, isn't she? Walks, talks, attacks. I guess it is pretty inviting." Kay looked back over her shoulder. "What are those monkeys called? The ones with the sassy red behinds? It would drive the sickie wild."

The sickie, Anna knew, was Rick, the man Kay had been living with off and on, but she couldn't tell what Kay thought of him. Almost the only facts she knew were that he read the Metro section of the papers looking for gory crimes and that he worked as a bartender. To raise extra money for coke he did organ gigs, mostly at weddings. Now and then he played with a band called The Rude

Awakening. To Anna he came across as another of Kay's cuties, but Kay was talking about something else now, about the girls Rick picked up and brought home. "Jailbait," Kay called them, "just another bunch of groupies." Kay only hinted at the details, and Anna saw how she was being watched.

"You look very prim sitting there in your rocker, Baby."

"I'm not so—"

"Kinky. Neither am I, Baby, neither am I. That stuff doesn't go down with me. Those years with the nuns really stick with you, I guess. When Rick found out he could get to me that way, there was no stopping the bastard."

"How come you stayed with him?"

"Come on, Baby. You know it doesn't work that way."

"Why'd you let something like that get started?"

"Because I'm romantic, like you."

When Kay grinned at her, Anna knew she was being teased, but not why exactly, and she wondered if there was any truth at all in what Kay was telling her. "What's so romantic about a family?"

"Cut it out. You're goo-goo about Steadman. Have you fucked anybody else since you've been married?"

"No."

"I didn't think so. Faithful Baby."

"What's wrong with that?"

"Nothing's wrong with it. I can see that it would take some doing out here. There aren't that many opportunities."

"It wouldn't matter if there were."

"Steadman's that terrific, huh?"

"I don't believe in that."

"In what?"

"Terrific studs."

"How would you know if you haven't balled anybody but Steadman for four years or five years or whatever it's been?"

"You know I slept with plenty of guys before that. It's nothing compared to—"

"To what? Don't be shy." Kay laughed at her. "This works you up, doesn't it. Baby's bliss. What does Steadman make of all this? Does he know how devoted you are?"

Anna could hardly get her breath. "Yes," she said.

"I'm happy for you, Baby, I really am."

Anna did not believe her for a second.

Kay got up and put on a Janis Joplin record. Anna told her to turn it down.

That night Anna dreamed. A green day, golden air, white blossoms floating in it. She was sitting on a polished stone bench. Her feet did not reach the ground and they were swinging under the stone. White socks, shiny black shoes, gold buckles. She held her feet in front of her and watched the waves and ripples of light on the black patent leather. Beneath the green hem of her dress her legs were ivory. Sun on the front of her, her bottom on the chilly stone. Her hands were in her lap—silver bracelet, perfect nails, perfect white crescents at top and bottom. She felt solemn, holy, beautiful.

And she woke terrified, for that was not a dream but a nightmare, not a nightmare but a memory.

That bench was in a cemetery and she was at her grandmother's funeral. She was—how old? Eight? Nine? It was the first time in her life that she had ever thought of herself as beautiful, the first time she understood the isolation of her body, the first time she had ever felt alone. She could not remember now, drenched in sweat, how she came by herself to that bench, but she remembered running— gravel slewing under her feet, turns in the path through the maze of shrubbery, spears of black iron, monuments shining like mirrors —when she saw herself reflected in the toes of her shoes, twin images, the warped silver specks of her faces, the wavering misshapen cones she recognized as her bodies. And she came to people, flowers, a pavilion, a bedecked coffin—and she recognized no one, no one, no one.

Later she was teased by Kay, by her father, for getting lost. It was not her grandmother's funeral she had returned to. A stranger—a man, short, puffing, chatty, holding her hand—brought her back to her own family.

Anna looked about her now—bright walls, silvered windows, the flat outline of Big Furnace across the panes, the flat mountain and the night sky framed in the window, joined like pieces of a puzzle. The only sound from Little Furnace was a whippoorwill. Anna was exhausted.

And she slept. When Maggie woke her she was mummified in the quilt and sheets. She was conscious of missing Steadman in the bed with them. Maggie was sitting in his place, her legs drawn up, nightie pulled down to her feet.

"Where's Daddy?"

Anna sloughed off the covers. "He's not back yet. Did you think he would come back so soon?"

"Sometimes he comes back when I'm in bed."

"He'll be gone for a few days. He called up last night and told me to give you a big hug."

Maggie did not want a hug. She pushed Anna away, climbed down off the bed, went back to her own room. Anna got dressed. Maggie had managed to pull her nightie off and she was struggling to pull on a pair of white tights.

"Are you going to wear those today?"

"Yes."

"Won't they be too warm?"

No answer. Maggie went to her bureau and opened a drawer. It stuck and screeched when she jerked on it.

"Hey, shhh. Kay's still asleep."

Maggie was not interested in playing a game of silence. She wanted to put on her best clothes, a long dress, her pumps. It occurred to Anna that she was dressing for a funeral.

"I don't think those are good clothes to work in, do you?"

"I don't want to work."

"But we have to work—we have to do all the work since Daddy's not here."

Maggie ignored her and tried to undo the buttons on her dress.

"Why don't you wear your shorts? That way we'll look alike."

"We don't look alike."

"Some people think we do. You remember what Amos said, don't you? He thought we did."

"You just look like Kay."

"Well, Kay's my sister. You can look like more than one person."

"I don't want to look like anybody."

Anna got on her knees so that she and Maggie were equal in height. "You don't look like anybody, you know. Just yourself, Maggie Steadman."

"Don't talk to me." Maggie stepped back.

"Why not, sweetie?"

"Because you're going to die."

Maggie's spite and rage were terrible to Anna. "Why do you say that?"

"Because everybody does and you will too."

"Not for a while," Anna said.

Maggie came close to her now and her voice was a hiss. "You're going to die."

Anna slapped Maggie hard. She heard the crack of her hand on Maggie's cheek. For an instant nothing happened. Maggie was just standing there looking at her, and then there was such an expression of grief on her face that Anna couldn't stand it. Maggie just fell down. She turned onto her stomach, black hair on her bare back. She was rigid; she wouldn't let Anna turn her over. "Maggie, sweetie, I'm so sorry." Anna had to pry Maggie's arm from her face, and when she did tilt her over she could still see the pale marks of her own fingers on Maggie's cheek. "Mama," Maggie said, bawling, reaching for her. Anna didn't know what all they were crying for, stretched out on the floor beside one another, but she did get Maggie on her feet after a bit, and dabbed her eyes with Kleenex. Maggie put on her shorts herself and had a silent tantrum when she couldn't do the button; by the time they got downstairs she was just grumpy. Over her Cheerios she said, "I hate to cry."

"Why's that?"

"Because it makes me feel all melted all over."

She was so emphatic that Anna laughed. Maggie looked at her angrily for a moment and then started laughing herself, right through her pout, and it seemed to be over. They chatted then, and fooled around in the kitchen, waiting for Kay. It was after nine when they finally heard her get out of bed. They heard footsteps, the water rising in the pipes, her coughs. When she came downstairs in nothing but that flannel shirt, naked below the waist, it struck Anna that Maggie'd had another reason for wanting to wear her tights. Kay complained that she hadn't been able to sleep. "Have a little disciplinary problem this morning?" she asked. Anna was holding a cup of coffee; she had to set it down. "The jitters, huh?" Anna looked at Maggie, her crayons spead out on the table, the indigo house she was coloring, orange faces at every window. Anna told Kay she needed a few things from Silesia. Kay didn't want to go along, and Anna asked if she could use her car. "Help yourself. You can't hurt the Cherry."

That car felt cramped and miniature after the Blazer, and all Anna bought in the store was toilet paper, coffee, and a fly swatter. Maggie had a Popsicle. The grouchy storekeeper, Nelson MacCray, a sixty-year-old who'd just married, had his toddling son with him for company and Anna had to inspect the kid's foot, stove up by a bee sting. Blanche Hammer came in, huffing about the heat, and Anna gabbed with her for a while. Maggie lost half her Popsicle when it fell off the stick and Anna let her have a Nutty Buddy.

On the way home she stopped at Xanaduc, where they were all watching the Senate hearings on TV. "Look who's here," Zep said. "When did you start making house calls?" They'd heard Steadman was in Bristol—from the Obenwalds, Anna guessed—and Anna was asked about Watts, but Rod said, "Hey, I want to hear this, okay? Rap somewhere else." Laurie took them into the kitchen, and when Maggie went out on the porch and played with the kittens, Anna asked about Kay. Laurie's account of the bad trip was worse than Steadman's. "It cleared the place out," Laurie said. The man who'd brought the angel dust had gone back to Philadelphia, and Peggy had left too. When Laurie asked her to have some lunch, Anna called Kay and let the phone ring and ring before Kay answered. Kay didn't want to join them. The record player was going. "I'm getting into a book," Kay said. "Enjoy yourself, Baby."

She ate with Laurie, and since Monday was one of Maggie's afternoons with Hope Byrd, Anna took her straight there. She ended up spending the afternoon with Mavis, making a batch of brownies. "Other's real particular about what he eats," said Mavis, a hefty woman with hair about the same color, shape, and texture as a cone of cotton candy. Other liked taters, hawg meat, and yogurt with a vanilla bean ground up in it. Anna said that Steadman was pretty fussy about food too. Other himself came into the kitchen and drank a glass of lemonade, and when Hope trotted to his knee, as she obviously was accustomed to do, Other, the great scowler, blushed to be witnessed in physical contact with his daughter.

When Anna took Maggie home at five, she heard the music before she reached the house, the Youngbloods now. In the kitchen the mayonnaise jar was open on the counter and a split avocado was turning brown. Kay had opened a can of frozen orange juice, made one glass, and left the rest to melt. The bread and cheese were out on the cutting board. Anna started cleaning up.

Kay came to the door. "Where've you been all day?"

"I stayed at—"

Kay didn't listen. "Around here where the fuck can you kill a whole day?"

She poured herself a glass of water and went back into the front room. Anna left her alone until she was about to make dinner. Kay said she wasn't hungry, but she tried to be agreeable. "I'm almost done with this book," she said, holding up *Play It As It Lays*. "Have you read it, Baby?"

"No. Steadman just got it. He was reading it the other day."

"Steadman was? That fucker'll surprise you."

Anna and Maggie ate alone, and after Maggie's stories and songs, Anna went to her own bedroom. She didn't go downstairs until Maggie was asleep. *Between the Buttons* was playing. "Do you mind if I turn this down a little, Kay?"

"Go ahead. I'm sick of it. You must have stopped buying records when you got married. I keep looking through them but it's the same old shit every time."

"I guess we haven't bought many records lately. We just set the record player up a few weeks ago."

"What do you listen to out here?"

"The radio, sometimes."

Kay laughed. "You crack me up, Baby, no shit. *The radio. Sometimes I listen to the radio.* You're like some little old auntie, sitting there in your rocker, getting your kicks from the radio. Where's your knitting, Auntie? Do you tune in some pretty wild stations out here?"

"I thought you meant—"

"Doesn't it get to you, Baby?"

Kay didn't have any clothes on, not even the shirt. She was stretched on her side on the couch, head in her hand, and the other hand, the bandaged hand—the gauze was dirty, bloody, hadn't been changed—lay on her hip. She looked amused, but her imitation of Anna's voice—mumbly, out of it—had been savage.

"It doesn't get to me any worse here than it did anywhere else."

"What do you *do*, Baby? I've been here—what? A week now. Weed the garden, eat a meal, play with Maggie, eat a meal, play with Steadman, go to sleep—that's about how it goes, isn't it? I left out the foxes."

"There's more to it than that. And it's been—a little different since you've been here."

"Yeah. I'm company. I remember."

Anna shrugged. "All I meant is that I haven't been doing what I usually do. There's still a lot of work in the house, and I've been drawing too."

"The bugs."

"Mostly flowers."

"I didn't see them, but I guess that follows."

"Don't be such a shit."

Kay laughed. "What did you say, Auntie? What was that naughty word?"

"I don't know what's wrong with you, Kay."

"Wrong with me? Jesus, Baby, wake up. Look around you. I'm not living out in the fucking sticks with diseased foxes running after me. I don't get up from the dinner table to go bawl out in the dark somewhere. I'm not drawing big bugs. I don't sit in my fucking rocker at night listening to the radio."

"Why do you have to make it sound like that? Why can't you try to see what it is?"

"What am I supposed to see?"

"What my life is."

"Don't break my heart, Baby. You're really on an emotional jag, aren't you?"

"Why do you have to belittle it all?"

"Because I see what's happening to you, that's why. I'm trying to wake you up, Baby. What are you doing here? With your friends Mr. and Mrs. Natural or whatever their fucking names are—don't tell me you like that big cow Diana."

"I do."

"Do you go out to the barn and moo with her? Or with those creeps at Xanaduc? All that piety down there is horseshit—they couldn't cut it in the city, that's all. You should have heard the earth rap I got down there—don't tell me you fall for it. Baby, I know you better than that."

"Don't twist everything."

"What am I twisting? You're so goddamn out of it you don't know what's twisted."

"Don't shout at me. I don't want Maggie to hear this."

"Do you hear that? Do you hear what you're saying? The earth doesn't revolve around your little girl."

"I don't want you to talk about her."

"I'm not talking about her, Baby. I'm talking about you."

"We don't see things the same way anymore, Kay."

"Yes, we do, Baby. You're trying to put one over on me and you can't even put it over on yourself. You can't do this number. Face it. It doesn't work for you."

"I try to make it work. I don't expect—"

"Try, try, try. You're not going to turn into a cow no matter how hard you try. You're in a trance."

"If I am it's because you're here."

"Oh yeah. That's when you started drawing the bugs? The monsters, that's what they are. And what about those lists? Make up the bed. Tie your shoes. Take out the garbage. I'm surprised you don't have to remind yourself to breathe."

"That list—"

"What about it?"

"It was kind of a joke between me and Steadman."

"Some joke, making yourself a little slavey."

"Kay, don't talk about Steadman."

"I can't talk about your kid, I can't talk about your husband—it's like the fucking relics in the tabernacle. He's not such a saint, you know. You should have stayed at that party, Baby."

Anna didn't speak, and Kay said, "Yeah, you know, don't you? You guessed. It was pretty hard to miss the way he came on to that little tramp."

"Peggy?"

"Don't act so innocent. You could see that those two were going to get it on from the minute you got there—and you couldn't stand it, could you?"

Anna, thinking of all that had happened when Steadman got home that night, said, "That's not why I left."

"Come on, Baby."

"I left because I heard you talking drugs with them. I left because I didn't want to see what was going to happen to you."

"Oh sure."

"That's true, Kay—but I should have stayed there."

"To protect me? That's what you mean, isn't it? Oh, that's cute. That's so fucking noble and wonderful. My little sister was going to look out for me when her husband was out in the bushes balling some teen-age Kewpie doll."

"He didn't do that."

"Wake up, Baby. Those two beat it as soon as they could. Her little pussy was pouting for it."

"It didn't happen. You weren't in a state to know."

"Is that what Steadman told you?"

"That's what Laurie told me."

"You've been checking up on me? Apologizing for me? Well, I didn't see him put it in her, but I knew what that gleam in Daddy's eye meant. I fucked Steadman once, you know."

Anna said, "You're lying," but it was almost the first thing Kay had said that she believed.

"I did," Kay said calmly.

"When? He wouldn't fuck you."

Kay grinned. "You think he saves it all for the one he loves?"

"When? You're lying to me."

"You don't really want to know, Baby."

"You can't tell me because it's a lie."

"What's a lie is your cozy little family. The night I fucked him you'd just had your baby and you were still in the hospital."

"That's not true."

"You know it's true, don't you? Don't you remember how we were there together one night when visiting hours ended? You remember, Baby. Steadman took me home. He walked me to the door like a gentleman. One thing led to another—you know how it is, Baby—and then he fucked me like a gentleman."

"If he did it was because of you."

Kay laughed. "Because of me? Who else could it have been because of?"

"I mean I blame you."

"Blame? We're not in the convent anymore. We're out in the shitstorm—everybody but you. I don't know where you are. And in the shitstorm, Baby, nobody's to blame."

"If he fucked you, it's because you tricked him."

"Tricked him? Baby, you're too much."

"I know what I mean, and so do you, Kay."

"Tell me then."

"I mean Steadman's not that cheap."

"And I am."

"Yes, Kay! Yes! Yes! You try to make everything low and smutty and cheap."

"And you're on some different plane, some high moral plane where you can judge me and put me down?"

"I'm not judging you."

"That's how it sounds."

"You're the one that's judging. You're the one that won't let things be what they are."

"Tell me, what are they?"

"Things have changed, Kay. It's all different. We're different. It's just not the same between us anymore. It can't be the same."

"It's the same for me, Baby."

"It isn't. You couldn't tell me the things you've told me if it was still. You couldn't be so cruel to me. You tell me I'm sick and twisted —oh Kay, what's wrong with you? What's happening to you?"

Anna was on her feet, and crying, and Kay, who'd been looking at her without any expression, turned slowly onto her stomach and brought her arms up to cover her face. Her ribs began to shake. Anna crossed the rug and knelt down beside the couch.

"Kay? Kay? Look at me, Kay. Kay, we don't have to fight like this."

Suddenly Kay did look, and her face was so sinister and hateful that Anna recoiled. "You'd fall for anything, Baby. Do you think the whole fucking world goes around in tears like you do? Do you think you could make me cry?"

Thirteen

Down in Bristol, Steadman couldn't shut up. He knew how loud and rude he was, but he couldn't help it. There was too much politeness, too many covered dishes in Corning Ware, too much scorekeeping —the number of condolences, the length of the obituaries, the size of the floral offerings. The governor had sent a wreath and a telegram, and Bunny Biggs, Steadman's old boss, was coming to the funeral. Rumors about the will circulated in confidential, solemn whispers. Steadman made it his business to be disruptive. No doubt his rudeness was seen as greed and gloating, but he didn't care. He made cracks about the flowers, the food, the register—a glossy white volume with gilt letters, "In Memory," that the undertaker had given Betty and she'd put out by the door to collect signatures—and about the funeral racket and about plumbing, for the septic system had backed up with all those people in the house, and Roto-Rooter had to be called, and in the midst of all the numbing observances a whistling workman was outside pumping sewage.

Steadman refused, not silently, to go to the funeral home to look at the body. He would not allow anyone to speak of the appearance of the corpse. "It's not a trip to a beauty parlor," he said to a daubed friend of Betty's. And yet the night before the funeral he did go, late, by himself. At once he felt gagged—drapes, rugs, upholstery, a thick smell of flowers and disinfectant—but he found the room and walked up to the open coffin. He thought, *he's dead, all right.* He turned and started to walk away as if that was what he'd come for. He fell down. He felt as if he'd been slammed across the shoulders. The weight stayed on him. He was on his hands and knees in the middle of the carpet, trying to lift himself up, and his arms gave way. *Get up, get up, get up off this floor.* He must have said it out loud, for a person who evidently worked at the place came into the room and helped him, with hands that felt like water-filled balloons, to his feet.

The funeral was as dismal and farcical as the rest of it. Everybody complained about the rain and counted the cars that went to the cemetery. The sagging green pavilion dripped. The senile old Presbyterian minister who conducted the service went gaga when drops kept spattering on his Bible. Most people, including Bunny Biggs, stayed in their cars during the service. The only ones who didn't were the men who'd worked for Watts, who'd sullied the procession with their beat-up trucks and Chevvies, who now stood there beside the grave, hats in their hands, getting drenched.

The business kept him in Bristol for a week. Talks with his father, talks with the lawyer. He stayed out at the lake with Betty, where there was usually company, and they ate their way through the cairn of covered dishes. Betty had asked him please to sort through all the things in the gun room, take what he wanted, decide what to do with the rest. She wouldn't have an idea how to get rid of those things. *Get rid of those things*—maybe she didn't mean to be so blunt, but that's what she said. Steadman parceled out the guns and fishing tackle, the souvenirs—the jug of pure corn whiskey that Watts had been proud of, the brass spittoons he bought when the courthouse decided that the era of tobacco-chewing had come to an end—to cousins, uncles, Watts's cronies. "What are we going to do with poor old Injun?" Betty kept asking him, which meant, he knew, that she didn't want to get stuck with a wheezing hound. One night a small nut-colored man, a bricklayer who'd worked for Watts, arrived to pay his respects. He'd only just heard of it, he said, and he'd driven four hours from Tennessee to stand there and feel awkward. Steadman took him back to the gun room to give him a framed photograph, Watts with his court of workmen. The man asked what was to become of Injun. "I don't mean to presume," he said, "but I remember how this one could flat run a coon. If he's in the way here . . ." Injun went to Tennessee.

The only things Steadman kept for himself were a railroad pocket watch that Watts had always carried, a few photographs, the packet of letters—all neatly filed in one of those cardboard wallets—that he'd written to Watts. They were all there, the postcards from the two summer trips he'd made to the Rockies, the letters from college consisting mostly of his praise, not very subtle, of himself as a scholar, political letters from Washington, cultural and culinary bulletins from Italy. Steadman didn't have the heart to read through all of them; he was struck by how hard he'd tried to impress Watts. He sorted through other correspondence, newspaper clippings, programs and papers and all the usual junk, throwing away most of it, stashing some of it in boxes, as he gathered he should, for there was already talk of the impossibility of Betty remaining in that house by herself. It was too big to look after, too expensive to keep up, too far from town. Mason—and it pained Steadman that his father was the executor of the estate, his father and the lawyer, though the necessity of that was clear to him—had said that it would be a shame if the house didn't remain in the family. When Mason added—relishing, Steadman thought, his own magnanimity—that there was a job for him in Bristol if he ever wanted it, he understood that the house was being offered to him. That offer, followed by the insult: "You may find that you want to look after your own affairs." Even that, Steadman knew, was only fair. Watts's assets were property, not cash, and the income designated for him depended on his father's management. Their detailed conversations were confined to business, but there was an embrace that took them both by surprise. After their last talk in his office Mason came around the desk to shake hands, for Steadman was leaving that afternoon; their hands did touch, and then they had their arms around each other. That was all. It was too peculiar to mention. "Well, come see us," Mason said. "I will."

A reconciliation, then, and there was a discovery too. Nothing was left to Joe Watt, the son who'd disappeared, but there was a bequest to his wife, Maude, and her two children. It turned out that Betty had been in touch with Joe, who was now a high school coach in

Arizona, divorced from Maude. Her children were about Steadman's age, and he dimly remembered playing with them. Maude he
remembered vividly. Jewelry, red hair, bright clothes. At that age
he was all in favor of extravagance; he remembered with humiliation
telling his plain mother that he wished she looked like Maude. But
in his confusion and anger and grief and nostalgia he did not think
much about the bequest, not until he came upon the wallet of letters
from Maude, as carefully put away as his own letters. There were
photographs too, one of Maude with her children by the fender of
a Buick convertible, a flashy car and a flashy woman. Another,
Maude in a bathing suit on a lawn chair in front of the screened
porch of a cabin, older, heavier, fleshier than Steadman had seen her.
She looked as if she had not wanted this photograph taken. She was
glowering, and she'd drawn her arms together, forcing a deep cleav-
age between her large breasts, a furrow to the throat. And the last
one, a nightclub photograph, Maude in a booth with Watts, eyes
hooded, mascara'ed, ratted hair, jewelry, a hardbitten honkytonk
veteran. Watts, his eyes dazzled by the flashbulb, had his arms
around her and his expression was the complete leer of the satyr.
Steadman didn't have to read the letters to learn that Maude's children were, or could have been, Watts's. He was going to throw out
the letters and photographs but couldn't, nor could he leave them
for Betty. He almost suspected her of having requested him to
empty the gun room so that the evidence could be—kept from her
eyes? Presented to his? Both, maybe. Not knowing what else to do
with it, he placed the packet of Maude's letters in his suitcase alongside the packet of his own and took it back to Zion County.

He drove through a thunderstorm near Roanoke and then
through a long, splendid mountain sunset. He was aware of clouds
like marzipan overhead, of fields and mountains in shadows green
as mint, of reflections that blazed on the St. Margaret's River, but
he concentrated mostly on the speeding road that followed the
bends of the water. Heading home, heading home: the geography
of this entire landscape seemed created to lead him home. Outside
the Silesia store there was a committee on the benches, familiar
figures who returned his wave as he passed. He crossed the iron truss
bridge over the river, followed the road hacked into the limestone
of Little Furnace, entered the valley, his own valley now, where the

deer were feeding in the fields of the Hammer place, where the shadow of Little Furnace had risen all the way to the peaks of Big Furnace opposite. In Panther Gap, under the thick pines and hemlocks, the full night had encroached. He turned on his headlights. Two curves, the lights of the Obenwalds' house, and away through the trees, beneath the mass of the mountain, the lights of his own house.

They're in there. Anna and Maggie are in that house.

Water splashing under the Blazer, bouncing on the stones of Prussian Creek. The kitchen where they'd just eaten, their footsteps. They were on their way down the stairs when he reached the hall, Maggie in her nightie, Anna behind her with her hands in the pockets of her shorts, her shoulder and bare arm skidding against the wall. Maggie sailed into his arms.

"Who's this?" he asked.

"What?"

"Are you my own darling daughter?"

"Yes," she said, but confused, shy.

"And who's that?"

"Who?"

"The one slinking against the wall?"

"Mama." She didn't know what to make of his questions and he just held her. He carried her back up the steps to where Anna stood. When he kissed her, he pinned her against the wall.

He put Maggie to bed. She wanted a story out of his mouth, not out of a book, and he told her one of the Grimm stories she never seemed to tire of. Anna sat behind him on the bed. He got a hand up inside her roomy shorts and kept it there during the storytelling and the bedtime song.

Then in the hallway Anna whispered, "Hey, we better not do this here. Maggie'll hear us."

They went downstairs and did it on the couch, and when his semen left him it was like a grouse flight out the ass—that sudden, that exhilarating, that clean a departure. But he was not too thrilled to know that Anna had been merely submissive. She stood up almost at once and began to dress, shivery and goose-bumped, against the light from the kitchen. She was furtive; sight was more threatening to her than touch. Light came through her legs, outlined the cleft protuberance, hung in the snarl of her hair. How bushy she was! That springy black patch, denser now because it was in shadow, was almost as large as his spread hand. She picked up her panties from the heap of clothes, but these panties, like most of hers, were disintegrating, the elastic parting from the nylon, and she had to hold them up to the light to straighten them out. Steadman watched how she stepped into them, the stresses of balance first in one leg and then the other, the ripple in the calves and the rolling on the bones of the ankles, the way she spread her weight on the edges of her feet. Those feet: they were broad and almost flat, and at the end of her long elegant legs they looked like a failure of evolution.

"Come here, Anna."

She obeyed dutifully, buttoning her shorts.

He took her hand and made her sit down beside him. "Let's not get off to a bad start. Something's bothering you."

"It's nothing."

"Did you have a hard time with Kay?"

"Hard enough."

"Tell me about it, Anna."

She blurted out, "Did you fuck her? Did you fuck that Peggy?" She was sitting over him, looking at him, and she put her hands on his shoulders, pinning him. "Did you? Why are you smiling?"

"Because you're so fierce."

"Tell me the truth, Steadman. Did you?"

"I told you what happened. I told you the truth. I didn't leave anything out."

"Did you want to fuck her?"

"No."

She removed her hands. "I don't see how you could. She's just—she's just a Big Mac."

Steadman laughed, but he sat up and put his arm around Anna. "You believe me, don't you? What's the trouble, Anna?"

"Oh, I believe you."

"What's this about then? What happened here, Anna? What happened between you and Kay? How long did she stay here?"

"Only a few days after you left. I told you that on the phone."

"We're not much good on the phone. Tell me what happened."

"Why talk about it? We're through, that's all. No more Kay. I sent her packing. That should please you—Steadman, I've been so miserable."

"Anna."

"I didn't want it to turn out like that, but Kay just wouldn't stop. She can be so cruel and terrible to me."

Against him now, Anna cried.

"I'm sorry, Anna. I am. I was worried about you two here together."

"She hates me now, Steadman."

"She doesn't hate you."

"You didn't see her. And it wasn't just Kay—I kept thinking of Watts, and Maggie was so sad, and you were gone—"

"Anna, Anna."

She rubbed her eyes hard. "I'll tell you one thing—this crying is going to stop. I made a vow while you were down there—no more tears. I'm turning into an adolescent. The next thing you know I'll have pimples."

She was determined to stand up and he didn't try to keep her on the couch. She got to her feet and pulled her jersey top over her head; he watched her shake back her hair and gather it, saw the flash of silver, the barrette in her mouth.

"Is there anything to eat in this house?" he asked, rising, dressing.

She'd kept dinner for him, a veal dish in cream. "Very fancy," he said, but she didn't want to be kidded. She still seemed withdrawn, and he did not press her to talk about Kay. Whatever had happened between them, Anna couldn't help blaming him in part—that much he understood. He did not resent that but he was disappointed to find Anna preoccupied with her own emotions. He had expected to be greeted with a sympathy in which he could unburden himself. But his disappointment was only faint, and the malicious satisfaction he took in hearing that Anna had broken with Kay was also faint. Watching Anna, for she'd made him sit at the table while she heated his dinner and fixed his plate, he thought he knew the extent of her loss. When she brought him a glass of wine he caught her wrist and kissed her hand. Her smile seemed wonderful to him.

They sat together at the table and talked while he ate the meal she'd made. He didn't think he exaggerated the excellent deportment in Bristol, not his but the others; he admitted that he'd been a wahoo. "Watts brought that out in you," Anna said tolerantly. Though he was on the verge of it several times, he didn't mention Maude. And he was dry-eyed when he told her about his last sight of Watts. They were talking quietly at the table, and Steadman said, feeling mawkish, "If anything happens to me, Anna, I want to be buried here, up there with the Argenstills. No preaching, no ceremony. Have me put in the ground in a plain wooden box. Get somebody to read 'Sunday Morning' over me."

Anna started. Steadman knew that she regarded herself as Stevens's chief appreciator. "I hope that doesn't interfere with any plans you had for the poem."

He was grateful when she smiled and said, "It must have been pretty gruesome in Bristol if it got you thinking about this."

"I thought of another Stevens poem driving home tonight."

"Poems now."

Stevens was one of the poets they'd read together in their first days, and Steadman quoted now, bashfully, from a poem they'd thought of as their own.

> *"She has composed, so long, a self with which to welcome him,*
> *Companion to his self for her, which she imagined,*
> *Two in a deep-founded sheltering, friend and dear friend."*

"How can you remember that?"

"It took me most of the way from Roanoke to remember one verse."

"It embarrasses me, Steadman."

"Pal, then. My dear pal."

But it was still too heroic. Anna got up and made coffee—for him only. She wasn't going to drink it after dinner anymore, she thought maybe she'd sleep better. While he drank his, he told her about Mason—"I'm glad you made it up," she said—and about the will.

"It's going to be possible to live here," he said.

"We do live here."

"We've been on a spree with my trust fund."

And as they talked he was watching Anna, the big dark eyes, the arms beginning to twitch a little as she felt the cold. He wondered how long she'd put off covering herself up with a sweater. He saw her glance once at those hands, the fingernails, and grimace, saw her scratch her back on the chair. He reached for her foot, still bare, and put it in his lap; she looked startled at first and then pretended not to know where she was treading. He loved her face when its severity was at odds with desire. She told him, her foot still moving, how Maggie had taken in this death, her outbursts, her play funerals, her new interest in God.

"Your toes are prehensile," he said. "They seize hold. Our next one will be a monkey."

"What next one?"

"If you want a next one."

Her foot stopped but he held it there. "Do you want another child, Anna?"

"I don't know. I haven't thought about it."

"If you do want more—"

"You do."

"Yes."

"What do you have in mind? A dynasty?"

"One more like you and Maggie."

"You're serious about this, aren't you?"

"Yes," he said, "but I think you're safe if you can bring me off with your foot."

Fourteen

They settled down to work. Zep came to help Steadman lay stone and Anna cleaned and treated the logs for the studio. She brushed them first with a wire brush to get rid of the lime and mud sticking to them, then chopped out the punky places with a hatchet, then soaked them with pentachlorophenol. Even out in the air its fumes made her dizzy and light-headed. She read the directions for the disposal of the can: punch holes in it, burn it in a hot fire, crush it beneath the wheels of a heavy vehicle, bury it at least three feet deep two miles away from any water source or livestock. "What is this poison?" she asked Steadman. "Just a bug killer."

He wanted to raise the walls on the Fourth of July, and once he started inviting people he couldn't stop. He asked Harry and Diana, of course, and the Xanaduc crowd and the others from around the county whom he now called their peer group. But he invited also the local people, the Byrds, and Duty Armstrong and his wife, Alice, and Blanche Hammer and the other widows, Sally Showalter and Lena Coy and Ruth Stewart, who all went to church together in Silesia and took their dinner these summer Sundays at a linen-covered table in the shade of Blanche's yard. He asked the bachelors too, the gang from the Silesia store, tiny Doc Hiner and his goon of a brother, Junior, and Leo Sullenbarger, who would probably bring his fishing rod—Anna had never seen him without it. He couldn't leave out Nelson MacCray, the old codger, and his new wife—because of her there now stood in that dark cave of a store a plastic rack shaped like a Christmas tree and loaded with silver balls, the eggs of L'eggs. And old Mr. Robinson, old Sugar Ray Robinson, Other called him, for he did have a phobia about black people—there was a black population of about twenty in the county —and the name fit otherwise too, for Mr. Robinson lived by himself up a fruitful hollow. He ran a small orchard and a huge garden and he was always complaining about the price of sugar; he used 300 pounds in putting up his preserves every summer. And Amos and Mrs. Argenstill, Buck and Toots—Anna was still shy around them, imagining they imagined they'd seen her naked—and some of the summer people. Johnny, the Englishman with gapped teeth, an importer in Washington, who'd come jogging up to the house one day, as he jogged, weekends, all over Zion County from his cabin in Barger's Mill, wearing a T-shirt that said "Chocolate City." And Jimmy, the manager of an IGA near Harrisonburg, a turkey hunter from one of the camps, who called his wife Angel, his teen-age son Bubba, and his pubescent daughter Beauty. Steadman invited Dan, a lawyer from Staunton whom he'd met fishing up on Jerkemtight, and his wife, Jenny, who'd had them to dinner; they had a little girl just Maggie's age. He asked Rufus Howell, too, and he asked Ben and Frances, the folklorists who appeared one day and took him to task for destroying the cabin; he said he wanted them to see it go back up.

The studio did go up, with cheers for each log. With all those people it was easy as piling up blocks. Steadman had marked the logs when he took them down, and they stacked right up the same way. The dovetail notches were good and tight, and Duty, looking for a way to praise the foundation Steadman had put under them, said he built about like the fairy-o's—meaning, Anna realized much later, the pharaohs. And everyone came, everyone Steadman had asked and more besides. Harry's parents were there, and Johnny's glamorous girl friend, Gwen, who started talking at once about the Guinness Book of Sexual Records and had Rufus at her side; the girl he'd brought got pestered by Zep. Duty's son came, an Air Force sergeant home on leave, with his two beautiful blond children and his German wife, Sigrid, who talked to the senior Obenwalds. And there were hangers-on from Xanaduc and among their peer group, but it was easy to keep the names straight, the men's names anyway; they were all called Gary.

After the logs were up they played softball in a field Harry had mowed for the occasion, with about fifteen players a side and a special first base for women, amid cries of "Don't cut your foot," which meant don't step in a cow plop. Old Sugar Ray held forth professorially on canning and preserving, and Amos got to meet the man who raised the yammers. Jimmy, the turkey hunter, and Junior Hiner got into an argument; Junior started it by saying the best way to hunt turkeys was to run over them with a truck. The folklorists split up to circulate among the crowd, and their conversations sounded to Anna like field work. Other and Dan, the lawyer, magnetized each other, and Jenny must have said to Anna three times, "I just can't believe she"—Mrs. Argenstill—"actually wears a bonnet. She's the dearest old soul." There were watermelons, hams, chickens, all kinds of salads and vegetables and breads, for everyone brought something, and after the softball Steadman organized other games, blowing his turkey caller instead of a whistle when he wanted attention, and clowning so that it was no loss of dignity to take part in the sack races, spoon races, three-legged races, wheelbarrow races. He took the burden of silliness on himself. And did so, Anna thought, with the right praise for the young children, and there were lots of them, who did feel observed and embarrassed when they dropped a potato, and the right jeers for the competitive Garys, who were toking up behind one of the sheds. The only ones nearly as loud as Steadman were Zep and Johnny, the Englishman, whose cries of "jolly good" and "hard cheese" and "well done" kept rising from the playing fields.

After dark they had fireworks, which Stan provided, a whole program of bursts, sprays, rockets, pinwheels. The hissing fuses, the bangs and pops, the fumes of powder, the dazzle of silver and gold and red and blue, the running sighs that lifted with each display, the oozes and awes, Steadman called them. Anna overheard Gwen say to Johnny, "God, I can't stand it, it's so sexy," and had a sexy vision of her own; all those sprays of color looked like brilliant sperm to her, short-lived throngs, each separate traveling spark dragging its wiggling tail behind it.

That night in bed, after everyone had finally gone, Anna admitted that it hadn't been the disaster she feared. She even told Steadman, when he began to kiss her, how the fireworks had appeared to her, and he said he didn't know if he could live up to that. She didn't say a word about her one bad moment of the day. Diana, whose secret was out now, who'd let it out during the party, had sniffed the logs once and asked, "Is that penta on them?" Anna said it was. "I'm not going to get near them. You know what that stuff does, don't you? It causes embryonic deformities. We used to use it around all the barns and pens till we found out, and we had some monsters too—yuck! I can't even stand to think of them."

With the walls of the studio up—and Anna liked the clean horizontal lines of the hewed logs, the openness of the unroofed enclosure—Steadman took a break and wrote a story. The roof could wait, he said, and his hands needed a rest; the mortar was caustic and had eaten his fingers raw. He joked about not being able to hold a pencil. He spent four long mornings in one of the downstairs rooms, a junk room where they'd stowed furniture they weren't using yet, but his desk was in there and he wasn't bothered so much by the racket. The racket—she and Maggie crept around the house and tried not to make a peep. When Steadman was writing his ears became very sensitive. Sometimes he came into the kitchen to get himself coffee, but if she asked a question or made a practical remark that happened to strike the wrong chord, he glared at her as if she were the enemy of literature. She wasn't, although she didn't read much fiction, never had. Even the writers she liked best, writers like Kafka and Flannery O'Connor, she'd read in a random, intermittent way. She didn't plow through novels as Steadman did. She was put off by thick novels—he'd tried for a year to get her to read *Parade's End*—and even when she liked them she often didn't finish them. She started *One Hundred Years of Solitude* and thought it was fabulous—but misplaced it and never managed to get another copy. She did like Steadman's saint of saints, Chekhov, and Steadman suspected her fondness: "You just like him because he never wrote anything long." She stuck mostly to her picture books, to the biographies of artists and to collections of their letters. It seemed to baffle and anger Steadman that she could read about writers—and she'd read a lot

about Virginia Woolf and Vita Sackville-West and the rest of them
—without feeling much curiosity about their books. She did love
some poets, particularly Stevens, who must have seen colors as she
once did; she turned through the volume of Stevens just as she
turned through the picture books, delighted just to look.

Steadman was trying, Anna saw, not to exaggerate the importance
of his story, trying to deflate it by calling it his *opusculum,* and trying
not to let the work of writing infect his other hours. He emerged
in the afternoons to take them swimming, or to till the garden, or
to mow the grass. But he was abstracted, his mind was on his writing,
and when she asked him a question she was likely to wait a few
minutes for him to reply, "What?" Anna knew, or remembered
anyway, what it was like to be absorbed in that way, and she was glad
to see Steadman at work again. He could be, when he did notice her
and Maggie, so tender and kind. One night after they'd eaten outside, just the three of them, and he was pushing Maggie in the swing
he'd hung in the maple, he said, "Isn't it wonderful to have time,
Anna? Doesn't it feel as if it's banked all around us? Time, anyway,
for the important things."

Anna watched the swing going back and forth, Maggie rising and
descending against Big Furnace, a clock ticking. She wondered if
that's what made him think of time, wondered what he meant by the
important things. He told her: "Time for love and work."

And so the night she listened to him typing his story—she was in
the kitchen and she was lapsing, drinking coffee after dinner—she
hoped she would think the story was splendid.

"Done," he said when he brought it to her.

"Shall I read it now?"

"It'll never be better or worse," he said. He went into the front
room and left her alone to read it.

---

*Lulu was digging. She'd scooped out little holes all over the potato patch
where the ground was loose and deep, but she was not planting. This year
she had no mind to garden at all, and the potatoes had never been her lookout
anyway, but Arlie's—and that was why she was here now. Because if he'd
been going to hide something from her, something he'd want to get at from
time to time, why then it would have to be somewhere she wouldn't discover*

it by chance and where he could put his hand on it without seeming to go out of his way. The potato patch was down the slope from the house, tucked out of sight in a little bowl all its own, and when she'd thought about it she remembered how he used to sit off to the side under the sugar tree. "Watching taters grow," he said, but it could have been something else he was watching.

The shovel made her foot hurt right through the sole of her blue U.S. Keds and it seemed like the ground was full of stones. Every time the blade thunked into one she thought she'd found the box and her hopes leaped right up like a mess of quail. Then when she saw it was just a stone—then it was crows that settled where the quail had been. And then she started another hole. She didn't reckon Arlie would dig very deep nor disturb many stones no matter what he was hiding. The box probably had a few inches of dirt over it, not more. Because there must have been times when he wanted to slip down to put a hand on it, and somebody would have seen him if he dug a pit.

The holes Lulu was digging were according to pattern. She didn't just spade the ground as the spirit moved her, oh no! Arlie had been a systematic man in his way, and what he did do, he did with a line and rule. If there was one thing he couldn't stand, it was crookedness—a crooked furrow, a crooked path, a crooked fence, a crooked bale. He'd saw down a tree sooner than allow a fence to stray from its line, and when he stacked wood it was all as straight and level as a brick building—and just let her take down a stick of it that made the stack uneven to his eye, he'd find a way to punish her. He liked things neat and straight and had even got so he moved that way, always walking as if he were stretching a wire tight and turning, when turn he must, in measured angles. More than once Lulu had seen him march right through a brier patch or step in a fresh green cow plop rather than stray from his course by one degree. A few scratches or a nasty shoe were nothing to a man with a brain like a compass. Arlie hated the mountains and his own humped-up fields, and he used to say he'd level them off like a table if he had a bulldozer like Duty Armstrong's. Bullnoser, he called it, and it was no use correcting him. He was that contrary. He wouldn't trust a cent of money to the bank either, which was why she was digging. There was money missing, had to be, because Arlie had sold off the 200 acres on the mountain to the state, and that was after selling the timber off it. She didn't know what the timber brought, but she remembered exactly what the state paid: $6,297, because she was standing beside him at the bank when he told Mr. Turner that he wanted the whole amount in cash. Nobody could reason with him. And he bought a new tractor, and a truck, and paid to have the water *brought into the house, but he must have hid thousands, and she knew what he must have hid them in—that black metal ammunition box his brother Amos had given him when he came back from overseas. Didn't he call it their treasure chest when they were first married? It had been many a year since she'd seen it, and she hadn't pestered Arlie about it, because the truth was, and she could admit it now, he had plumb worn her down. With Charles, the son she named for her own father, killed in the war, and her own family dead or scattered, she didn't care for the money, for she had no wishes of any kind.*

But Arlie dropped dead and things were different. There was no earthly reason for her to stay here now on a place that was never hers anyway, and it was Arlie's last way of tormenting her, making her hunt the money he'd hid. He was taking his sweet revenging pleasure watching her turn up the potato patch, not that she actually believed he was watching. She hadn't been brought up superstitious like these people out here. She'd seen strange things since Arlie died, a kind of glow up on the mountain where he was buried, and heard strange noises—but nothing was going to run her off till she found what was rightfully hers.

Her holes. She'd lined them up with the landmarks. The first one she dug where a line from the sugar tree to the gate in the picket fence, and another from the big walnut tree to the power pole, would have intersected. That was almost dead center of the patch, and she dug a right big hole—no box. So she tried again, using the sugar tree and a corner of the barn, the walnut tree and the pitcher pump on the dry well, as her reference points. Again nothing, nothing but those dang stones. Go on, laugh, *she said out loud, even though she didn't think Arlie's spirit, if there was such a thing, would be out in daylight. But now that she'd been at it for a time, now that her feet ached and the hot sun was binding her shoulders, now that she, Lulu Cutler Argenstill, was so warm that sweat made the inside of her hatband slippery, now that she felt herself being stabbed right through by straight black lines that radiated from every fixed object—well, it eased her to talk out loud.*

"Mrs. Argenstill?"

He would call like that, ever so polite and false-humble, using his name, her married name. She never had felt like an Argenstill, and he knew it. She never had dropped the Cutler from her full name, and no matter how many years she lived there under that mountain she always felt that her true home was the one in town where she grew up. Arlie resented that.

"Mrs. Argenstill?"

He could croon her name all he wanted, he wasn't going to run her off. She stepped down hard on the shovel. This was the first time he'd called out to her by name, but he might not be trying to run her off, he might just be there for spite, just to watch her scrape and strain. She'd always differed with him about what was woman's work, she wasn't about to haul and carry all day long the way he thought she should, she wasn't born to it, and she told him so before they married. Her daddy owned the Cutler Hardware Store on Main Street in Zion, and a house with a great big yard and the white porch swing hung from the elm tree. That was the house she married from, and hadn't she brought barrels of china and trunks of linen with her? Some china anyway, and a tablecloth with that Swiss lace as fine and regular as any spider's work. She wasn't raised to hang off the end of a shovel, and she never had in Arlie's lifetime. She had that satisfaction even if he was making her toil now.

Oh, Lord, he was walking. He took steps right down the slope. She dug faster. Wouldn't it be just like him to come pick up the box from right under her feet and glide away with it? She might not could whack him with the shovel, but she resolved that she would hammer on that box if he tried to take it. It was metal and it would take a blow even if Arlie wasn't nothing more than light.

The gate opened and shut. Lord preserve her, he threw a shadow. It was all around her feet broken up in the dirt and it made a pool in the hole she was digging. If he . . .

"MRS. ARGENSTILL."

It was loud as a tree falling on her, but she jumped out from under it and got ready to swing the shovel like an ax if need be.

The other jumped too, and sure enough he had the box. It was swinging from a strap around his neck. Somehow it didn't look big enough, and it was leather. She studied it close . . . it was nothing but a dang camera.

"Excuse me, ma'am . . . I never . . ."

She didn't know what to do with the shovel, she was so ashamed and embarrassed. She let it fall out of her hands. This was no angel addressing her, it was nothing but a person. Well, he'd caught her in the act. For an awful moment she wished she hadn't dropped her shovel, because without it she was at this stranger's mercy . . . but if he meant to rob her, it was just as well he'd come when he did, before she found anything.

"*. . . wanted to look around the place if you wouldn't mind. The Oben-walds said . . .*"

The Obenwalds. Maybe they'd seen Arlie with it? The man—he was hardly a man, just a tall boy—stopped talking and smiled at her. Teeth shining like a bunch of spring onions, blooms in his cheeks like roses. She sucked in her cheeks and remembered that her own teeth were up at the house on the dresser. They were irritating to wear when she worked. They had fit perfect when she got them but her mouth must have shrunk, they were too big now, they felt like two whole octaves of piano keys. Without them, however, she whistled when she talked and her lips just naturally tucked back into her mouth.

"I'm sorry, Mrs. Argenstill. I seem to have come at a bad time."

Not only were her teeth in the jar on the dresser but she was wet as a beaver with her own sweat, and the ribbons of her hat were loose, and the dust clung to the sweat . . . yes indeed he came at a bad time, but she didn't say a word.

"Harry told me that you might be thinking of selling, and, well, I didn't get you when I called. . . . I just walked over the bridge."

He looked mighty young to be a buyer, but he said he came from the Obenwalds, and they had money enough. Hadn't been there a year before they had new trucks and tractors, a brand-new kitchen in the house, sheep that cost more than bulls. And that was after they paid for the farm in ready money. She wished she hadn't rared back at this nice-appearing young man with her shovel, but on second thought it might be an advantage if he thought he was dealing with a helpless mute. She wondered if she ought to keep playing dumb and had half a mind to, but she could feel her lips and tongue stiffening and before she knew it she ventured to say, "$40,000." It came out clear enough even if she did whistle like a tea kettle.

Well, he busted right out with his life story. He was living in Charlottesville, he really didn't know how much he could afford, he had a wife and daughter to look out for, he was still in school, was she going to sell soon? She set her hat straight and tied the ribbons. She arranged her next speech down at the root of her tongue and when he stopped talking she let it come forward a word at a time. "You look around. I'll be up at the house." It sounded fine, except for house, *which sailed out like the first note of the white-throated sparrow. Lulu decided to leave the shovel in the garden, even though it meant a special trip back, but the young man stooped down and picked it up. He did have good manners, except for his shouting. She watched him strut off toward the creek with the shovel on his shoulder like a soldier on parade, and she thought that if he was too innocent to guess what she'd been doing in the potato patch, he might be the very one to sell to.*

She made herself as respectable as she could. She peeled off her dress and sponged herself from top to bottom, but she was still fearful warm. Her heart was running like a chick's, and her mirror told her she had splotches in her cheeks. She was even a little bit dizzy, or maybe her eyes didn't adjust right off to the dimness in the house, but her rose and white image flickered in the wavy green depths of the glass, and every time she raked the comb through her hair the strands of it streamed up and whirled electrically. What she really wanted to do was lie down for a rest until this heat had passed from her, but she had to get dressed. So she clamped her hair down with two big tortoiseshell barrettes, one on either side of her head, and she put on her good lilac dress right over the damp slip, and the black shoes that were still in the box with the tissue. When she'd worried her teeth into place she felt some better, even though the barrettes stuck out like the ears on a bear cub. Well, they'd just have to. She intended to sit down in the rocker right here in the cool bedroom, not on the porch, and compose herself before that young man returned. She folded her hands in her lap and rested her head back and closed her eyes and rocked, rocked, rocked. It felt as if there was a breeze in the room; it was cooler and cooler, as cool and restful as a bank, and there was Mr. Turner, the bank president, fanning her with a big feathery peacock fan. She was gliding past the teller's windows, gliding like a cloud toward the coolest place of all, the vault. Mr. Turner scooted ahead of her and opened the big shining door. Out of the mouths of the tellers arose a hymn, a sweet hosanna . . .

"MRS. ARGENSTILL."

She flew out of her chair, ready for glory, but here was no vault, no fan, no heavenly music. She was all alone in her room, and she heard a rapping. If that young man screeched her name one more time, she was going to take that shovel back and drive him right into the ground with it like a fence post. She straightened her dress, patted her barrettes, clapped her teeth to set them securely. All right, she was coming, and she meant to talk business.

The first thing he said was how beautiful it was.

Devious now, she agreed. She lifted up her arm to take in the view from the porch. "It seems like it changes every single day of the year, like every day it's just a little different from what it was before. It's a sight to behold."

"How often does the creek get up too high to ford?"

"It depends. We got water inside the house. First house in the valley to have it. It's not a drop of iron in the water nor any of the bad smell. It's limestone water, pure as pure. You couldn't set a price on it."

"Where is the spring?"

"Up above. It never has run dry. . . ." She was about to tell him how long she'd lived there, but she held back in time. *"An eternal flow,"* she said, and, struck by the poetic sound of the words, she repeated them twice more. *"Yes, I'll miss that water, indeed I shall miss it, I'll miss it sorely."* Lulu could hardly believe that this language ran out of her just as fluid as a preacher's. She felt as though she could sell the Brooklyn Bridge.

"Would it be all right if I walked up to look around? I'd like to see how far up the mountain the property goes."

"It's like a bower there, flowers and honeybees buzzing. Grapes and berries! Ladies' slippers and wild flags, little violet ones with yellow flames in them! The deer come down to drink—coons, turkey, bear! And just as gentle as ever they were in Eden!" She had a moment's regret she'd mentioned bear, because it wasn't strictly true. *"It does cast my spirit down to part from all this."*

"Well then, I'll have a look up above."

He stood the shovel up against the wall and started right off. Lulu was disappointed to have her eloquence ignored. She too stepped off the porch, and she watched her customer make his way upward.

"Wait!"

He was going in the wrong direction, toward the graveyard instead of the spring. That was the one place she didn't want him to go. Arlie knew her all right; he knew she'd look for the money anywhere before she went up there to look for it, but she was sure that's where it was, and she was just working up her nerve by looking elsewhere. It wouldn't do for this boy to go up there.

She ran after him, holding her dress off her knees so that she could move faster. He finally turned round. *"Yonder's the spring."*

"Oh."

Thank goodness he was dumb.

"That up there is the Argenstill burying place."

"Up there?"

"Inside the fence there. It's nothing to see up there."

"I'm just going to walk past it. That looks like the easiest way up."

"It's nothing but weeds up there."

She knew she had to act fast.

"My, my, the sun's got to work, hasn't it? It's a warm morning to walk up the mountain."

"I don't mind the heat on a day like this."

"This is the kind of heat that brings the snakes out and sets 'em crawling." *Right away she wished she hadn't said that; she didn't want him to think this was a viper's den.*

"I'll keep an eye out for them."

She didn't have any choice. She looked at the sod; at least it was clean, and the worst it could do was stain her dress. She closed her eyes and let herself sway, hoping this boy was quick enough to catch her before she toppled. "Fainting . . ." she said, to give him a clue.

There. He'd got her, and she just relaxed. He could figure out that he ought to carry her to the house. He cussed and she almost laughed out. It was like being a bride to get carried down the slope, riding in his arms with her ear right against his heart. How it drummed! Right through his flesh and bone it was saying something like money money money.

When Anna finished reading she hesitated for just a moment before going into the front room. "I like it better than anything you've ever written," she said to Steadman.

He put down his book. "I was only pretending to read. I was listening."

"To me reading? How did I sound?"

"I heard a few chuckles."

"It is funny, some of it. I laughed at the line about his busting out with his life story, and about driving him into the ground like a fence post. It's more—good-natured than some things you've written. But—"

"Now the interesting part."

"No, no. I just wondered if it really happened. I know Lulu found the money and all, and she fainted the first time you came over here to talk to her, but is this really the way it was?"

"It's never *really* like what happened."

"You know what I mean."

"I'm not sure I do."

"I just wondered if you believed Lulu thought those things, in those words."

"It's not that literal. Lulu is more—a field of force, something like that. I just guessed at what she might have thought, but she did have an outburst of flowery language. You look doubtful."

"You knew her better than I did, but—I don't know, Steadman, it seems kind of mean somehow."

"I thought you just said it was good-natured."

"Well, it is, but you laugh at Lulu."

"Is that mean or good-natured?"

"I probably wouldn't think about it if Lulu wasn't somebody I'd met. But I got the impression you really didn't like her that much."

"What gave you that impression?"

"All that stuff about her teeth, and how she's greedy, and she doesn't really know what she thinks about anything."

"Isn't all that true about Lulu?"

"I guess so, but even though the whole situation is funny, she's so pathetic."

"Wasn't Lulu?"

"Yes, but . . . I don't know what I mean."

"You began by saying you liked it."

"I do, Steadman, but it makes me uncomfortable—I guess it's because of the ghost. Because she can't make up her mind about the ghost."

"She does at the end. She believes in it. She's just successful at deceiving herself."

"Do you think she really did?"

"Really believed in it? You've heard what Blanche says about her."

"I know, but—what do you think, Steadman? You don't think there's a ghost."

"What does that have to do with the story?"

"It matters, because if the ghost was real Lulu wouldn't seem so foolish."

"Do you think it's real, Anna?"

She didn't answer.

Steadman reached out his hand. "Can I have the story, please?"

Anna, still standing, gave it to him.

"You think you're Lulu, don't you?" he said.

"It occurred to me when he gets peeved about her disturbing the woodpile."

"It's not the woodpile, it's the superstition that bothers you. I hoped you were over that by now."

"I don't look for ghosts."

"Neither does Lulu. She just dreads them."

"I don't dread them either."

"But you believe in them."

"Not in ghosts, Steadman—but I believe in something."

"In what?"

Anna didn't know what she could say.

Steadman said, "That's the problem, isn't it? It might as well be a goddamn ghost if you're the only one who knows about it, if it's too private and mystical to talk about."

"I was only trying to tell you what I thought about the story."

"And if the story makes fun of Lulu, it makes fun of you, right?"

"I didn't say it made fun of her."

"You said it was mean. It comes to about the same thing."

"It is about me, isn't it?"

"Try to be a little more modest, Anna. It may be possible for me to imagine something without your image dictating to me."

Fifteen

What the baler said:
Ka-boom
Ka-boom
Ka-boom
or something like that. Harry Obenwald tried occasionally to interpret the noise and got cartoon, Khartoum, barroom, blue moon . . . but he did not require intelligible conversation from his baler. Lodged sideways in the seat of his green Oliver diesel tractor, watching the intake of the windrow, a continuous airy line of clover, concentric and unbroken, looped and whorled like his meadow's green thumbprint, he thought that deeds sufficed. The clover marched right up the ramp and into the enclosure, where it was hammered into a rectangle and sliced into a dozen uniform sections, where the whirring knotter bound it in loops of twine, where the loose grass was translated into blocks of feed, ka-boom.

Harry loved the baler. It was a new, red Massey Ferguson, squat, complex, and functional. It reminded Harry of some kind of armored animal. It would never appeal to aesthetes. Some bearded guy who called himself a sculptor had once stopped and offered to buy the old combine and buggy rake, but Harry was not expecting bids on the baler. He did not require beauty from his machinery any more than he required conversation. In the division of energy, as he saw it, nature was responsible for beauty; men and machines were supposed to get the work done.

The bales still had to be got up, but on this late-July day there was no chance of rain. It was astonishing, really, that the weather had conspired with him for the three days he'd needed to cut, ted, condition, rake, and bale the hay. For once the weather had held clear and dry, for once the machinery had all worked, for once he'd gambled and cut a whole field, for once the gamble had paid off. He'd trusted the forecast—he could trust it now that he owned a shortwave radio. He kept it tuned to the weather band, which gave meteorological reports for aviators, and not only had he learned to understand the jargon, he'd come to regard the North American continent from the point of view of a satellite, gazing down upon it through its enveloping mists and swirls. Weather! The poor planet was swaddled in it like a fiery jewel in plush excelsior. He liked this sort of day when the texture of space was the same at the surface of the earth as it was, he supposed, beyond Jupiter. He was going to get the bales in without mishap.

As soon as the baler stopped, the setters Wig and Thump were out of the house. Diana and Steadman followed. Steadman leaped the bales as if they were hurdles, landed on one, sang.

> *Oh Lordy, pick a bale of cotton*
> *Oh Lordy, pick a bale of hay*
> *Oh Lordy . . .*

"You're not Odetta."

"No?" Steadman pulled a bandanna out of his pocket and knotted it into a skullcap. "How's that? Oh Lordy, pick a whole lotta bales."

"About four hundred, Aunt Jemima," said Harry.

Steadman pulled on his gloves and helped him hitch the wagon to the tractor. Diana climbed up into the seat, and they began: the hot regular toil, the feeling of substance almost miraculously confined by the thin twine, the bite of the twine across the palm, the thrust of thigh that helped sail the bales onto the wagon, the plummeting flights all around them of the barn swallows, the loping dogs, the daggers of sweat, the lofty smell of the barn. Steadman continued to be a horse's ass. He pretended to collapse under the weight of the bales, climbed the ladder in the barn to leap into the stack, hid in it, came up covered with particles, ran out and jumped into the creek, splashed Wig, put ice from the water jug down Diana's shirt, crawled around and bellowed like a bull, bleated like a sheep, squawked like a gander. Yet when Harry was on the wagon stacking, the bales came up close and tight, Steadman never got ahead of him, he made it easy for him, he laid them up so that Harry could get his hands right away on the twines, tossing them so that the bales almost stayed in motion from the ground to their place in the stack.

By the third wagonload he did slow down. The tonnage began to tell. The tractor kept the pace up, for it had to move at a certain speed or stall, and Steadman turned his energies to the hay. This was the silent, rhythmic exertion that Harry preferred. He didn't think of much except the numbers—272, the tally for this cutting, and 1948, the total of bales in the barn. 272-1949 . . . bale 2000! This was the labor that made a show. All the seeding, liming, fertilizing, mowing, tedding, conditioning, and raking were now expressed in those real numbers that ticked each time he grabbed a bale, expressed in the stack built like a Titan's staircase.

"Done," he said at last, not with entire happiness, for once the work had found its momentum he felt it could go on forever, and he almost wished that it had. At the same time he felt a battered tranquillity, peace solid as an ingot; his body, resting, was knit integrally from the work, and legs, arms, torso, even head, were joined together like . . . well, like a baler. *Man, with his many muscles, the significant leverage of his upright stance, was made to move hay.* Steadman might have said something like that, but Harry wouldn't dream of it. But even Steadman was quiet now, seated on the empty wagon, soaking not with creek water—the sun had dried that—but with his own sweat, and he was filmed with chaff. Diana sat beside him, also grinning and glowing, her fresh color visible even in the dim light of the barn. The sun shot in sheets through the cracks in the siding high above the stack, and whole constellations of motes moved through the light. Harry, looking up, let himself lean against one of the hewn timbers. The particles floated against the golden pine, across the human architecture of mortise and tenon. He felt grateful —for this moment, these bales, this barn, his body and the two others near his.

"Water," Steadman said.

"Water?" Diana questioned, the word sounding as though her tongue had never felt it.

"Who'll race me to the Lime Pool?"

"I'm a little too"—with her hands she made a globe before her belly—"for racing."

"Harry?"

"Let's just stroll."

They did. Across the road, down the bank, along the path through sycamore and cedar, beside the creek running black over the slate, into the deeper woods where hemlocks and pines crowded the way. Wig and Thump scooted ahead of them. The path opened on a shoal of smooth rocks, and the deeper water was coppery green. They stripped and entered it, and when Steadman splashed down to the end of the pool with the dogs, Harry let himself sink into the cold depths, eyes open so that above him he observed the suspended form of his wife, the pale floating shape, the dark patch shaking where the naked legs forked. She swam until she was looking down at him, big and vivid and trembling and spectral, against the lighted filigree of overhanging limbs and the sky beyond.

Harry surfaced, breathed.

"You looked drowned down there all splayed out on the rocks," Diana said.

Harry paddled around her making a perfect gurgling imitation of an outboard diesel motor.

Sixteen

Anna studied the calendar on the kitchen wall. It was one of those almanac calendars that made weather predictions, kept track of the planets, gave the phases of the moon, the hours of moonset and moonrise and the times of the tides, recommended methods of canning and grafting. Printed in red and black, each square was crammed with stuff—a moon, a fish, a crab, a part of a disemboweled man, an umbrella, or a cloud. In the corner of the page there was an advertisement for a product called *Rough on Rats,* and a picture of a rat turned belly up; at the bottom of the page there was an advertisement for a laxative with bile salts and a picture of a purged woman sitting in her bed with musical notes coming from her head. Anna studied this writ.

August 6. Her period was already two weeks late.

She had not told Steadman. Neither of them had told the other much of anything since their difference about his story. Steadman was still closing himself in the junk room every morning to write, but he hadn't even referred to his work, let alone asked her to look at it. He treated her with painful courtesy, painful because it didn't come anywhere near hiding his disappointment in her. Of course he didn't want to hide it. She was supposed to know how she'd failed him. Poor Steadman, he could not bare his soul to her, for *her* soul did not travel in the same exalted orbit. Nobly, he did not complain of her deficiency.

Well, she could be just as petty as he was. She had her secret too. At first she didn't think of it as much of a secret. After all, she had an IUD, and she knew that she was just the sort who magnified every symptom. She thought that her period was bound to begin any day. She'd just make a fool of herself if she told Steadman it was late. And she wasn't going to weasel out of their sullen little feud that way— she knew exactly what effect it would have on Steadman if she announced that the stork was coming. He'd started the feud, and he could end it too.

One day after he'd been fishing he brought her back a plant, a single lovely green-veined flower with heart-shaped leaves on the stem. They had to look in the book to find its name: Grass of Parnassus. That was just the sort of discovery that delighted and uplifted Steadman and made him feel responsible for the glory of creation. With a certain grim foreboding she watched him take out his rapture on Maggie. Anna knew what to expect. She prolonged Maggie's bedtime ritual, but sure enough he was waiting for her outside Maggie's door with a hard-on. He thought fucking was the sovereign remedy. Well, he'd been fucking her all along, and she didn't have much choice this time but to spread for him. He shoved his dick in and out of her and she felt like a trussed dead bird with stuffing being crammed into its cavity.

And so she knew. The abomination she felt was not incidental. This was no hysterical pregnancy, it was the real thing, and she'd just been stringing herself along by refusing to admit it. Her body hadn't been fooled. Lying inches from Steadman, who naturally subsided at once into his gratified oblivion, she understood exactly why she'd nursed her resentment. She'd done her bit to prolong their feud because she didn't want to have to contend with his pride and joy. If she'd told him she'd missed her period he would not only have forgiven her, he would have worshiped her, his vessel. That night it all seemed very clear and dire, and the phrase that kept occurring to her was the Biblical phrase: *I am with child.* On that high bed, watching the stars hover like insects beyond the window and listening to the mountain's predatory wails, she felt as if she were being carted to some hideous sacrifice.

The next morning she was nauseous for the first time and her breasts were tight and sore, but at least, in daylight, it was just a matter of biology. That she could deal with. She was not afraid. It was not her fate bearing down on her but something that seemed much simpler, her life. *I am with child*—the knowledge, because it was hers alone, even brought with it a sense of power and freedom.

Then the whimwhams began. That's what Steadman, who'd never had them, had named her night terror and panic. The whimwhams —he must have thought her accounts were amusing. But now she didn't tell him about these and never woke him. Beside him on the bed she moaned and writhed and blubbered, but he snoozed on. Sometimes her blood felt not liquid but solid, like hot thin needles her pounding heart was stitching through her arteries. She felt utterly cut off from all mercy. By morning she was worn out and sick to her stomach and disgusted with herself. She went into the bathroom and puked and looked at herself in the mirror. "You fucking baby," she said.

August 6. She studied the calendar. She knew she was not mistaken about the signs. She was going to have to do something soon.

That afternoon—hot, fat summer air—she took Maggie berry-picking. Steadman had gone with Duty Armstrong in Duty's big truck to buy the rafters and boards for the roof of the studio. "I guess I'd better get the fucking roof on while we still have weather to work in." She understood this to mean that he regarded the studio—his idea in the first place, not hers, his big gesture—as getting in the way of his writing and blamed her for it. *Prick,* she thought.

She made Maggie put on overalls so she wouldn't get too scratched up in the briers, and she put on her own overalls and tied a bandanna over her hair. They started picking along the edges of the brushy fields down by the creek, but they hadn't been there long when they heard a clanging and banging—two canoes scraping the rocks. There was a couple in each, college kids by the look of them. "Hey, where's the water?" one of the boys called.

"You're in it," she said.

"We're running out. Is it deeper than this downstream?"

"There're pools. It's August, you know."

"Hey, look, they're picking blackberries," one of the girls said.

"We left one of the cars down at Silesia. Do you think we can make it that far?"

"It's about like this all the way," Anna said. "The only deep water is in the pools."

"Shit, this is a drag."

"Let's just pick some berries and go back and get the car."

"We can get there."

"It's not your fucking canoe, man. These rocks are grinding the bottom out."

"Ask her if we can pick some berries."

"You ask her."

"She might come after me with that stick she's got."

A giggle. These jerks thought they were whispering.

"She reminds me of something out of *Deliverance.*"

"Well, ask her. I want some blackberries."

"Let's decide what we're doing, okay?"

"Hey, is this your land?"

"Yes," Anna said.

"Do you mind if we pick some berries? Just a few to eat? We wouldn't carry any off or anything."

"Go ahead," Anna said, and she got out of there. She took Maggie's hand and headed for the mountain, leaving the fields to these canoeists, their beers and their radio. There were plenty of berries on the slope of the mountain at the upper edge of the pastures, and the cows were out of the way, down at their shady shitty wallow along the creek. The only things moving were the deerflies and Anna got stung twice on the same shoulder, right through her shirt, stings that felt like being vaccinated with a nail. She kept expecting to put her hand on a copperhead; she kept picking.

She heard something. She waited, heard it again. She asked Maggie, "Do you hear anything?"

"Some grunts," Maggie said. Her hands were purple, her shirt was purple, her tongue was purple.

They were picking along the edge of a dense thicket and Anna saw nothing in it. She looked, waited. More grunts. She was about to leave when a black shape heaved right up in the middle of the thicket —a cow, just one of Amos's cows. She threw a rock at it and was surprised when she hit it. It went barging and groaning through the briers. When it got down to the field it looked back up at them and retched out a moo. Anna tried to laugh. "Why do you think that cow was in the briers?"

"I guess it was hiding."

Something about this cow looked peculiar to Anna. It stood there at the edge of the field, all four legs angled and braced stiff under its body. Its black flanks were shaggy, mucky—it must have been on its side down at the creek. Why was it in the berry patch? It kept mooing and mooing. It sounded as if something was wrong with it, but cows always sounded catastrophic to her.

"What do you think, Maggie? Had enough?"

And as they left Anna gave the cow plenty of room but it jogged toward them, stopped, jogged again. "It's coming after us," Maggie said. Anna turned and raised her stick. The animal was close: wet flecked nostrils, stems and leaves stuck to the bristly hair over the brow, a flank running with green muck, flies fizzing along the spine. "Go on, beat it, leave us alone." She whacked it hard and when it turned, the tail still swishing at the flies, she saw in the midst of the filth of its rump, in the rim of folded swollen pink, the dainty hooves, the curled shiny lip, the purple tongue of a calf.

"It's trying to have a baby," Maggie said.

Anna, running, dragged Maggie back to the house. She called the Obenwalds first. No answer. Then she called Amos's number and got Mrs. Argenstill. "I believe Buck is up your way somewhere," she said. "He might check directly. He said he might before he come home. He was to the dentist this evening. His teeth have been bothering him right much."

"Should I call the vet?"

"Lord, no, honey, we don't use the vet, not for birthing. They generally do for themselves."

"But this is an emergency."

Mrs. Argenstill laughed. "Honey, I'll tell Buck just as soon as he gets back."

Anna called the Obenwalds again. This time Harry answered.

"Where were you?"

"Outside," he said.

"There's a cow trying to have a calf here."

"Is anything wrong?"

194

"The calf's sticking out."
"Is it hung?"
"What?"
"Hung."
"I don't know."
"How much of it can you see?"
"Harry, will you come over here?"
"I just saw Amos drive by. I don't know whether he stopped at the ford."
"Harry, please come over here."
"I'll be there soon."
She went to the window and she did see Amos crossing the field. "You stay here," she told Maggie and she ran across the fields—it took minutes and she was panting—to meet him. "It's a hot un, all right," he said. "Too hot to be running."
"Did you see the cow?"
"That little Angus heifer? I did. She's hung tight, ain't she. It's her first calf, mind, and I believe it's a whopper. That Charolais bull I got throws some big calfs, that he does. And that little heifer's done got shy, which reminds me: is it a rope somewhere handy? I can't go chasing her all over the meadow."
"There's a rope up at the house."
"I thought maybe I ought to see could I lead her into one of the barns and quiet her some, you know. They turn into rogues running loose this way."
"I'll go get a rope."
"I'd appreciate it. You go a whole lot better than I do. I'll just set down under that walnut tree and keep a eye on her till you come back."
So Anna ran back to the house, meeting Maggie on her way.
"I told you to wait."
"I want to see the baby."
"You go back inside."
"No."
And Maggie took off running as hard as she could away from Anna. Anna let her go. She got the rope out of the garden shed. Under the tree Maggie was laughing at Amos, who was showing her

his new cap, bright red with a yellow emblem, an ear of corn, and the words *Funk's Hybrid.*

"This one's been in the berries, ain't she? I was just telling her I got my clappers checked to get ready to eat some corn." He took the cigar out of his mouth to show her his straight white teeth. "They ain't mine but I call 'em mine since I paid for 'em."

"Here's the rope."

"Thank you, ma'am. I never would of been so quick. I'd still be getting there but by golly you flew."

He tied a knot in the rope, slipped the end through, made a lasso —which he swung once and tossed over Maggie. The loop fell around her without touching her. "I ain't lost my touch altogether," he said. "Now let's see if we can't catch us a cow."

"Do you want me to come?"

"Fine," Amos said, "that'd be just fine."

And so she followed Amos and helped him back the cow against the fence. "Easy now, don't move sudden, just let her touch agin the wire and learn where she's at. Stand off that way—we don't want her to take a notion to fly up the mountain." He kept talking to the cow, trying to charm her, and just as she turned and started to move along the fence the noose flicked out and over her head. Amos didn't even have to pull to tighten it; her plunge cinched it tight. "Whoa, now, whoa, whoa there, Nellie, just where do you think you're going to?" And the cow did stop, didn't struggle, just trembled. She let herself be led across the field to the big barn. Every few steps she balked and made that congested grunt, and Amos just twitched the rope and led her on.

"Is it any more where you come from?" he said to Harry who met them in the field. "We might need some weight on the end of this rope directly. She's done got down tight on this calf."

Harry went round behind the cow and looked. "It's in the right position."

"She ain't but a little heifer though. I got an idea this calf when we drag it out'll be dang near as big as she is. Toots told me, I bet she told me a hundred times, I never should of put that Charolais bull in with the heifers."

At the barn Amos said, "Now then, let's ease her in if she's agreeable. Maybe when we get her fixed we'll turn over a rock and see can't we find some of that money Arlie hid. He was a close one, all right." He slipped his hand along the rope until he held it just below the knot. Harry opened the door to one of the stalls. The heifer shook her head and lifted Amos up. There was a foot of air between his boots and the ground. "Hup now, Nellie, this ain't a dang rodeo." Then the heifer wouldn't budge. Maggie and Anna were behind her now, and Maggie was taking it all in. "I believe we're going to have to give her a push," Amos said. "We could just shove her down right here, I reckon, but they do lie quieter inside. You don't see a stout board in there, do you?"

Harry found a board.

"Now, ma'am, if you wouldn't mind getting at the head of her, you might can guide her into that stall."

Anna took the rope and Amos and Harry crossed the board across the cow's haunches.

"There. We moved her some." The cow's forehooves were on the threshold beam. "Give another lift."

And when they did the cow plunged forward into the dim stall. Anna dropped the rope and pressed herself against the wall of the partition. The dim confined stall, the black barging animal. The heifer bumped hard against the trough, spun, faced the entrance in that braced, angled stance. "Now ain't she a rogue? I do hate to hurry a heifer, but it looked to me like she was bearing down right hard on that calf. I don't like to see a calf's tongue swole up that way, indeed I don't. You reckon we can throw her?"

"If we can get her away from that wall," Harry said.

They got behind her and shoved. Anna was holding the rope again and the cow pivoted away from the wall and when she was in the middle of the stall they reached under her and tripped her somehow and fell on top of her when she hit with a dull massive thud. "Do you reckon you can hold her head?" Amos asked her. "I don't believe she'll try to rise, but a body before her might make her feel better looked after."

Anna knelt down and put her hand on the black ledge of the brow. It was shaking. Amos did something with the rope, the head lifted, came down with its full weight in Anna's lap. The flanks were heaving now, and the huge hot head jerked against her belly. The mouth was dripping.

"Daddy's coming with Duty," Maggie said. She had climbed up to watch over the partition.

"How fast is he coming? Between us and this heifer we're about to choke this calf. We ain't budged it a hair."

Harry went to the door and called.

"I thought I saw somebody down here," Steadman said.

"She's hung all right," Duty said.

"She's closed down tight as a bank," Amos said. "I don't know but that calf's already choked. We can't do nothing but pull."

They did pull. The four of them strained on the rope and hauled the heifer out of Anna's lap before the rope slipped and they tumbled back upon one another. There was a furrow in the dirt of the stall where the heifer's head had dragged. Anna crawled forward and cradled the head again. "What's the matter? Why can't you get it out?"

"It's slick, and it ain't a good place to fasten to yet. See can you fix that rope on there some way, Duty."

Duty crouched down, his cheek all pouched out with tobacco. "It ain't hardly room to reach your hand in there, is it? It's drove in there like a wedge. This un may have to come out in pieces."

"Is it alive?" Anna said. "Is it still alive?"

"It ain't had time to die yet," Amos said. "It ain't never been born."

When they pulled again she heard it and felt it, the drawn-out slurping puckered sound, the force and rigid weight across her lap. The knob of one eye dug into her thigh; the other was on her in jellied anguish.

"Oh, she'll come now."

"We ain't going to hang on the hips, are we?"

"She'll slip. Let me see if I can't work her loose here. There now, you all pull away. There she comes, by golly. It's a bull calf and ain't it a dandy, though?"

"Is it alive? Is it all right?"

It was drenched, bloody, black. Amos stuck his hand in its mouth, patted it around the shoulders. "It's going all right. How about that? The little feller's going."

Most of the placenta had come with it, drooling and glutinous. The heifer now struggled to her feet and turned, bloody integument hanging out of her, and began lapping the wet huddled thing. "By golly, she's owning it too, and I wouldn't have blamed her one bit if she'd bolted right out of here."

The men were all grinning. "I feel like the city feller at the birthing," Amos said. "You heard that one, ain't you? City feller watched the calf hauled out and then he says, Lord have mercy, how fast was that calf going when it run into this poor cow?"

Anna was on her feet. Steadman reached out a hand to stop her but she pushed by him. She got out the door of the stall and around the corner of the barn before her nausea doubled her over.

Corn, beans, squash, cucumbers, tomatoes, beets, eggplant—everything in the garden was coming at once. Steadman had what he called a conflict with a family of coons who were shredding the corn. He bought several traps, baited them with honey, set them around the edges of the garden, and caught two small coons. He shot them with a .22, the varmint gun, and cut off their ringed tails. The big coon got into a trap one night and chewed its leg off to escape.

Anna put up food for the winter, frozen packets of beans and peppers and beets, cans of tomatoes and pickles. She helped Steadman put the roof on the studio, leaving two big openings for skylights. She told him she thought she should visit her family. It had been months since she saw her mother, father, Papi. Maggie said she wanted to go too.

And Steadman said, "Maybe we all need a vacation. Why don't you go to Washington for a few days if you want, and then we'll all drive down to the Outer Banks after Labor Day. After all, it'll be our anniversary."

They'd spent their honeymoon on the Outer Banks.

"We don't have to do that."

"I'd like to do that. It's been a long pull. I'd like to look at the ocean. I want to catch a big fish."

She gave in. Steadman drove her to Staunton, where she and Maggie caught a bus to Washington. The next day, Thursday, she left Maggie with a friend who had two little boys while she went to the clinic, her urine specimen in a pocketbook. A pocketbook—she

never carried one and thought everyone who saw her must know
what was in it. She was pregnant. The woman, not dressed like a
nurse, told her she really should have had her IUD checked. And
when she told the woman she was married, she had to explain why
she wanted the abortion. "My husband's unemployed," she said. She
was told she couldn't have an appointment until the middle of the
next week, Wednesday the fifth—her anniversary. "I can't wait that
long. I'm from out of town."

"That's the best we can do."

"But I can't wait that long."

"We're already overbooked. Everyone's going back to school,
you know, and we've just been swamped."

"Can't I have it tomorrow?"

"I'd say yes if I could. I'm terribly sorry."

That night she called Steadman and told him she wouldn't be able
to leave when they'd planned. "It's just family stuff," she said. "I
walked right into the middle of it."

"Kay?"

"Yeah. And I just can't walk away from it. I wish I could."

"Call me, okay, as soon as you think you can go."

"I will."

He didn't ask her to explain. "Do you want me to come up
there?"

"No. You shouldn't have to bother with this."

She got the money from her father. He owned a few restaurants,
just greasy spoons; all he ever seemed to do was clean out the cash
registers. He played horses and cards, drove big cars, wore flashy
clothes, always had cash in his wallet. "So Baby's broke, huh? Steadman not looking after you right?"

"I want to get something for him."

"Right, right—your anniversary. So how much?"

"Two hundred dollars."

He whistled. "You think a lot of this guy, huh? So what are you
giving him?"

"An electric typewriter."

He laughed as he counted out the bills. "Yeah, the famous
writer."

"Thank you, Papa."

But she didn't call Steadman back, couldn't, and finally on Monday night he called her. "I can't leave yet," she said.

"The fifth is Wednesday," he said.

"I just can't leave."

"No sentiment," he said. "What about Friday? Suppose I plan to come up on Friday? I miss you, Anna."

"Friday's okay."

On Wednesday she dumped Maggie at the same friend's, a woman she knew from drawing classes. At the clinic she seemed to be assigned to a tiny woman with a pinched face who jabbered while Anna waited. She had a blood test, waited. The woman talked about birth control and tried to be chummy. Anna was told again she ought to have her IUD checked regularly. The woman told her how fit she looked and tried to get her to talk. Anna said something about the garden, the mountains. "It sounds like a good healthy life," the woman said. Finally Anna was on her back, her feet in the stirrups, and the doctor, a man, got busy on her. The woman was still beside her. She'd already explained everything and she explained it all again as it happened. The doctor gave her a shot of novocaine and took out the IUD, a loop. This surprised the woman, who was sure that Anna must have passed it. "Gee, you're unlucky," she said. The doctor put the tubes in her to dilate her cervix and he stuck the hose in her. She had some cramps. The hose went into the wall. There was a mechanical noise but no mess. When the doctor left she sat up and saw nothing but a little blood on the white paper. No mess. "You better not try to stand up yet," the woman said. Anna felt dizzy and wavering and lay back again. Her whole belly felt like cunt, but there was no mess.

In the lounge the woman brought her a cup of ginger ale and a cracker. "You should try to eat something." She'd been told to bring something to eat but hadn't. Next to her a black woman was eating grapes and Brie; she offered her some. Anna shook her head and realized she hadn't spoken for a long time. Maybe that's why the woman seemed worried. She made herself talk. "It's not so bad, is it? Nobody even sees it.".

"Lie back down, dear, and just rest a bit longer."

They kept her there for a long time, and when she left at last she walked several blocks and found herself on Wisconsin Avenue in

Georgetown. She went into a drugstore and bought a box of Modess but she couldn't ask the druggist—fat, bald-headed—for the goo she was supposed to use with the diaphragm they'd given her. On the sidewalk people kept bumping into her, all kids or tourists. She got out of the crowd in the recessed entrance of a clothing store, where there were bins of blouses that had been pawed over.

"Hey, we got tops inside that would look terrific on you."

The man was short, dark, hairy. His shiny shirt was open halfway down; there was a jeweled scarab hanging from a silver chain. Tight salmon pants, lump in the groin. Cork platform shoes below huge cuffs.

"This is trash out here, Babe, just junk. You want something with class, something that'll look great on you, come inside."

He was beside her, shorter than she was. "Come on in. Listen, I run this place, I can make you a good price. I get tired of two-bit stuff, you know? Fucking T-shirts. They're for kids, slobs. You could dress, Babe, I could dress you so you'd blow their eyes out. Look at this stuff." His hand ran along a rack of blouses like feathers. "You got the structure, elegant, you know? Hey, what are you doing in that cowboy shirt? I mean, it's okay, but a body like yours, show it off, what the hell. Look at this." He held a piece of fabric, blue and black swirls, the size of an envelope. "Tell you what, you try this on, you like it, it's yours. On the house. I want to look out and see a chick like you go by dressed right. That's what it's about, babe. Come on, you try it on. Listen, you come back here and try it on. I like to see a chick's back, you know what I mean?"

She was in a dingy office, file cabinets, a closet, papers strewn all over a desk. "Go ahead, try it on. Hey, Babe, don't be so shy. Turn around if you want to. I just want to see you in it. I'm giving it to you, I want to look, you know? What gets me off is beautiful chicks, beautiful chicks in beautiful clothes. So I look at you, I think, shit, do something about it, dress this chick right, bring her out. So try it on. You like it, I'll get you some pants too, shoes, the works. I got it all right here."

Anna stood there holding a box of Modess under her arm.

"I get it, I get it. You don't trust me. Look, this is my place, I rent, but my place. I can give you everything in it. I can treat you right. Look at this." He reached in the closet and brought out a metal box.

"Who's got the key to the cash? I got it, that's who." He took the key out of his pocket and opened the box. He lifted out a tray with a pistol in it and started pulling out bills. "You think this is some two-bit operation, huh? You want to count this? Look at this. I'm hauling it in. This is yesterday and today, and look at it—it comes easy, no sweat. So I feel like giving something away, I give it away. You need bread? Take it. Help yourself. What the fuck. There's plenty coming in."

"I can't take any. I don't want any." Anna put the blue and black top down on the desk.

"Come on, hey, try it on. I'm not asking for anything, babe, nothing. I'm giving, you dig?"

Anna tried to open the door of the office. It was locked.

"Let me out of here."

"So what'd you come back here for anyway? Hey, listen, what did you think was going down? I give, you give a little too. No asking, Babe, giving."

"I have to go."

"So now you got an appointment. Babe, you get to me, you know it? I don't like a chick that runs at the mouth. I like a little fucking class. Quality, Babe, quality. You got it. You're a class chick."

"You dumb fucker! You dumb blind fucker! I just got up from an abortion! You want to fuck me? You want to see what's pouring out of my cunt?"

He put his hands up in front of him. "Hey, Babe, don't lay that on me. Hey, come on now." He stuffed the top with swirls into the paper bag with the box of Modess, he unlocked the door, and Anna was on the street again, bumping into people.

When she went home with Maggie in a cab, Kay's crumpled red car was parked on the street in front of the brick duplex. Anna took Maggie inside and sat her down in front of the TV. Her mother switched channels to get "Sesame Street."

"Where's Kay?" Anna asked.

"Upstairs."

Kay was waiting in their bedroom. "So, Baby. You've been in town for a week, I hear."

"How did you find out I was here?"

"I talk to Mama now and then. We're not completely estranged. We still like to yell at each other. What brings you to town?"

"I just came for a visit."

"On a shopping spree. What does the country girl buy when she gets to the city?"

Kay was too fast. Anna couldn't keep her from seeing into the bag. For a strange moment it looked as if Kay was going to cry, but her expression became one of such bitterness that Anna shrank from it.

"You came up here for an abortion."

"No I didn't."

"You liar. You never used a Modess in your life. So that's what all that family shit comes to, a fucking abortion. You asked for it, Baby, you had it coming."

Kay laughed. "You know, I almost didn't come in to see you, but I wouldn't have missed this for anything. Welcome to the shitstorm, Baby. Come look me up when you get used to it. You may be human after all."

Kay left the house.

Seventeen

Harry was making hay on shares for Blanche Hammer, who ran a few sheep and cows. On the Thursday before Labor Day he listened to his radio, looked at the sky, and decided to mow all ten acres. The hay wasn't much—it hadn't been cut all summer, it had gone to seed, the stems would be about as nutritive as cardboard—but Blanche was counting on it to feed her stock through the winter. And it was thick; Harry made a pass through the fields on Friday with the tedder to turn it over so that it would dry. On Saturday stratocumulus clouds began skimming over Little Furnace and Harry, listening to his shortwave, learned that scattered showers were likely in the mountains. This meant to Harry that it would rain on Blanche's hay. He called Steadman, who'd already said he would help get the hay up, and asked how soon he could start. Any time, Steadman said. "As soon as the dew burns off I'm going to start baling," Harry said. "There'll be twelve or fifteen hundred bales anyway. I'm going to call Zep too, and maybe you two could start getting the bales up right behind me."

By noon they had three hundred bales in Blanche's barn. There were a thousand more bales in the field. Harry looked at the sky and said, "Showers, my ass. In about an hour the bottom's going to fall out." The clouds were piling up now and the breeze had moved round to the south.

"We ought to have a big periscope," Steadman said, "so we could see what's behind Little Furnace."

"I'll tell you what's behind there—a pisser of a storm that's just cruising along looking for this field to unload in."

He asked Zep if he could get help from Xanaduc.

They all came, including Peggy. "Hey," she said to Steadman, "how you been?" *Ha ya bin,* that southern accent.

"Getting by," he said. "Zep told me you were on your way up north. School starts early."

She smiled, that damn promiscuous smile. He was flattered enough to let a competition develop between him and Zep. There was a lot of monkey business as they hustled to stay ahead of the storm. "Those are your typical nimbostratus," Harry told them, pointing skyward at the violet swirls dragging over the mountaintop. But the rain held off until all but a hundred or so bales were up— and then a cold swell blasted up the valley, the first big drops started bursting around them like eggs, and they took shelter in the barn. It sounded, Zep said, like Mr. Ringo Starr himself going bananas on the tin roof, and they all stood—Rod, Val, Stan, Laurie, Peggy, Harry, Diana, Zep—crowded in the entrance watching when the thunder and lightning moved through the gap at Silesia and started up the valley. The bolts were big neon hooks, the sky looked as solid as the earth, the thunder really did make them shudder.

"That was a *C,*" Steadman said after one flash and crack.

"A what?"

"A big *C.* I think we're getting a message."

"What do you think this is? Ouija?"

Another dazzle and boom.

"That was an *R.*"

"You'd be a great cheerleader, Steadman."

"Pay attention. The sky is spelling."

"I notice it's spelling in our direction. I hope we're not the period at the end of the sentence."

"*A,*" Steadman said. "Did you see how that one was forked?"

"That one was close."

There was no interval now between thunder and lightning.

"*C* again."

"Jesus. I don't like this."

"I saw that one hit."

WHAM!

"Holy shit."

"Did you see that? Did you fucking see that?"

"The goddamn ground jumped."

"I got a shock in my feet."

"Goddamn."

"That fucker hit right there by the gate."

"Dynamite! What was that one, Steadman?"

"That was a *T. C-R-A-C-T.* This storm can't spell."

"It missed us," Harry said, "but not by a hell of a lot. The next one will be farther off."

And he was right, the storm did move off. The truck and wagon, both loaded, were in the barn, but these bales were to go to Harry's, and the Xanaduc people were leaving when Laurie said to the Obenwalds and Steadman, "Why don't you come to supper?"

They went back to Harry's first, when the rain had turned to a leaky drizzle, and stacked the bales in Harry's barn—apart from Harry's own good sheep hay; this stuff was just mulch and bedding as far as he was concerned—and Steadman went back to his house to shower and change. Naked under the needles of water, he thought of Peggy—the red hair, the freckles that descended only as far as the shoulders, the short compact spherical body, cream and ivory, that looked so unsullied beneath the gaudy head—and watched his cock begin to thicken and curl.

But he thought he was going to stay home, that he was going to call Laurie and tell her he couldn't make it, until he dried himself off and began to shave. He picked up his razor—Anna must have used it before she went to Washington. She never got around to buying her own damn razor to shave her legs. The razor cartridge was clogged with her black hair. There were no new cartridges left in the pack. He looked again at the clogged Trac II and felt like a witness to his own anger when he said out loud, "What a fucking mess she is."

He sat across from Peggy at the Xanaduc table chomping away on yellow ears of corn. Peggy was talking about used cars, which she'd sold that summer at her father's agency. Pre-owned, she had to call them—the sales manager laid down the law at the morning meetings, and he didn't let them forget that they were selling class items. In her underplayed way—despite the accent she was no gusher—she let them know she'd "moved a heap of scrap," and she was not unaware of the advantages she had, a young sexy woman, in moving it. As it happened, she knew something about engines and cars, but the buyers of pre-owned Cadillacs were more interested in accessories and appointments than in the horses under the hood. Peggy had to beat back arguments from Rod, who said the used-car business was a rip-off; Peggy said he might not feel so charitable if he'd met some of her customers. And Val said that Peggy had been exploited as a woman, meaning, of course, that Peggy herself had exploited her sex; "I declare," Peggy said in a lush accent, "that never even occurred to me." Val was irritated by the sarcasm, but when she said, "Listen, cutie, I'm holding all the aces in this argument," Peggy replied, "If I were you I'd play them. People might think you're bluffing." Laurie tried to make peace.

Peggy asked Steadman, "Have you not-written a lot this summer?"

"I've got him there," Zep said. "I've not-written two novels. This fucker has got a not-writing block now. He can't do anything but write."

"I can't keep up with Zep anymore," Steadman said. "It's true."

"He's sucking my dust."

"It was a terrible falling off."

"Yeah, but I envy you in a way," Zep said. "Every couple months I like to have something to burn. Burn! Burn! Burn! It's one of those rituals I used to look forward to, the pages crackling and curling in the fire, outtasight! I miss it, fuckin A!"

"I read your story," Peggy said.

"What story?"

"The one about the lovers in Assisi." Ah-seezy, she said. The lovers in that story were Steadman and Anna.

"I thought the waste-paper collectors had recycled that one by now."

"I found it in a library. I had to look."

This declaration was unmistakable. Nevertheless, when they went down to the swing after dinner—in the darkness, through the damp fields, under cloud-huddled stars—Zep accompanied them. And when he made his roaring takeoff, imitating not a Boeing but something more like a walrus as he ran along the brow of the bluff, when he sailed over the edge and disappeared against the shadow of Big Furnace, Steadman touched Peggy's arm. "Shall we make a run for it?"

They did. They ran for the nearest cover and crouched there in a thicket of sycamores. They weren't hiding, really, and Zep understood that. When he thumped back to the bank and chuffed up to the top, he said in a normal voice which carried clearly, "I get it. Hide-and-seek time now. Cat-and-mouse time—but I ain't the pussy. Cock-and-tail time—but I ain't the cock either." He laughed, his jovial big-man's laugh. Out there in the starlight he began humming *The Blue Danube* and waltzing through the dew, his arm around an imaginary partner, waltzing, large and stately, across the field and back toward the house.

"The ground is kinda wet," said Peggy, and so they went, when Zep was inside, up to the small barn where the Xanaduc hay was stored. A few sheep started out of the shadows, and the three goats were munching away across the fence. The barn was dark and low-ceilinged, and Steadman bumped his head. He found a canvas tarp in one of the pens and carried it up the ladder when he followed Peggy into the loft. "A roll in the hay," she laughed amid the sounds of unfastening—and Steadman somehow had the notion of buttons popping like champagne corks, of zippers rent asunder. There seemed to be more of her naked—to him, in that light, she was a pale blob—than her clothing could possibly have contained.

"We're lucky we found the tarp. Hay is about as comfortable as a bed of nails."

She touched him, pulled on his cock like a lever, let it slap against his belly. "A real boing."

"A what?"

"A boing."

"That's a new one on me."

"It is? That's the first word I learned for it."

They spread the tarp. "And what do you call that?" he asked her.

"That's my little nubbin. That's how it was known around the house."

"It's not so little anymore. It's more like—a hummock."

"That's a new one on me," she said. "A boing and a hummock. Is this going to work?"

"It usually does."

He got in her. "Uh-oh, you're not a virgin, are you?"

She laughed. "Do I feel like one?"

"You're very dainty. I thought probably you'd be more—pre-owned."

"How does it feel? Tell me."

"It feels—well, solid."

"Solid?"

"Semi-solid. Sort of like pâté, like molten pâté. It's all one nice round mass. It doesn't feel like there's a passage in it yet."

"Do you like that?"

"Pâté?"

"The way it feels."

"Yeah. It feels like a nice juicy roast and I'm the spit it's turning on."

"Don't you think about anything but food?"

"Well, yes."

"What?"

"Right now I'm thinking I'm about to have a premature ejaculation. What you're doing is not exactly virginal."

She kept it up. "I'm about to deposit my truffle," he said.

He did. She laughed at him.

"You're going to make me self-conscious," he said.

"That was fun. I liked the talking. Most men don't talk."

"No? What do they do?"

"Oh, you know. You're still hard."

"That was just a truffle. I'm not going to give up my place in line for that."

"Who's behind you?"

"I don't know, but I'm staying right where I am. Have you ever heard of the *trou normand?*"

"What's that?"

"It's when you pause between courses of a meal. Usually you take a sip of brandy to clear the pipes. Literally, it means the Norman hole. Well, I'm in it, the Norman hole."

"More food," she said.

"That's terrific when you laugh. It sort of shakes—it sort of nibbles in there."

She laughed again.

"How do I taste?" he asked.

She thought a bit. "Like a strawberry."

"This is like making butter," he said.

"How do you mean?"

"Haven't you ever churned butter? Laurie has a churn."

"How do you do it?"

"Well, you stick the plunger down in the cream and you dash it and dash it and dash it."

"That's dashing, huh."

"And it gets thicker and thicker and thicker."

"Oh yeah?"

"And you sing a little song when you dash it, just to keep time."

"How does it go?"

> "Come butter come,
> Come butter come.
> Peter's waiting at the gate,
> Waiting for a butter cake,
> Come butter come,
> Come butter come . . ."

"This butter's about to come."

"Yeah? That'll make us even."

"This fucking talking has really got me going."

"Am I about to crack this safe? I think I feel the tumblers falling into place."

"Shut up and just fuck now, okay?"

He did and she came off, not in hard shudders the way Anna did but as if a man with a hammer—not Steadman but a small inner man of her own—was using her diaphragm as a gong and setting off sympathetic reverberations elsewhere in her torso. Anna gave blows with the bones of her ilium, but Peggy's quiver was deep and private and internal—and Steadman, over her, did not feel much involved in them. The talking had detached him, as, he supposed now, he meant it to. Listening to himself had made him more spectator than participant, made this fucking safe somehow, and now he was not just a spectator but a voyeur: Peggy kept coming. He was connected to her all right, but his penis felt as inert as an ax handle. Its presence in her must have been enough to keep her going. If the contractions —more like palpitations really—had not seemed so involuntary, he would have doubted the authenticity of this prolonged orgasm. He hardly moved in her, for she did not seem to require it; she made sounds like the cooing and fluttering of doves as they settle to roost; he watched in the darkness. This went on for minutes, it seemed. "Come inside me," she said. He started shoving harder then, and somewhere down in his perineum he felt a wad of semen as hard as a bullet. It didn't want to budge. He kept at it, sweating now, and moved this lodged load forward millimeter by millimeter, and when he finally discharged it a long pulsing stream was brought out in its train, a strand of stuff that felt like it would yank his prostate out like an onion.

Peggy went home with him that night—in the Blazer, for he didn't want anyone to see her Opel, loaded with books and a desk lamp and a wastebasket and all the other things students transport, parked at the ford—and they fucked some more on the couch in the front room, listening most of the night to records and to each other. Peggy understood about the car and the sofa—"my married man," she called him. They listened to music and they talked. Talk talk talk— that was probably the greatest delight a lover conferred, Steadman thought, this loosening of the tongue, this dusting off and revising of the biography, this invention and presentation of a fictive self. He talked, always kidding but kidding-on-the-level, about writing, and was told by Peggy, sincerely, that he had talent; he didn't, tried not to, value her opinion but knew he was flattered, just as he was flattered by her frank admiration of his body. He was so fit, she said, and took hold of his ankle and flexed his leg and told him it looked like a frog's leg, that long and springy. He found it hard to praise her in return, though he did admire her, and his compliments were worked up; he said her freckles reminded him of pebbles at the bottom of a clear stream.

As far as he could make out, at first, she regarded her body as a source of delight, to be gratified and pampered without any shame, a lovely curiosity she was still exploring. Yet the way she held in her body when she stood or sat, the way she lifted her large breasts, were signs of self-consciousness, and her talk of experience—experience, the great word with her now; she was going to Columbia for the experience of New York; she'd sold cars for the experience; and he was, though she didn't say it outright, an experience—didn't convince him. She told him she'd been attracted to him right away, and why should she not act on her desire? Steadman didn't try to answer the question, but it didn't convince him either. Peggy's comments about other men made him aware that the charm being worked on him was anything but artless, but he still knew that he was getting the best of this. He was getting fresh butter; she was getting an onion.

Peggy stayed two nights, till Labor Day. Steadman had not been on such a sexual binge since Washington, and he'd forgotten how easily excess generates itself. Part of it was physical—he was plain pussy-whipped. During their long couplings, while they waited, as he said, for talking was a feature of this binge, for his sperm to undergo a complete life cycle, all the way from their hatching out to their journey hence and the fulfillment of their destiny, which was disappointment and death against her copper seven, anything became possible. And part of it was talking, the need for new images and words, for new postures and stimulations to provide these. Peggy had studied the sex manuals. She suggested many of these experiments, but for all her show of expertise, all her experience, Steadman was sure that she was often hesitant; he was sure too that she would have gone much further, further than he had any wish to go. The best of the sex for him was not the calculated extremity but the physical extremity, the exhaustion, the lush smacking odors, the long stretches when they got way beyond desire and talk and just fucked and fucked, slippery, sweaty, sloppy, racks of tumultuous organs, maps of blood and nerves.

And after one of these fucks, Peggy said, "Sometimes fucking feels holy, doesn't it?"

Steadman didn't answer right away. He finally said, "If you starve yourself you begin to feel holy too."

"You son of a bitch," she said, but she didn't hold it against him for long. She knew the terms: no emotion.

She knew the terms. She called him her married man but she had not mentioned Anna by name. Neither had Steadman. *Anna. Anna.* In the bathroom, pissing, he saw a hairbrush she'd left behind on the shelf over the toilet. There were red hairs in it, Peggy's. He pulled them out and flushed them down the toilet. He realized that he was going to tell Anna about Peggy. He put the brush back on the shelf beside the silver barrette she used to pin back her hair and the vision of Anna—shaking the black hair over her shoulders, her arms lifted, holding the barrette in her lips—made him cover his face with his hands.

No emotion: he was just cheating everybody.

Peggy was, he imagined, as glad to be gone as he was to see her gone, although her voice got throaty when he drove her back to Xanaduc and let her out of the Blazer. "Well," she said, blinking in the sun, "that ended the summer with a bang. We did some fierce fucking."

"Yep." He was at the wheel of the Blazer, his window down; her small hands rested on the door. He looked down the road and raced the engine.

"Well, thanks a bunch," she said, the accent thick and caustic.

"I hope you meet a lot of nice Yankees. You'll be able to pick and choose up there."

"I always pick and choose," she said.

Why, he thought as he drove off and left her standing beside her loaded Opel, why? Why do I fuck everything up? He was thinking of Peggy, whom he saw in his rear-view mirror, her hair fiery in the sun, but when he rounded a curve and she disappeared he was thinking only of Anna.

Anna, Anna, Anna.

Eighteen

They went to the Outer Banks for five days. Steadman kept talking about seafood. He kept gazing at Anna and kissing her with a fervor that struck her as dramatic. They couldn't fuck—the Modess. When he asked her about it she told him she'd finally gone to a doctor and had her IUD removed and she was a little bloodier and tenderer than usual. The way he clutched her then she knew that he thought she'd done it so that they could have a baby. "I'm glad you got rid of that thing," he said. "I never thought it was safe. I never liked it."

What the fuck did he think it had to do with him?

At night she got up in the refrigerated motel room and passed gouts of blood. Steadman didn't even wake up.

When he asked her about Washington she told him they were all upset about Kay. She probably blew it all out of proportion, she said; it wasn't a real crisis, but she hadn't seen her family for so long that she'd forgotten how they screamed at each other. That seemed to content him.

He played with Maggie. He took her swimming in the ocean and took her for long walks down the shore looking for shells. They walked until they were specks in the distance. Sometimes they just disappeared. Anna wasn't surprised. After so much time in the mountains the beach and sea and sky looked amorphous to her. She could see why Prussian Creek stayed in its banks but not why the ocean did. The meeting of the shore and sea was an illusion, just like the meeting of sea and sky, the horizon.

A bug got in her ear. It made a noise boring into her skull. She thought of the powder-post beetles that chewed on the logs in the house and the fine dust trailing from the holes they drilled. Steadman came back from his walk and kissed her navel. "What a lovely warm belly." He and Maggie started arranging shells on it. When she told him about the bug he tore a page out of a book and rolled it into a tube. He pushed back her hair and put the tube to her ear and sucked the bug out. "Glug! I almost swallowed it." He blew the bug back out through the tube. "A simple operation," he said.

He and Maggie went fishing on a long pier. Anna started out the pier with them but there were fish flopping on the planks, fanning their crimson gills, drowning in air. There were scales glittering and blood. Anna told them she'd wait for them on the beach. Hours later they came romping up to her, Steadman dragging a string of fish, Maggie jabbering, hopping up and down, telling her about the fish she caught herself. Maggie in a long-billed cap, sunglasses that kept slipping down on her nose, her hair stiff with salt, bouncing around, laughing. Steadman with the dead fish, laughing. It occurred to her that they were happy.

Happy, what an idea.

She had to start fucking him again. He licked her cunt and told her it was tangy. He put his whole mouth on it and there was nothing she could do about it.

They drove back to Zion County on Wednesday. In the Blazer Steadman asked her what she wanted for her birthday.

"I don't know. Nothing."

He smiled.

"The trip was enough," she said.

He put his hand on her thigh. "I don't mind getting old. Not yet, anyway."

She was afraid he was going to stop when they drove over Big Furnace, and he did. The sun was setting and Maggie was going to sleep in the back seat. He pulled off at the scenic overlook, got out, came around, and opened her door.

"In the mountains, there you feel free," he spouted. "And in the ocean, there you feel—wet. Anna? Anna? It does feel like home, doesn't it?"

She refused to look at him or the mountains, but she said, "I'm sorry, Steadman. I guess I had a worse time than I thought. Thanks for being so patient—I just feel like such a zombie."

He kissed her. There was nothing she could do about it.

They found a dead bird in the house, a female wood duck. It had come down the chimney and left its hard crusting shit everywhere. Steadman tracked it upstairs and found it stiff under Maggie's bed. "This stuff's like barnacles," he said when he tried to clean up the shit.

In the garden the tomatoes had fallen off the vines and split open and the pulp was oozing out of the shriveled skins. The bean pods were a foot long, swollen with lumps like tumors. The zucchini were gross and dark, donkey dicks.

Anna went to an orchard on Hoot Mountain to pick peaches with Diana and Val and Laurie and Maggie. They brought bushels back, and when they were sitting in the kitchen at Xanaduc, drinking Red Zinger tea, Val started talking about how it fucked your mind to be on an artificial cycle. She talked about September and going back to school and the calendar of the school year. She mentioned Peggy and paused.

"Oh, was Peggy through here?" Anna asked.

Val said, "I thought Steadman had probably told you."

"You bitch," Laurie said, "you goddamn bitch."

Anna made peach preserves and chutneys. She canned tomatoes and fucked Steadman.

Sunday, September 17, her birthday. Steadman and Maggie spent most of the morning making her a carrot cake. Maggie wouldn't let Anna come into the kitchen. They took a walk and went swimming. Steadman threw huge sticks into the creek for Otto to retrieve and laughed when they dragged him downstream.

When Anna came home she went into the bathroom and passed blood, a jellied hunk of it. Through the V of her legs she watched it disintegrate along the edges and stain the water in the toilet bowl. That was the last of it, she thought. They told her this might happen, she might discharge whatever they hadn't got out, she shouldn't be alarmed. The last of it. She felt drops hitting on her naked thighs.

Tears. Sitting on the toilet, weeping. She made fists and hit her thighs with all her strength. She wiped off her cunt. She wiped off her face. She studied the mirror, extended her hand. The smooth cool surface. The reflection was deep and far away and her fingers did not disturb it. The last of it. The last of the tears.

Steadman cooked for hours. They ate outside. September, and they had to wear sweaters. Cold drafts came down in the shadow of Little Furnace. The whole valley seemed to be full of migrating nighthawks, bullbats Steadman called them, swooping and feeding on air, making their strange, exultant cries. Maggie brought out the cake and they sang Happy Birthday to her. "Make a wish." She blew out the candles. Maggie's presents were socks and panties. U-trou, she called them, copying Steadman. She had picked them out herself because Anna needed them. Steadman gave her a cased book, the Duc de Berry's *Très Riches Heures*. A book of hours, plates illustrating the months of the year. She could see that the plates were gorgeous, but in the decreasing light she noticed mostly how the gilt bulged on the gloss. Steadman was sitting beside her pointing out the things he liked best in the pictures. The phone started ringing in the house.

"Don't get it," Anna said.

"It's probably for you. It's probably your mother."

"Don't answer it."

It kept ringing. He said, "Ah, I can't stand to listen to it. She'll let the damn thing ring forever."

But it stopped before he got to it. It started again before he got back to the table. This time he ran to it.

"It's for you, Anna."

"Mama?"

He shrugged. "It's your father."

Her father said, "Baby, Baby."

"What, Papa?"

"Baby, I told her to get rid of that damn Jap car, I told her it was nothing but a goddamn tin can."

He was sobbing, her father was sobbing.

Anna said, "Kay's dead."

"Baby, she never knew what hit her."

Details. She was on the Beltway where they were working on it. There were lane crossovers. Kay missed one and hit an abutment.

Nobody with her, no other cars involved. They couldn't find any identification. They had to trace the license plate. Her father, sobbing. "Twenty-seven years old, her birthday. Baby, Baby, you come home as soon as you can, okay?"

She hung up and waited for Steadman. He came before long. "What is it, Anna? Is everything all right?"

She watched the movements playing on his face.

"Has something happened?"

"She did it."

"Kay?" He made a noise, a puff. "What, Anna?"

"What do you think, you stupid fucker? She killed herself."

Tears came to his eyes. They came slowly but they came.

"Don't you cry, you fucker. I won't watch you cry."

Anna went upstairs to the bedroom and sat down on the bed. She untied her boots and then undressed completely. She lay on her back, arms straight at her sides. She closed her eyes and lay on her back, naked and perfectly still, and waited. She made her wish.

She waited. She could feel nothing now and the silence was absolute, but she could not get rid of the sensation of sight. Her eyes were closed but the shadows would not stop flickering on her eyelids. Shadows, and dusts of light. Then the silence was broken: crickets, croaking. And then she was thinking in words, words were in her mind, fixed, those words Steadman liked to quote about crickets, chirping bugs: *The poetry of earth is never dead.*

God damn him. God damn him.

She heard him moving now, clearing the table outside, the rattle of plates and utensils. The screen door opened and closed, didn't bang. He must have stopped it with his foot. Otto yelped; Maggie was teasing him. Whimpers, snapping noises, Maggie's giggle. She'd thrown the rubber ball in the lilac bush and he was trying to get it. Then Maggie's command. *Give. I said Give.*

She couldn't even remember how Kay looked. She couldn't remember anything but the scar.

Anna shivered. She opened her eyes. She felt cold now, and she was goose-bumped. She could feel her heart trembling as if it were made of feathers.

She got up and dressed and sat down on the bed and waited, this time for Steadman. She heard him scraping the plates. The water ran in the sink. Maggie was talking. Steadman came up the stairs by himself and stood in the hallway outside the closed door. He knocked lightly. She didn't answer but he opened the door.

"Anna? Anna?"

"What?"

"Will you talk to Maggie, Anna? She's confused—you didn't eat your cake."

"Cake. Shit."

"Anna, she doesn't understand."

"She's your fucking daughter. You tell her. Explain it to her."

He started to come into the room.

"Leave me alone."

"Anna, Anna, I love you, Anna."

"Get the fuck away from me. Close the door."

He closed it and went downstairs. The dishes thudded in the water in the sink. Voices, his and Maggie's, indistinct. Otto scratching the screen, wanting to get in. "Bad dog," Maggie said. Then they came upstairs. Water in the bathroom, Maggie brushing her teeth. Rustling in her bed, Steadman telling her a story, "Rapunzel." Then a song, his voice low, Maggie enunciating each word clearly so that it shivered the door.

> *Oh, the fox went out on a chilly night*
> *And he prayed to the moon to give him light*
> *For he'd many a mile to go that night*
> *Before he reached the town-o, town-o, town-o,*
> *He'd many a mile to go that night*
> *Before he reached the town-o.*

God damn him.

They went through every verse.

Maggie's clear voice, singing.

> *Oh, he ran till he came to his cozy den,*
> *There were the little ones eight, nine, ten,*
> *They said, Daddy, you'd better go back again*
> *For it must be a mighty fine town-o, town-o, town-o,*
> *They said, Daddy, better go back again*
> *For it must be a mighty fine town-o.*

Oh, the fox and his wife without any strife,
They cut up the goose with a fork and a knife.
They'd never had such a supper in their life
And the little ones chewed on the bones-o, bones-o, bones-o,
They'd never had such a supper in their life
And the little ones chewed on the bones-o.

Then whispers. He walked and stood at Maggie's door and switched off the light. "Good night, Maggie. I love you." He wanted me to hear that, Anna thought.

"Good night, Daddy."

He went downstairs. Maggie stirred, got up once, walked barefoot into the hallway, got back into bed. Anna waited. She waited until Maggie was asleep and then she went down to the kitchen. Steadman was at the table drinking coffee.

"I'm going to Washington."

"Do you want me to come with you?"

"I'm leaving. I'm leaving you for good."

She looked at him until he bowed his head and put a hand up to shade his eyes.

"Anna, I haven't asked you what happened in Washington. Will you please tell me?"

"It doesn't concern you."

"It does if it makes you leave me."

"You hated Kay."

"Oh Anna, you're wrong."

"I am not wrong."

"You don't know how I pitied her."

"Pitied her? Who are you to pity anybody? How are you so perfect that you can pity the whole world?"

"Please, Anna."

"*Please, Anna,*" she mocked. "Don't think I'm going to fall for this fake emotion. It's just like those fucking birds you kill, and the deer and the fish and all the other things. You pity all of them when they're dead. Why can't you love something instead of pitying it?"

His lips were pressed together and drawn in. His hand was over his eyes. "Maybe I'm not very good at loving things."

"How can you fake like this? *I'm not very good at loving things.*" She imitated his choked voice. "When did you ever try? Don't you pretend to be sorry for Kay."

"I am sorry."

"Why? Because there's one less cunt for you?"

"Anna."

"I know you fucked her."

"I didn't."

"Oh, you liar, you fucking liar. Tell me now you never fucked Peggy either."

"I thought you might have heard about that."

"You thought. And you expect me to believe you never touched Kay."

"I didn't, Anna. I would have told you about Peggy."

"This makes you look up, huh? Not so teary now."

"I was going to tell you, Anna, but you seemed—"

"What?"

"So unhappy."

"So you were going to wait until I was happy. Oh, thanks, thanks. You're so fucking kind."

"I was going to wait until I thought—you'd forgive me."

"What about with Kay? Have you been waiting four years for just the right moment to make your act of contrition?"

"That never happened."

"You're lying, you're just lying. And you lied about Peggy—and oh, God, when I think about that night when you came back from fucking her! That night Watts died! Oh shit, I believed you, you fucker, but no more!"

"I didn't, Anna."

"I won't listen to this."

"Nothing happened that night, and nothing happened between me and Kay. Did she tell you it did?"

"Yes, she told me. Deny it."

"Couldn't you see that she had reasons for telling you that?"

"I saw her reasons. She wanted to get me out of this shithole."

"And first she wanted to make you believe that it was a shithole. Anna, Kay needed help."

"What do you mean? Do you mean a psychiatrist?"

"Yes."

"You think everything can be explained. You think you just walk up to some stranger and talk to him and he tells you what's wrong with you and then you're all better. You're stupid. You're stupid, stupid, stupid."

"Anna, don't blame yourself for what Kay did."

"I don't have to. She blamed me. She made it clear. Even you should see that, you stupid fucker. Why do you think she killed herself on our birthday? Just to make her life come out even?"

"You did as much for her as you could."

"You don't know anything."

"What could you have done? What did Kay tell you, Anna? Did she want you to leave here? What happened in Washington?"

"What does it matter? You got what you wanted, didn't you? I'm back here. I'm back here and Kay's dead."

"Anna, I know—"

"You don't know anything. I could have made a difference to Kay. I'm not shit to you. Kay, Peggy, who else? Who else have you been fucking? Have you fucked Diana yet?"

"Anna, stop."

"You're too stupid to know what fucking's about. Why wouldn't you fuck Diana? She's another cunt, right? You don't know what anything's about unless you can fuck it or kill it or eat it."

"Anna, please stop."

"But you can't do anything about what people think or what they feel. You don't know shit about that. That doesn't exist, does it?"

"I know it does."

"You think it's all superstition. At least I believe in something. At least I believe that things can mean something. At least I know there's more to it than cunts and blood and meat and chewing it up and shitting it all out and starting all over again."

"I know that, Anna."

"Why don't you do something about it?"

"I try to."

"How do you try—oh, you write about it. Your precious writing. What does that do? Written anything lately? How do you find time to write with all your fucking?"

"This is pointless, Anna."

"This gets to you, huh? One word about your precious writing—

you aren't faking now, are you? That's what you care about. *I love you, Maggie*—I heard you putting her to bed tonight and it's all a big lie. You want to write because it's all you, just you, and everybody will love you and you can pity all of them."

"You don't know about my writing, Anna."

"No, I can't understand it. It's too fucking profound for a dumb cunt like me. It's such great art. My drawing was just a little hobby. I don't know about great art."

"I didn't think your drawing was a hobby."

"You didn't say it but you thought it. You think saying things is so important, you think it doesn't exist unless somebody says it. But it does, it does, and there are all kinds of things I see and feel and never say, and they're real too. You didn't have to tell me what you thought."

Steadman had stood up from the table and walked to the end of it where Anna had been standing the whole time. "Anna, please stop this now."

"Why? Why? You can't stop me now because I'm leaving you. I'm leaving, you fucker, and I'm going to say whatever I feel like."

"You've said enough."

"I haven't said anything."

"I'm going to leave, then."

"You're leaving. I thought you were tough. You're the tough fucker who can take anything. You know something? I pity you. I pity you, you poor bastard. You know why? Because you're going to end up like Watts."

"Stop."

"You're going to end up just like him, a bully with nobody but your kids to boss around, and anybody poorer than you. And when your kids get too old you'll go to work on your grandchildren just like he did, trying to find somebody who'll still adore you even if you are a fucker."

"That's all, Anna."

"You won't last long here. Your funeral! Ha! Telling me you want to be buried here. You'll sell this place when you run out of things to keep you from writing, and you'll make a profit, and then you'll go to Bristol and play the rich hillbilly, just like Watts, but you—"

At last he hit her. She couldn't believe how quick it was, how suddenly it was happening. The blows, on her ribs and shoulders, moved her back against the wall. She was standing against the wall looking at him as his face just crumpled, just crumpled the way Maggie's did when she cried.

He ran out the door and into the night.

She felt herself and realized that he hadn't hit her hard. He'd just pushed her back. *He tried not to hurt me,* she thought.

She thought, *I couldn't tell him about the abortion.*

Nineteen

Maggie woke Steadman before dawn. She came to the high bed, as she often did, groggy and wobbling, and slipped in beside him under the quilt. She slept again. He watched the light change. November now, the gray neutral dawn, a translucence in which the mountain, its ridges and trees, gradually resolved itself. Inside the room the light had the same ambiguous, potential quality. Against the white walls the outlines of the furnishings were distinct—wardrobe, dresser, bookcase—but they were outlines, not substances. Steadman waited, watched, his breath an issue of white in the cold room.

On this day he was to see Anna again for the first time in two months.

He had spoken to her several times on the phone, to her or her mother, who often told him Anna was out—a lie, he was sure. Anna never answered the phone herself, but when she did speak to him she was so distant and tentative that he had never been able to say what he always meant to say: Please come back. He told her what he and Maggie had been doing as if she were merely away on a visit. She said nothing about herself. Finally he said he thought she should see Maggie soon. She replied immediately, "I'll pick her up at that place outside Charlottesville, that truck stop, the one we always used to stop at."

"You've thought this over, haven't you?" he said, hoping she'd laugh.

"I can't come there, and I don't think you should come up here now."

She was so decided that he did not try to change her mind then. A truck stop. He didn't care.

He was going to see Anna.

Maggie began to wake, flutters first of the lips and eyes, rearrangements of the body, the drawing back of the lids, huge, startled pupils. One of her arms was slung across his cheek. She moved it, felt the stubble of beard on the inside of her wrist, said her first words of the day, "You better shave for Mama."

"What about you? Anna won't recognize you if I don't scrub you up."

He shouldn't have said it. Maggie took it into her head that she had to be spotless. She was in the bathtub while he shaved, and he had to wash her hair and scrub her neck and brush her fingernails. Then she insisted on wearing her patent-leather party shoes, the long green dress with red hearts embroidered on it, a red bow in her hair. It all had to be just right. Her fussiness exasperated him a little, but when satisfied at last she looked at him with such humility and uncertainty that he was ashamed: she thought she wouldn't be loved if she wasn't beautiful.

Since daybreak they'd been hearing gunfire. At breakfast Steadman tried to explain that the hunting season had begun. The men they'd seen in the trailers and orange suits were all out hunting. They heard a shot just up the mountain, close enough to make them flinch. Steadman went to the window at the back of the kitchen. Just above the small log barn a spike buck was trying to cross the open slope. It must have been hip-shot; it couldn't keep its back legs under it. Another shot. Steadman heard the bullet whang through the tin roof of the garden shed. A third shot, and the buck staggered to the ground. It sprang up once, then fell again, collapsed on its jerking legs.

"You stay here," Steadman said to Maggie, pulling on his jacket.

One hunter had already come out of the woods, a boy, and another was blundering through the woods after him.

"Did you shoot it?" Steadman asked. The boy looked horrified. He was about eleven or twelve years old, Steadman thought, and felt his anger giving way. He was about that age when, with Watts, he killed his own first deer.

"I didn't—" the boy said, choking.

"Well, Jesus Christ." This was a man, puffing, overweight.

The buck was still struggling. The first shot had gone through the hams and crippled it and the second shot was in the lung.

"Kill the goddamn thing," Steadman said to the man.

"What?"

"Kill it, for Christ's sake. It's lung-shot. It's drowning in its own blood."

"You mean stand here and shoot it again? Up close like this? It's just about dead anyway."

Steadman looked at the man more carefully now—brand-new jacket and corduroys and boots, cheap gun.

He said to the boy, "Shoot it in the head."

The boy looked at the man.

"If you don't I'll shoot it, goddamnit."

The boy shot it and wept.

"Who the hell do you think you are?" the man said.

"I live right there, you dumb son of a bitch. You almost shot into the house. Don't you know what the fuck you're doing?"

"I just brought the boy hunting," the man said.

The weeping boy, trying to stand up straight, this man with his hand on his son's shoulders, the dead deer at their feet. The last shot had blown away the back of the head. "I'm sorry," Steadman said, "but goddamn it, you've got to look where you shoot."

"I haven't been out here before," the man said, and Steadman realized that the accent wasn't local. "I just brought the boy. I guess I never thought he'd get one. But he had to go. Hey, Ronny, look —you got one."

The boy wiped his face on his sleeve.

"It's a good big spike buck," Steadman said. "Did you have much of a shot at it?"

"It was running and then it stopped. I don't know. I saw it had spikes and then I shot."

"Somebody else must have spooked it. There are a lot of hunters out this morning."

"Yes, sir."

"Where was it?"

"In the woods there." The boy pointed.

"Where were you?"

"We were up above the Game Commission line," the man said. "We weren't on your property. I never even saw the house."

"It must have been a good long shot," he said. "You've got open sights on that gun."

"Yes, sir."

Steadman asked the man, "How'd you come in?"

"Along the mountain here." He pointed north.

"Is your truck parked up there on the road?"

"I got a Vega. It's up past the bridge."

Steadman said, "The easiest way to get it out of here would be to take it across the ford."

"The ford?"

"That's the only way to drive up here."

"I guess I never counted on us getting one," the man said.

"You go ahead and dress it out, then," Steadman said, "and just drag it down the slope here and I'll take it across the creek for you. Your Vega won't get across. You can dress it out right at the edge of the woods there."

The boy said, "I never dressed a deer before."

The man said, "This is the first one either of us killed."

Steadman helped them drag the deer to the edge of the woods and told the boy how to run his knife up the belly so that he didn't puncture the stomach, how to remove the scrotum, how to cut the intestine free from the anus. The boy's bloody hand was shaking. The hot guts steamed on the leaves. The father stuck his hands in to help pull them out.

"How do I blood him?" he said.

"He's bloody already," Steadman said.

"I mean the way you're supposed to do it."

"Just touch him, then. That's all you have to do."

The man hesitated and the boy stood up straight and faced him.

The man put forth his hand and left blood on both his son's cheeks. Walking back to the house Steadman saw Maggie's face close to the window.

The man and the boy came in with him. They rinsed off their hands and Steadman wrapped up the deer's liver for them. He gave them a cup of coffee. Voluble now, the man said they'd just moved to the area, he'd never hunted before but all his boy's friends were out hunting. They just came out to see what it was like. He said he'd never heard of a place where the kids got out of school to go hunting. He told Steadman to send him a bill for repairing the roof. Steadman took them and their deer across the creek in the Blazer. He came back to the house, changed his pants, for they'd got bloody, packed a suitcase and some toys for Maggie, and then, giving in to his own hope, packed a few things for himself.

"I'll be surprised if Anna's here yet," he said when, at noon, he pulled into the enormous parking lot of the truck stop.

"She is here," Maggie said, and pointed out her father's car, a big blue sedan. Steadman parked the Blazer beside it. He unstrapped Maggie from her safety seat. Acres of pavement, gray sky, Interstate traffic. Halfway between Washington and Zion County. Maggie ran toward the building, stopped, waited for him, slid her mittened hand into his.

They stepped onto the concrete walk and passed before the big green aquatic panes of glass, looking in. They saw their own wavy reflections and within, dimmer, the outlines of booths and tables. Maggie tugged his hand hard. "She really is here." Steadman saw the pale shimmer of her face and saw her slender form moving behind the glass. She was going toward the door.

He walked slowly. He felt Maggie's hand turning, slip away; he was still clutching her mitten. She ran a few steps toward the door and stopped. Anna came out. Steadman stopped. For a moment they were all still, Steadman and Anna with Maggie between them. Anna's hair was cut shorter, her arms were folded as if she was cold. Maggie shoved her hands into the pockets of her coat and looked down at the concrete. Steadman and Anna looked at each other over her head. Then Maggie ran to Anna across the concrete, and Anna stooped, lifted her, bent back to get her legs under her weight.

"You're so big, you're so big, Maggie. And so dressed up—did you put that ribbon in your hair?"

Maggie nodded her head into Anna's shoulder.

"Hello, Anna."

Anna looked at the ribbon in Maggie's hair.

"Let's go in. It's chilly out here." He held open the door and followed them inside. Anna was wearing clogs that clopped on the floor. She slipped in beside Maggie on one side of the padded booth, opposite Steadman. Her face was thinner, paler. There were circles under her eyes. She kept her arms folded.

"Will you eat something? Maggie and I have been counting on a meal. We were up early."

"You have pretty new clothes, Mama."

"And so do you—not new, but you wore your best clothes, didn't you?"

A waitress brought menus. Under the plastic covers there were lurid illustrations of platters named the White Line Special and Mason-Dixon Dandy. Steadman tried to interpret this to Maggie. After they'd ordered—Anna wanted only coffee—Maggie reached out and touched her face so that Anna would look at her. "Diana has to get twenty shots," she said, making it sound as horrible as she could, "all over her, with a great big needle, and they hurt so much she has to get them in a different place every time."

Anna started to turn to Steadman but Maggie reached and touched her cheek again. "And so does Harry, but he says they don't hurt—but I think they really do hurt, a lot."

Anna said, "What happened, Steadman?"

Maggie said, "The fox killed two of their sheep and it could have been the same fox even though it was so long ago."

Steadman explained. Two of the Obenwalds' sheep—two rams, purebreds—had acted as if they had some obstruction in their throats, and Diana and Harry had both fished around to try to remove it. The rams died of rabies. Evidently they'd been bitten, but they were pastured with a group of rams, and they were always scuffling and banged up, and neither Harry nor Diana had noticed anything unusual. Nobody had seen a fox. The incubation period of the virus could be weeks or months. The rams' brains had been sent to a lab for analysis. They had just got the report and decided, even though the risk was remote, that they'd better take the shots.

Anna listened silently and said, "How can Diana take the shots the way she is?"

"She's only had two so far," Steadman said. "They were both in the bottom."

Their food came. Maggie said Diana had helped her bake an applecake for Steadman's birthday. "We got the apples on the mountain," she said. Steadman told Anna they'd gone up Little Furnace to pick wild apples in those orchards. They'd pressed some cider.

"The apples rolled and rolled," Maggie said. "We couldn't catch them all. Harry shook the tree and Daddy lied down on the ground and let them bump him."

"The bees did the backstroke in the cider," Steadman said.

"We made a leaf book, Mama."

"What kind of book?"

"A leaf book, with some real leaves and some prints of leaves and some traces of leaves. And we made a college too."

Anna smiled.

Maggie caught her mistake and clapped her hand over her mouth. "I can't remember that word."

"A collage."

"A collage, a big one, with pictures on it, and feathers, and some beads and strings and you know what else? Some beer cans we fixed so you could see little pictures inside. And Otto caught a fish!"

"What?"

"He caught a fish and brought it home."

"He did catch a big fish, one of those silver falls fish. I have a fish dog, not a bird dog."

"Otto was funny, wasn't he, Daddy? It was a great big fish, Mama, and he wanted to keep it."

"I tried to chink a few courses in the studio," Steadman said. "Those damn skylights still haven't arrived yet. I'd like to close that roof up before we get any real winter weather."

"It sounds like you've stayed busy."

"We had our spells. The first couple of days we'd get up and get dressed and have breakfast and do the dishes—"

"We have to do them right after we eat." Maggie made a face.

"And then we'd read or play a few games of Uncle Wiggily and build castles with the blocks and go through the Brothers Grimm and then, when we were ready for lunch, I'd look to see what time it was—and it still wasn't ten."

Anna looked at Maggie's plate. "You certainly have a big appetite."

Maggie took this as praise and stabbed with her fork at the remains of a turkey sandwich in a pool of greenish gravy. "I'm still hungry," she said. "I want some of that pie too."

She scrambled over Anna's lap out to the counter to study the plaster wedges of pie on display in a case. "She's all wound up," Steadman said. "She has been all morning. So have I, Anna."

"What have you told her?"

"About what?"

"About us."

"I haven't told her anything. I haven't known what to tell her. Come back, Anna."

She shook her head.

"Anna, can't I see you? Will you see me if I come to Washington?"

"Don't come."

'I want that one," Maggie said, and pointed it out to the waitress when she came. She sat with her elbows on the table, turning from Steadman to Anna. She settled on Anna. "Harry says Diana's baby is going to be an alarm clock," she said. "It's going to be an alarm clock because it will wake them up all the time. Do you see, Mama? It will cry and wake them up and that's why it will be an alarm clock. And Daddy's going to help him get the lambs because Diana won't be able to because that's when she's going to have a baby. Mama, Mama?" Maggie reached out and touched her cheek again.

"I'm listening, sweetie."

"You weren't looking."

"I was thinking about Diana."

"Daddy says I'm an alarm clock too because I wake him up, but I don't cry. I don't cry, do I, Daddy?"

"Here comes your pie," Steadman said. "Yikes! You got the biggest one they had."

"Soooo delicious," said Maggie, but after her first bite she just pushed it around with her spoon. She said, "Daddy helped the man and a boy take a deer apart this morning. The man said he wouldn't know how to do it without Daddy."

"What deer?"

"The dead one the boy shot."

"What is this, Steadman?"

"Hunting season opened today. A kid shot a deer out behind the house."

"How did Maggie see it?"

"She couldn't help seeing it. It ran out into the field."

"Why did you let her?"

"Anna, I couldn't do much about it."

"He just helped them," Maggie said. "He let them come in afterward to wash off the blood."

"Couldn't you stay inside with her?"

"I just wanted to get the thing out of there."

"Yum yum yum," Maggie said, taking another bite of the pie. She got a gob of Miracle Whip on her nose.

She didn't wipe it off. Instead she laughed with mock sophistication and spooned up another tuft of it and put it deliberately on her cheek. She kept laughing, making them watch her. Another tuft on her cheek. "I love to eat with my face," she said. "It's how I eat all the time, ha ha." She ducked her face into the pie and covered it with whipping. She fluffed the stuff daintily with her fingertips. She lifted the spoon and started to move the whipping around, humming, pretending to shave.

"Stop her," Anna said. "Make her stop."

"All right, Maggie, you can't fool me. I know you don't have real whiskers."

"Oh, god damn your jokes."

She dabbed at Maggie's face with a napkin. When Maggie began to sob she took her to the ladies' room.

Steadman paid the bill. Before he left the truck stop he put Maggie's things in Anna's car and he left a note on the seat.

Anna—

Maybe I shouldn't leave you this way now, but I don't know what I can do. Is there anything?

He was going to write, *I love you, Anna,* but he thought she would not believe it. It didn't seem to make much difference anyway.

Twenty

Dear Anna,

You've heard the good news. Diana told me she phoned you, and since she's not bashful about her ecstasy I doubt there's much I can add to her report. There we were in the Gorge, the road a sheet of ice, sleet pelting the Blazer, the wind screeching, and Harry in the back with Diana with his veterinary supplies, ready to make the delivery on the spot—and Diana just giggled each time she had a pain. It was happening to her at last! "Here comes one," she'd sing out, with such wonder and surprise each time that Harry gave up trying to coach her. Duty, as usual, comes out the hero of the story, the knight on the bulldozer, although he didn't need the bulldozer, just his chain saw and cant hook, to get the tree out of the road. The elements, the weather, and the scenery, all made the adventure more splendid to Diana, and she was so delighted through it all that it was a grand joyride. And of course it ended just the way it should have ended, with Baby Ben, the alarm clock, arriving in time to toll in the new year. The Spirit of '74! Diana thinks it is only right that she and Ben have been photographed for the newspapers and showered with detergents, frozen pizzas, car wax, et cetera, by the Staunton merchants.

Meanwhile the first lambs have been born without mishap, though I have been midwife to some of them. Harry has hired me, more or less, to help him during the lambing, and it's settled that my pay will be one ram and two ewe lambs. Harry really is a kind of Johnny Sheepseed. He's managed to fix *it at last so that I'll have to start a flock. A gift, of course, for I don't think I'll be much real help. I have instructions to wake Harry if anything at all goes wrong during my watch.*

My tiny flock—it may come to that, or it may not. Down in Bristol at Christmas Mason was excited, in his way, about his doings and he made me feel that he would be glad to have me there with him. He's come forth a little, I think, but it may be that I took in more than I usually do down there. We were all subdued—how I missed Watts! His memory presided, as you'd imagine, but we seemed knit together in other ways too. There was much kindness toward me, anyhow. A little confession—I didn't tell anyone in Bristol until just before I went that you and Maggie wouldn't be with me this year. The story I let out was that you thought you should be with your family, but when I got to Bristol, and they all asked about you—I couldn't keep up the pretense. So your presents and Maggie's were sent late and should be reaching you soon. It didn't sound as if Maggie missed them much when I talked to her on the phone. A Mickey Mouse record player and a Barbie Doll! How did you let Santa—who had to be your mother—get away with it?

But Maggie sounded thrilled and you sounded—about the same. So did I, probably. We're no good on the phone. I hear your voice and think of all the things I want to say, think of them but can't say them, and feel as if I'm choking on two hundred miles of Bell Co. wire. All I want to tell you is that I love you, and I end up choking. And I wonder if it's love at all if it does so little good to anyone.

So I'm writing, and I see that I already have more of a letter than I've been able to write since I saw you at the truck stop. It seems to me that I've spent most of this time composing letters to you, some raging and some pathetic, but all of them with the same purpose—to bring you back. They were never written, but it is time to write now. The year's begun, the lambs are coming, and we have to do something with ourselves—and I will not meet you again at any truck stop to discuss this! I had better write what I can.

More than anything I want to live with you and Maggie again, here if you will come back here. If not, then anywhere. And if you won't live with me at all—well, you won't, and I would just as soon know that now. Maybe that is why I am writing to you now after all this time: because I think that now I can get by if it is over between us.

After I saw you and came back here I believed it was over. That time was desolate for me. I didn't know what to do except the things I have always done. I went out and chased the birds, the grouse and turkeys. I wandered around the mountains with Otto. There was no joy in it. For me the flash and racket of a grouse getting up has always been an elation, more than an elation; when a grouse flew I felt as if I'd cornered the mountain and forced its secret out into the open air. There, suddenly, was the magnificent bird, made manifest for me, actual in its feathers but to me a revelation—yes, a spirit. And of course I was too thrilled to be much of a shot. This season I couldn't miss. It got so I dreaded seeing the grouse fly. It seemed that I had forever to cover them, that they sat there on the bead of the gun. I shot, they fell. Thump. When they hit the ground they were meat.

There was that dread and not much else, not even much pleasure in watching Otto discover his instincts, his passion. There was that dread, but I kept going out, kept going harder and farther, afraid of what would happen to me if I stopped doing the one thing I knew how to do. I went as far as I could. I tried to get lost. Those woodcraft books, my scripture, are never so lyrical as when they take up the art of getting lost. Survival, they call it. I went as deep into the mountains as I could and tried to sleep in hemlock lairs, listening to cold streams clank on ice and stone, listening to hoots and howls, smelling the cold and embers of my fires. It didn't work. I'd lie awake and watch my breath rise in the cold, the little white vanishing feather of my breath. And I would think, this is how it will be for me for the rest of my life. It's gone, all gone, all but these tiny white puffs out of my mouth.

And it was all gone because you were gone, Anna. If loving you came to nothing, it all came to nothing. I'm done for, I thought. That seemed to be just a fact like any other—and then I would wake up here in the house in the middle of the night and feel the whole bed trembling under me. It felt as if the bed was trembling. It felt as if the bed and the whole world depended on my shaking heart, that small defective organ. The bed shook, the house shook, the mountains shook, the sky shook—and the world was in a bad way if it depended on me. And the only thing that terrified me was that this world that seemed on the point of dissolving contained you and Maggie. It seemed to me that if I could not love you, if my heart failed, then you would be blown to atoms. And so I'd pray, let them live, let them live, because I felt so helpless and singled out and so judged and damned and dying that it was too awful not to believe in a compensating mercy.

When I think now, Anna, how I kidded you about your sleeplessness, I wonder what it is in me that resists so strongly, for whatever it is that resists these terrors also resists love. Just nerves, I used to tell you. And maybe it is *just nerves—but we would never love one another if we were just nerves. We would have nothing to fear. Anna, Anna, I know you have always been more alive to the terror of our changes than I have been, and when I believed that you were afraid of them, and scorned you for it—I was just resisting, as usual.*

And I'm still resisting, though in a different way. Now when I wake up with the whimwhams I get up off that damn bed and I go downstairs and huddle by the stove and dose myself with coffee and read—I'm reading Hardy now, those fortifying books—and if that doesn't work I get dressed and walk outside and cross the creek and make my rounds through the sheep. There they are in the fields, snuffling, bedded down, and I swear that sometimes I don't know what keeps them from sailing out among the stars. They are so unprotected, nothing but fleece between them and infinite spaces. But they are confident of the few feet of earth they're pressing down, and I begin to be more confident by and by. I plod through them and I am not metamorphosed. I seem to be thermodynamically sound; I do not fizz into a billion swirling particles. I bump into things. And I know that you're alive, you and Maggie, somewhere else on this same globe under these same stars, and that some of my terrors are just vanities, after all.

Life is sturdier than I imagine, sturdier and more relentless. Anyway I kept on puffing and plodding. And then on the morning after the first snow I woke up late, it was full day, the snow had stopped falling, the sky was absolutely clear, and Big Furnace was standing in the window—standing there, as if the falling snow had eliminated the intervening air. I went downstairs and fixed waffles for breakfast and drenched them with your thick syrup. And then it was a mess of plain ordinary birds, junkos and sparrows, that gave me a lift. They were outside hopping around in the snow. They looked like punctuation on a clean page—and a cardinal flashed into the midst of them, a streaking red exclamation! And I realized that the first snow was a kind of anniversary, the end of a year here, one complete turn of the seasons—and that started it.

That was the first drop of joy—plink! Because of your syrup I think now of how the sugar water sounds when it drops into the bucket, how astonishing it is that the sweet stuff runs in the bare trees. And I began to run too—oh Anna, what a crying jag I had! Bucketfuls! The veins of joy did open, and I sank taps everywhere. Suddenly everything moved me and I moped around the house looking at the jars of tomatoes and jams and chutneys you put up, the reds and purples of the berries, the cobalt blue and mossy green glazes of the jars, your neat labels and the way you dated them, 16.VIII.73, the month in Roman, as if they'd been put down to age, to be broken out in our plentiful future—and of course I bawled. I looked through that leaf book I made with Maggie, and bawled, and looked through the book of your flowers —those clear lovely drawings, bloodroot and showy orchis and wild columbine and wood sorrel, the names and dates written under them—more bawling. And God help me, I'd do anything to keep the tears coming. I'd play Satie's Trois Gymnopédies *and sit listening to it and marveling at how exquisite that music is, and thinking that it really did sound as if it came from on high—as the record jacket said—and thinking that, after all, beauty was loose everywhere and weeping, for myself, that I could sense it. I was weeping and glorying in my tears too, proud of myself for being so moved by things and grateful that I have been given such a portion of happiness that I can grieve for its loss.*

And this indulgence of tears seems to have done a work of erosion. Another vein begins to show, this one a vein in stone. I feel presumptuous when I write that, since everything seems so ephemeral, moods and emotions most ephemeral of all—but still, a vein in stone. The vein forks, branches, keeps running through the stone. It keeps running. It carries us forward and finds us out. I see how brief, after all, that spell of desolation was, and how little it took to dissipate it. And I see, or think I see, that our veins converge, Anna, yours and mine, for a time yet to come. It is strange to me how little choice I feel in loving you. It is as if, like Maggie, you were the one given me.

With all the birthing going on around here, I've had to remember Maggie's birth and how protective and complacent I felt when your pains began. I was so proud of myself! And the pains went on and on. They kept trying to get you to take pills and you wouldn't. You wanted to be awake, you said. I would feel your hand tighten on my arm and I'd say, Breathe. *You would have breathed whether or not I said it. After the first day you were so exhausted, so gone in your pain and labor, so gone in yourself—and there was nothing I could do then, nothing, nothing, nothing.* Breathe, *I'd say, and feel your hand strong on my arm, and you'd open your eyes and create my happiness with your sight, with your words, "Thank you, Steadman." How could you say that? My happiness was all in that, my happiness and my horror. When they finally took you into the delivery room to try to turn the baby, the doctor told me that they might have to do a Caesarean. He said you might be too worn out for a natural birth. I walked around outside in the parking lot and all I could think was* let her live, let her live. *Why* is it, Anna, that in extremities love separates us and reduces us to these simple prayers?

Then I saw Maggie, not Maggie yet, not to me, a swaddled thing with black spiky hair. And then I saw you. The stretcher was being wheeled down the corridor. I saw your black hair beyond the white wrappings. Your eyes were open. You were close enough for me to touch. Your hand was around mine. You squeezed hard. You smiled at me, Anna.

That was it.

That was it, and now, after being here, I know how to put what I felt then. I owned you. I mean that just as Diana or Amos or Duty would mean it if they said that a ewe had owned a lamb, had recognized it as her own. This one is mine, I thought. I had no more choice in it than a ewe has. You were the one given me. I went and looked at Maggie again. Another gift. Neither of you were mine for the keeping, only in trust. Gifts, both of you. Gifts, love and life both.

Anna, my lamb. Maggie, my other lamb. Steadman, the ewe. I know how dopey I sound, but maybe the hour forgives me. It's late and I'm nodding. Finishing this is a race against sleep—but it is finished, isn't it? Let her live, let them live. And if you can forgive me, if you can live with me again, Anna—well, I would prepare for that event by going out and buying a lot of Kleenex to sop up the overflow of those veins of joy. And then, when I stopped bawling, we would have—just time, rich hours and poor ones, as before.

Good night, my lamb, my love.

Steadman

January 12

Dear Steadman,

I just read your letter tonight. It got here two days ago but it was so thick that I was afraid to open it and read it. I didn't know what it might say. Tonight Mama was watching the news and telling me I had to start taking an interest in life and Papa blew up at her and told her to leave me alone—and I knew I had to get out of this house. I came upstairs and read the letter.

I will try to answer you, Steadman. I dreaded those phone calls too because it was impossible for me to say the things that crowded me so when I talked to you. I didn't know how I would ever say them.

I am starting now, Steadman.

It is hard for me to describe what I felt those first months after Kay was dead.

I can't remember what I was like as a little girl. I only remember what Kay was like. It was Kay I saw and heard and watched. She was real for me, she was the one who existed in the world. I was like a shadow, nothing but a shadow. If Kay had been taken away I wouldn't have existed. I knew what I was by seeing Kay. Everything else I saw or felt was shared with her. I remember looking at her for long minutes and never saying a word and believing that everything in my mind was in hers, and everything in hers was in mine, and feeling the composition of our minds change together. It was as if our minds together were one sky and our thoughts were the weather in that sky. That is the only way I can explain it now. I have thought about how I would try to explain it to you. There was such a sympathy between us that when it began to come apart we could not bear to talk about it. We made believe that it was still there. It was there once, Steadman.

I thought I had my own life apart from Kay. I had my own life with you and Maggie, but nothing I felt was as encompassing as that sympathy I remembered with Kay. When she killed herself I was alone as I had never been. I was nothing, a negative. When I looked in the mirror I could not see anything, not me, just not-Kay. I looked at my hands and didn't see my hands. They just weren't Kay's hands. Steadman, do you understand? I was alive but I wasn't Kay, I was not-Kay. I was all that was left of her but I wasn't her. I had a body now and Kay didn't. The body did not belong to me. It did not belong to anybody. It was just not-Kay. If she was not real in the world, then how could I be real?

As I try to explain this I think of what you said about the hard vein, the vein that forks and branches. I do not know how Kay and I grew apart, but the vein forked. I do not know how I got through the time of that terrible estrangement, but I think I am through it, the worst of it anyway. I feel grief and sorrow now, not estrangement. I am in the mirror again, Steadman.

When I feel this terrible grief I want more than anything to be with you. I would have come back, Steadman, but I could not tell you that I

*had an abortion when I came to Washington in September. I thought you
would hate me. I was afraid I would lose you and Maggie if I told you.
Steadman, I believe you will love me.*

*Now I try not to think of how different things might be if I had told
you. I think of you in our house writing to me. For a while I've been
walking around and wondering what would become of us all, wondering
because there didn't seem to be anything I could do about it. I'd look at
people here in the city and try to imagine their lives. I couldn't. I couldn't
imagine any life, not for them or for me. And then I read your letter and
thought of you in our house, and imagined the way it looks and sounds
there, minute by minute. I thought of the life that went on in that place.
Steadman, I believe that we were in love and that between us we invented
our lives. We are real, all right, and that place is real. We have our blood
and our beating hearts. The mountains have their grouse and deer. And
our griefs are real and our deaths will be real. We do not have to invent
them. But the rest of it, minute by minute in the precious minutes left, is
up to us.*

*I had to stop writing there for a while. I am in my old room and Maggie
has been asleep, but she'd kicked off her covers and when I went to sort
her out she woke up. She told me she had a picture in her mind and I asked
her what it was—and she couldn't remember. It just popped out of my
head, she said. I tucked her in again and we talked for a while. She was
wide awake and she looked me over—you know how she can fix you with
those eyes. She told me that I was not so gloomy tonight and she asked me
why. I told her I was writing to you. She said, "We're going to live with
him again, aren't we?"*

Steadman, I told her Yes.

And in the room in Washington, her daughter sleeping now,
she looked at the letter she was about to fold and send. She
realized that she had not completed it. Her hand was shaking
when she wrote the last words.

Love, Anna.

Printed in the United States
132685LV00002B/115/A

9 780813 918778